Lincoln's Senior Generals

President Abraham Lincoln *carte de visite* taken on February 9, 1864, by Anthony Berger of the Brady Studio in Washington. Author's collection.

Lincoln's Senior Generals Photographs and Biographical Sketches of the Major Generals of the Union Army

Thomas Glass

Schiffer Military History
Atglen, PA

Acknowledgments

The author would like to acknowledge the encouragement and assistance given him to complete this book. First, thanks to Howard Norton for providing the author an opportunity to purchase many of the *cartes de visite* shown in this book. Thanks also to Dan Weinberg of the Abraham Lincoln Bookstore in Chicago for twenty-six years of friendship and encouraging the author to become a Civil War photography collector. Very importantly, the author wishes to acknowledge and thank Jim Hayes for his permission to use the signatures of union major-generals as they appear in his book, *War Between the States: Autographs and Biographical Sketches*. Finally, thanks to my wife Patricia for tolerating a quarter century of Civil War book and photograph collecting.

Book Design by Ian Robertson.

Copyright © 2012 by Thomas Glass.
Library of Congress Control Number: 2012934762

All rights reserved. No part of this work may be reproduced or used in any form or by any means—graphic, electronic, or mechanical, including photocopying or information storage and retrieval systems—without written permission from the publisher.

The scanning, uploading and distribution of this book or any part thereof via the Internet or via any other means without the permission of the publisher is illegal and punishable by law. Please purchase only authorized editions and do not participate in or encourage the electronic piracy of copyrighted materials.

"Schiffer," "Schiffer Publishing Ltd. & Design," and the "Design of pen and inkwell" are registered trademarks of Schiffer Publishing Ltd.

Printed in China.
ISBN: 978-0-7643-4035-2

We are interested in hearing from authors with book ideas on related topics.

Published by Schiffer Publishing Ltd.
4880 Lower Valley Road
Atglen, PA 19310
Phone: (610) 593-1777
FAX: (610) 593-2002
E-mail: Info@schifferbooks.com.
Visit our web site at: www.schifferbooks.com
Please write for a free catalog.
This book may be purchased from the publisher.
Try your bookstore first.

In Europe, Schiffer books are distributed by:
Bushwood Books
6 Marksbury Avenue
Kew Gardens
Surrey TW9 4JF, England
Phone: 44 (0) 20 8392-8585
FAX: 44 (0) 20 8392-9876
E-mail: Info@bushwoodbooks.co.uk.
Visit our website at: www.bushwoodbooks.co.uk

Contents

Introduction 6

Lincoln Becomes President and Commander-in-Chief 8

The Photographic Image Captures the Civil War 17

Lincoln's Major-Generals: Their Military Careers and Lives 22

President Lincoln, Cabinet Officers, and Governors 382

Bibliographic Sources for the Sketches of the Generals 399

Introduction

The Union Army in the Civil War was led by the largest number of general officers in American military history. Depending on the definition of what might constitute a "substantive" general, between April 1861 and May 1865, some 583 union officers were appointed as a major-general or brigadier general. Nearly another thousand senior rank union officers were breveted as a brigadier-general or major general. These "honorary" generals sometimes received their brevet promotions for gallantry in action and sometimes as a political reward.

The rapid buildup in 1861 of the union volunteer army presented newly elected President Abraham Lincoln with an enormous problem in quickly finding hundreds of generals to put in command of divisions and brigades. At the beginning of the war in 1861 the federal army had only five serving generals. Three were over the age of seventy and the youngest was fifty-three. The existing military pool for Lincoln to draw from to fill all officer positions consisted of about 750 West Point trained officers and another hundred West Point trained officers willing to return to active service from civilian life.

By existing army regulations and protocol, officers serving as major-generals held higher levels of command than single star brigadier generals. Usually they were appointed a major-general after demonstrating abilities in the field to lead large military combat operations. However, a few of the hundred and thirty-three appointed union army-major generals were assigned to administrative staff duties and saw little or no action in the field during the war.

An examination of the personalities, experiences and performance of the one hundred and thirty-three major-generals provides a candid picture, both good and bad, of the union army leadership between 1861 and 1865. Many major-generals were former civilians, political office holders, and business leaders before and after the war. Others were lawyers, professionals, farmers, educators, and clergy responding to their country's call to arms.

A majority of the one hundred and thirty-three major-generals possessed prior experience in the regular army mostly at the rank of lieutenant or captain. These experienced regular army officers were to provide the senior military leadership for the army during and after the Civil War. Some of the major-generals constituting senior army leadership were Ulysses Grant, William Tecumseh Sherman, Philip Sheridan, John Schofield, John Pope, George Thomas, George Meade, George Crook, and Winfield Scott Hancock. One, Ulysses Grant, became President, and two others (George McClellan and Winfield Scott Hancock) were presidential candidates for the Democratic Party. Another President, James Garfield, was appointed a major-general, but his appointment was never fully confirmed by the Senate.

This book portrays the men serving as union army major-generals through the medium of period albumen photographs and brief biographical sketches. Each general's military career is briefly outlined, along with other interesting events in his life. The photographs are *cartes de visite*, which are small albumen images mounted on card stock similar in size to a nineteenth-century lady's or gentleman's visiting card. They were printed from glass plate negatives, many of which survive and are located today in the National Archives and Library of Congress.

For a fee the National Archives and other institutions holding collections of Civil War photography will usually provide high quality photographic copies taken from these plates or other period images. Unfortunately, original glass plate negatives for many of the major-generals do not survive. Therefore, *cartes de visite* and other printed images on engravings taken from lost plates are the only means we have of knowing what the generals looked like during the Civil War. Post-Civil War cabinet cards (a larger photographic format than a *carte de visite*) are sometimes available. Relatively few images of Civil War generals exist on daguerreotypes, ambrotypes, or tintypes because these early forms of photography were one of a kind, meaning there were no copies other than the original negative.

The images shown in this book are all original Civil War vintage *cartes de visite*. The *cartes de visite* of many of the pictured major-generals can still be purchased by collectors. Although some of the *cartes* used in the book are not in pristine condition, they are representative of most hundred and fifty year old albumen photographs.

Lincoln Becomes President and Commander-in-Chief

After decades of sectional conflict, the 1860 election of Abraham Lincoln brought about the final "impending" crisis between the south and north. Almost immediately after Lincoln's election southern states began to secede and prepare "defense" forces to protect their "independence". War was now certain, the only question being when and where the first shot would be fired.

Abraham Lincoln, in his inaugural address on March 4, 1861, assured citizens in southern and border states his new administration had no desire to interfere with the institution of slavery. His greatest concern at the time was to prevent further dissolution of the union by the secession of the border states.

Lincoln hoped the efforts of many influential southerners opposing secession could be strengthened if they could assure their constituents the new Republican administration would make no effort to eliminate their "peculiar institution".

Preserving the union through conciliation would be Lincoln's primary political objective, and in order to achieve this he was willing to continue a divided national political structure half free and half enslaved. Such a situation at the time was bearable to Lincoln, as the only other option seemed to be armed conflict.

To his shock, a few hours after his inauguration Acting Secretary of War Joseph Holt briefed him on the deteriorating conditions at Fort Sumter, situated in Charleston harbor. Major Robert Anderson, a southern born officer, commanded the small federal garrison facing much larger South Carolina state militia forces. Holt informed Lincoln that South Carolina had officially cut off the garrison's ability to purchase provisions in Charleston, meaning the fort had foodstuffs for no more than two weeks. In addition, numerous new batteries of artillery had been mounted facing the partially completed fort. Major Anderson stated in a communication just received by Holt during the day of March 4th that he was likely to have to surrender within the next ten days. The only question seemed to be if and when South Carolina would begin firing on Fort Sumter.

Lincoln, after the briefing with Holt, probably appreciated a comment made by former President Buchanan and heard by White House staff that "he was the last President of the United States". Lincoln's option to maintain the union through conciliation with southern states would be shattered by the firing on Fort Sumter by South Carolina forces at 4:30 AM on April, 12, 1861.

When war finally came, the military resources available to President Lincoln were meager and scattered. The Army consisted of between 15,000 and 16,000 men largely stationed in small forts throughout the west protecting against Indian depredations. Other units were stationed in shoreline artillery posts, arsenals, and in various Army administrative staff bureaus. The army had not been engaged in large scale regimental and division size field engagements since the cessation of Mexican War hostilities in 1848.

Americans in 1861 were suspicious and distrustful of a professional military, and even the need for specialized military knowledge. Reliance for protection of citizens had been largely left to the states and their usually poorly organized and supplied citizen militias. The size of the Navy was relatively small, considering the United States was a leading commercial maritime nation. Unlike England and France, the United States had been slow in building steam warships and had totally rejected the construction of ironclad vessels. Most Americans simply had not seen the need nor desirability of financing a military establishment.

The Army in 1861

The Army in 1861 was led by Brevet-Lieutenant General Winfield Scott, a seventy-four year old officer unable to mount a horse and lead an army in the field. Another senior general was Brevet Major-General John Ellis Wool, two years older than Scott. Other colonels, later to be generals, were Edwin Vose (Bull) Sumner, Phillip St. George Cooke, and William Harney, all experienced Indian war fighters but out of their element commanding thousands of inexperienced officers and men. Most other senior colonels lacked extensive field experience, as their careers had been primarily in staff bureau positions. The dearth of younger senior officers was partially attributable to a seniority system lacking retirement pensions, causing officers to remain on active duty until disability or death, whichever came first. Accentuating the problem of senior officer supply was the resignation of many experienced and highly competent southern-born officers. Of 1,098 commissioned officers in the army on January 1861, fully 333 resigned and joined their state, and later the Confederate forces.

In general, a majority of remaining active senior officers were too old to assume prolonged field assignments and few possessed prior experience in leading larger than company size operations. A very few had been in regimental command during the Mexican War, where the total number of troops in action never exceeded 20,000. To make the situation worse, many experienced and younger regular army officers desired assignment in state volunteer units for appointments at higher rank. Who would lead the largely volunteer union army in the impending civil war? The answer would be a mixture of former regular army officers returning from civilian occupations, political appointees, and regular officers leaving the regular army and accepting volunteer appointments made by state governors. A few would be chosen directly by President Lincoln.

Putting the Union Army in the Field

When hostilities erupted in armed conflict, Lincoln had an immediate problem of centralizing the nation's scattered armed forces to locations where armed action was likely to occur. In April 1861, the Lincoln administration strongly felt that a Confederate movement on the capital, located between Maryland and Virginia—both slave holding states—was eminent. Prior to the surrender of Fort Sumter in April 1861, General Scott had informed President Lincoln only one or two regiments of regular infantry and several batteries of artillery could be immediately assembled to defend Washington. After the surrender of Fort Sumter, the formation of the union army began with an initial call to the states for 75,000 ninety day volunteers. This call for state troops by the national government was received with enthusiasm in states such as Massachusetts and bitterness in border states, such as Kentucky and Missouri. The rapid build-up of the Army from 16,000 men in April 1861 to nearly 575,000 by December 1861 put a tremendous administrative burden on state governors, the Secretary of War, and President Lincoln. The build-up of the huge federal army did not always go smoothly.

The basic organization of the 1861 Army prescribed by rules and regulations was a thousand men to a regiment, one hundred men in a company, and two to twelve regiments in a brigade. A division was to contain two to five brigades, and the Army was to contain as many divisions as necessary. The number of officers assigned to staff bureaus was also spelled out in the regulations, and in many respects the staff bureaus were a parallel organization under the command of their chiefs, who reported directly to the Secretary of War, not to the general-in-chief of the army.

The senior officer ranks consisted of full colonels to lead infantry regiments assisted by a lieutenant colonel and three majors. A senior colonel or brigadier-general was to lead a brigade. A division commander was to be a senior brigadier or a major-general. Senior major-generals were to lead forces larger than a division, usually an entire army. Later in the war, the creation of the corps structure changed the command ranks to include major-generals commanding a corps containing usually two to six divisions. The initial rapid expansion of the 1861 Army created an immediate need for dozens of brigadier generals and at least a dozen or more major-generals.

Lincoln quickly found the role of Commander-in-Chief of the Army and Navy to be one with few precedents and few if any written policies. Precisely what were the limits placed on the president to conduct a war voted on and funded by Congress? Fortunately after the surrender of Fort Sumter Congress was in recess, and Lincoln was able to utilize unprecedented executive initiatives in building a federal war machine to counter the rapid military build-up in states already or about ready to secede from the union.

The first call for 75,000 volunteers was, in actuality, a levy on the remaining states for military manpower. Each governor received a quota for his state in terms of men and regiments. The result was the establishment of recruiting efforts in each state accompanied by the construction of training installations supervised from the governor's office. The initial call for 75,000 volunteers was met within several weeks, and thousands of troops were immediately ordered to the defense of Washington.

Governors and the Call for Volunteers

Governors were the chief recruiters in organizing volunteer units. They appointed colonels to raise state regiments, or appointed colonels of regiments already raised often by those same colonels. In many instances they appointed former state militia colonels to lead regiments in state and later federal service. A few militia officers were appointed to be generals in state service. The process, in most if not all states, was haphazard and prone to extreme politics. Some regimental colonels were selected from older officers having served long ago as company grade officers in the Mexican War. Other colonels appointed were West Point educated, having left the Army prior to the beginning of the Civil War. Colonels and field grade officers were governor appointed, but many officers were democratically elected by the vote of soldiers in their company or regiment. This was not an illogical practice, considering that most Americans did not feel that a military education and experience was necessary to be a qualified field commander.

Most appointees possessed an absolute minimum of military and field experience. Many governors used military appointments to reward political supporters, or to gain the support of political opponents. In states like New York, Pennsylvania, Wisconsin, and Illinois, immigrant groups of Germans and Irish were influential voter groups, and governors courted them with regimental colonel appointments. Many of these Irish and German colonels would later become generals. Governors needed to use political patronage to not only solidify their positions as "war" governors, but also to draw into the Army significant numbers of senior officers, often leaders in their towns and counties not particularly favoring the war prior to the firing on Fort Sumter. This was especially true in states with large numbers of Democratic voters. Many Democrats were strongly opposed to secession but not strongly opposed to slavery. Some Democrats viewed the war as a Republican war brought about by radical abolitionist sentiment in New England states. The governors were very mindful of the patriotism of men answering the call to the colors, while at the same time seeking the support of those skeptical about the war. An effective strategy to bring in the skeptics was to appoint leaders in their community to raise and lead local regiments despite them knowing little or anything about soldiering and warfare.

Many of the regiment level colonels appointed in the first 1861 call for volunteers would go on and become major-generals later in the war, leading brigades, divisions, and even corps. Others for reasons such as age, health, business interests, and political ambitions served only a few months and resigned after the first ninety day call up. A good number of these civilian colonels resigned once they saw how lacking they were in qualifications and taste for military campaigns and hardships. Their places were often filled by younger lieutenant-colonels and majors often possessing prior military education and background

In the early weeks and months of the war General-in-Chief Winfield Scott and the War Department, under Secretary of War Simon Cameron, would seldom allow officers in the regular army to transfer to state raised volunteer units; their rationale being the war was going to be of short duration, and regular army officers were needed to serve with their regiments as they expanded. Only later did the government realize that regular officers possessed the skills and experiences to quickly and better prepare for battle the hundreds of state raised regiments. These same junior grade officers often later became brigade and division commanders in the volunteer forces. Officers remaining with regular army regiments for the course of the war were relatively few. The regular army units were not able to successfully recruit due to stricter discipline, longer enlistment periods, and a lack of bonus incentives offered by most states. Their low numbers also restricted the promotion of officers.

Although governors appointed regimental colonels prior to the regiment being accepted into national service, only the president could appoint and the Senate confirm general officers to serve in state volunteer units mustered into federal service. This did not discourage many of the governors from placing political pressure on the Lincoln administration, the Secretary of War, and their state's congressional delegation to appoint and confirm favored candidates. These were officers residing in their state or those already serving in a state regiment. Oftentimes Democratic governors urged the appointment of Democratic officers, and Republican governors looked for officers with political feelings akin to those of the Republicans in their state. As mentioned earlier, in some states governors catered to immigrant groups and made sure that Irish and German regiments had popular and politically connected Irish and German colonels.

The governors often used their appointing powers to also reward lesser party faithfuls to the lower officer ranks. In summary, the initial call up began the process that would recruit and draft eventually 2,300,000 men to bear arms in the Federal army.

Union Generals

There is no precise count as to how many substantive general officers served in the union army. This is due to the rapidity of appointments and slowness and confusion in the confirmation process. The use of brevet rank also confuses a final tabulation of the number of generals. A few extraordinary cases exist where an officer served in a position reserved for a general without obtaining presidential appointment or Senate confirmation, but nonetheless is referred to as a general in historical sources. The best current source citing who and who was not a full substantive general officer in the union army is *Civil War High Commanders*, authored and compiled by John Eicher and David Eicher. The numbers given by the Eichers is between 554 and 564. Ezra Warner, in his classic work *Generals in Blue*, identifies and writes biographical sketches on 583 union generals. The lists of Warner and the Eichers do not always agree with each other as to who was fully appointed and confirmed. Both Warner and the Eichers do not include the very few state militia generals that served in regular assignments but were never fully mustered into federal volunteer service.

Brevet Rank

The use of brevet rank is one of the most confusing aspects of identifying full substantive general officers. Brevet (nominal) rank was conferred upon officers for army command efficiency, valor and extraordinary service. Additional pay usually accompanied the brevet. Occasionally, brevet rank was given an officer so he could temporarily serve in a position calling for general rank, or to avoid having subordinates possessing similar rank or more seniority. In these cases the brevet system was used by senior commanders to avoid the slowness of "bureaucracy" in Washington. Federal officers receiving brevet promotions were allowed to wear that rank insignia and be addressed by that rank. Many times it was confusing to know what real rank an officer actually held.

Roger Hunt, in *Brevet Brigadier Generals in Blue*, found 1,367 union officers receiving brevets as generals but never given full substantive rank. Many of these promotions occurred during the omnibus promotions in March 1865 or shortly after the end of the war. Some were awarded posthumously, some for gallantry, and others for exceptional service in staff bureaus. A good many were awarded for political reasons, an example being of an officer never serving above the rank of major being breveted a brigadier-general. Each of the officers listed by Hunt was never confirmed with full rank as a brigadier-general. However, each step of the appointment and confirmation process was taken by President Lincoln (or President Andrew Johnson) and the Senate in awarding them the brevet rank of brigadier-general. Some officers receiving the brevet rank of brigadier-general also received a brevet as a major-general. Many confirmed brigadier-generals with full substantive rank also received brevets as a major-general. The bulk of the brevets awarded for brigadier-generals and major-generals were in the volunteer service, rather than the regular Army. In 1865, a number of full rank major-generals in the volunteers with West Point backgrounds received brevets in the regular Army. Many of these officers remained in the army after the Civil War commanding regiments, departments, or serving in staff assignments.

Many Civil War writers criticize the use of brevet ranks, as they were often used to reward officers with political supporters during and after the war. Actually, many times they provided the government flexibility in officer assignments and provided rewards and reinforcement for exemplary service. At the time of the Civil War, the federal army had few medals for gallantry or service for officers, and a brevet was an effective reward for meritorious conduct or bravery.

Appointment Process Leading to Conformation for Brigadier and Major Generals

The formal recommendation for an officer to be made a general by regulations originated with superior officers. However governors, congressmen, and cabinet officers frequently petitioned President Lincoln and the Secretary of War to make an appointment. The recommendations from senior officers were accompanied by letters of support. The proposals were forwarded to the General-in-Chief of the Army and later in the war to Major-General Henry Halleck in his role as Chief of Staff. The General-in-Chief then either endorsed the appointment proposal or sent it to the Secretary of War without a supporting endorsement. The two wartime Secretaries of War, Simon Cameron and Edwin Stanton, were the gatekeepers for appointments. If the Secretary of War did not accept the endorsement of the General-in-Chief the appointment was usually dead and buried. In a number of cases President Lincoln, directly with or without conferring with the Secretary of War, appointed generals.

An example of President Lincoln making a unilateral appointment was the deathbed appointment of Gettysburg hero Brigadier-General John Buford. Posthumous appointments were not uncommon, as Lincoln often desired to reward officers gallantly making a final sacrifice for their country.

In most cases the Senate confirmed President Lincoln's appointments. The number of regular appointments was fewer than brevet appointments. A number of general officer appointments early in the war were made on a non-procedural basis, meaning that normal protocols were not always followed. Chaos is perhaps the most appropriate word to describe Army personnel actions during the first months of the war.

Early in the war Lincoln made numerous direct brigadier-general appointments subject to much later Senate confirmation, as the number of brigades needing general officers increased almost weekly. The Senate confirmation process was slow and tedious, and never kept pace with the need of providing general officers for the army in the field. It was not uncommon for one of President Lincoln's appointments to expire, as there was a set period of time required for the confirmation to be made by the Senate. Sometimes Lincoln resubmitted the nomination to the Senate, and on several occasions the Senate ignored time limits so as to effectively disqualify an appointee.

General officers were frequently seriously wounded, contracted serious illnesses, or resigned. The number of wounds suffered by some federal major-generals clearly demonstrates they were leading their divisions and corps from the front. The high casualty rates among all general officers resulted in a high turnover rate and an opportunity for President Lincoln to appoint generals from a pool of recommended colonels. Occasionally, a brigadier-general would be appointed from below the rank of colonel. An excellent example of Lincoln accepting a field commander's recommendation for promotion of lower rank officers is the promotion of Captains George Custer, Elon Farnsworth, and Wesley Merritt, all appointed brigadier-generals upon the recommendation of General Alfred Pleasanton, Chief of Cavalry for the Army of the Potomac. President Lincoln agreed with Pleasanton that the Army of Potomac cavalry needed a strong injection of youth into its regimental leadership ranks.

The last step in the proposal/appointment process was the acceptance of the appointment by the candidate. This was usually done in a written document sworn to by the applicant. Once the acceptance document was received by the Secretary of War the nomination process was complete and the Senate confirmation process was initiated.

The Confirmation Process

While steps in the appointment process might be disregarded on rare occasion, the steps to confirm the appointee were adhered to as they were specified in statute. Some nominations went through the confirmation process quickly and easily, while others created political furor and suffered long delays.

The first step in the formal confirmation process was the formal nomination by the President. This was a written request to the Senate Committee on Military Affairs, chaired during the war by Senator Henry Wilson of Massachusetts. The nomination then received a committee hearing and vote before being forwarded to the full Senate. The usual outcome was Senate support for Lincoln's nominations, especially for major-generals. Lincoln, the consummate politician, usually knew when a nomination would be dead on arrival in the Senate. Of the major-generals, one hundred-twenty-four were appointed and fully confirmed. Nine of Lincoln's major-general appointments were withdrawn, revoked, or not confirmed. Several appointments to major- general were not confirmed until after the end of hostilities in April 1865.

Following a confirmation vote by the Senate, the Adjutant General of the Army engrossed and registered the appointment and forwarded it to the Secretary of War for sealing and signature by President Lincoln.

The Political Process

Governors usually appointed officers in state units above the rank of captain before the unit was mustered into federal service. These appointments were entirely state affairs. However, once a colonel in federal service was proposed to President Lincoln for a general's star by a senior federal officer, there often occurred lobbying by the prospective general's state governor, his friends back home, and even national political party leaders. The lobbying not only was directed at President Lincoln and the Secretary of War, but also toward the state congressional delegation. During the war, the Senate contained only thirty-four members, with six serving on the Military Affairs Committee.

Most of the "war" governors desired to have as many native sons as possible serving as general officers in corps, divisions, and brigades containing regiments from their respective states. The governors also needed at times to have high profile general officers from their states journey home and assist in raising new regiments and garner votes for state and congressional elections. In 1864, many popular generals returned home and campaigned for Lincoln's reelection. Popular major-generals also possessed political influence that could be used to continue support of the war effort in their state and influence national policy debates.

An example was Republican Illinois Governor Richard Yates' periodic leave requests for Major-Generals John Logan and John McClernand. Logan, an early war Democrat, was instrumental in keeping southern Illinois loyal to the union. McClernand, also a Democrat, was a strong influence in recruiting and keeping a steady flow of manpower from Illinois to the Union army. Both supported Lincoln's reelection.

Lincoln's cabinet officers often acted as lobbyists for appointment and confirmation of major-generals of their choice. Even more often they lobbied Lincoln to make command changes involving major-generals. A good example of a cabinet officer lobbying for an appointment is that of Secretary of the Treasury Salmon Chase's support for General George McClellan. An example of Lincoln's cabinet officers' involvement in a command change was after the Battle of Antietam, when Secretary of War Edwin Stanton, Secretary of State William Seward, Postmaster Montgomery Blair, and Chase all lobbied Lincoln to remove McClellan as the commander of the Army of the Potomac.

Of a less positive nature was the influence and frequent interference in the appointment, confirmation, and assignment of generals by the Congressional Committee on the Conduct of the War led by Senators Benjamin Wade of Ohio and Zachariah Chandler of Michigan. Members of the committee were influential in forcing the Lincoln Administration to remove Army of the Potomac Commanders George McClellan and Ambrose Burnside. After Burnsides' removal they strongly advocated the appointment of General Joseph Hooker to command the Army of the Potomac. Following Hooker's failure at the Battle of Chancellorsville, Lincoln ignored the committee in selecting General George Meade to lead the Army of the Potomac.

After the federal victory at the Battle of Gettysburg, the Committee severely criticized and nearly caused the removal of General George Meade for his not pursuing Lee's army. In a series of committee hearings shortly after the battle, committee members who were strong supporters of General Dan Sickles, a vociferous critic of Meade's generalship at Gettysburg, castigated Meade and demanded that Lincoln replace him. The intrusion of the committee likely distracted Meade from his eventual campaign to follow Lee into Virginia. Another outcome was the committee's influence in holding up Meade's promotion to full major-general rank until it was demanded in 1864 by General-in-Chief Ulysses Grant. Through the device of committee hearings the committee was able to censure selected federal commanders and place blame on these commanders for battlefield losses.

Once Major-General Ulysses Grant was appointed and confirmed as General-in-Chief of the Army, interference with the appointment of generals by the Committee on the Conduct of the War diminished. Federal victories by Grant and the Army of the Potomac, along with the victories at Vicksburg, Chattanooga, and Atlanta blunted the fangs and power of the committee. However, Michigan general Orlando Wilcox complained that the hostility of Senator Zachariah Chandler, also of Michigan, and a key committee member kept him from being promoted to major-general during the war.

Fortunately for President Lincoln, appointments of major-generals were, for the most part, promotions based on successful performance in the field or in a prominent staff role. Excellent performances by political or civilian generals John Logan, Francis Blair, John McClernand, David Birney, Francis Barlow, and Jacob Cox clearly demonstrated civilians could be effective fighting generals. On the other hand, political appointees such as Nathaniel Banks, Benjamin Butler, Franz Sigel, Robert Schenck, Robert Milroy, James Shields, David Hunter, and John Fremont showed that civilian and political appointees could be incompetent major-generals in the field, even though possessing some prior military experience.

A frequent lobby effort for the appointment to general rank was by the officers themselves. Army tradition and regulations discouraged officers lobbying for promotion, but few prospective generals did not, at some time, write directly to their state governors, congressmen, and even President Lincoln asking for support for promotion or for new field commands. Officers having served in the regular army appeared to do less of this than officers with civilian backgrounds. In some cases regular army officers not willing to blow their own horns were slow to gain promotions.

Some like Major-General Robert Milroy of Indiana constantly badgered Lincoln first for promotion, and then for a new field command after being soundly defeated at the Second Battle of Winchester. Milroy thought that Henry Halleck, then General-in-Chief, hated him. Another Indiana Major General, Lew Wallace, felt that General Ulysses Grant's personal animosity kept him from being assigned to an important field command after making a grave error in judgment at the Battle of Shiloh.

All through the war Lincoln was reminded daily that not only were states' rights a political issue in the south, but also in the northern states when it came to which Army officers should be appointed to be generals and which units they should command. Governors, Republican and Democratic Party officials, members of Congress, business men, and even prominent clergy lobbied for the interests of their favorite generals.

The Photographic Image Captures the Civil War

The American Civil War was the first to be extensively photographed. Prior to 1860, photography had been limited to one-of-a-kind daguerreotypes, ambrotypes, and tintypes. With the development of a camera that could take a glass plate from which a number of images could be cheaply printed, the millions of printed cartes de visite *provided a contemporary visual picture of the war and its participants. The* cartes de visite *took the battlefield into homes both in the north and the south.*

The Civil War period photographs illustrated in this book are all original period *cartes de visite*. A *carte de visite* (cdv) is an albumen paper photographic print pasted on a cardstock about two and three-quarter inches by four inches. The image size is about two and an eighth inches by three and a half inches. The popular *carte de visite* originated in France before its introduction in America between 1855-1860. These photographic images the size of a typical French visiting card became immensely popular throughout America, as friends and families exchanged cards, often placing them in specially made albums. Earlier forms of photography, such as the daguerreotype and the ambrotype, were more expensive and very fragile. Another inexpensive image was that of the tintype. However, it could not be reproduced in quantity. Many soldiers had only one tintype made. The paper mounted *carte de visite* was inexpensive and easy to store, and could be safely sent through the mail. Today, they are a popular collectible for Civil War and photographic collectors.

The Civil War CDV *Carte de Visite*

By the beginning of the Civil War, a number of regular army and naval officers had sat for a *carte de visite*. Some had instructed photographers to transfer their image from a daguerreotype or ambrotype into a *carte* print. A good example of a general sitting for an early *carte* was General Winfield Scott, who posed for Matthew Brady in 1860. The popular hero of Fort Sumter, Major Robert Anderson's *carte* was produced by the thousands in the first months of the war.

Once thousands of soldiers both north and south joined the ranks, loved ones and friends wanted to have a "likeness" taken. Newly enlisted soldiers by the thousands had their *cartes* taken to leave behind with family and friends. In the south, where there were fewer photographers, soldiers were less likely to leave an image behind for their families and friends to remember them by. Also, more of the images that Confederate soldiers took to war were older types of photography, such as the ambrotype or tintype.

Not only did soldiers and officers have their *carte de visite* image taken in a hometown studio, but also in locations where they served in garrison. There were many photographers that traveled by wagon with the army. Perhaps a majority of *cartes* of generals available today, and seen in Civil War publications, were published by a handful of well-known photographic studios in Washington, New York, Boston, and Philadelphia. Studios in Louisville, Chicago, Cincinnati, Columbus, St. Louis, and Nashville also published and distributed *cartes* of generals in the western theater, but in fewer numbers than in the populous east.

Often soldiers sent home *cartes de visite* of messmates and their regimental officers and favorite commanding generals for the family to put into either a company or regimental album. Most of these albums contain *cartes de visite* of one or more popular generals. The *cartes* of early in the war popular generals, such as McClellan and Burnside, were often purchased by family members from fancy goods stores. It seems as if almost every album contains a *carte* of General George McClellan, Army of the Potomac Commander, who was very popular with his soldiers, even though very unpopular with the Lincoln administration.

Many generals were quite delighted to have commercial photographers selling large numbers of images showing them in uniform. This was especially true for elected politicians now serving as general officers. Two excellent examples of politicians turned generals were Benjamin Butler and Nathaniel Banks. Their *cartes* are among the most common and least expensive. Though most generals were happy to see their photographs distributed across the country, there were a few, usually career officers, who were reluctant to frequently sit for commercial photographers. The number of major-generals in this group is small, and collectors may only be able to find one or two views that were commercially distributed.

By the beginning of the Civil War, *cartes de visite* were being commercially made and widely sold by photographic studios in New York, Boston, Philadelphia, Washington, Chicago, Louisville, New Orleans, Savannah, Charleston, Baltimore and Richmond. Some of the most encountered photographic studios selling images of Union major-generals were: Brady, Gardner, Whitehurst, and Addis in Washington; Gutenorst and Appleton in Philadelphia; Black and Whipple in Boston; Fredricks and Gurney in New York; Webster in Louisville; Fassett in Chicago; and Morse in Nashville.

Correspondence by federal generals and other officers sometimes mention sending or receiving *cartes* of fellow officers. Often mentioned is the sending of *cartes* home, or asking those at home to have more copies of their *carte* made. The *cartes* were usually purchased by the dozen. An officer could usually buy a dozen cards costing from a dollar to three dollars. The commercial cards produced by dealers like E.H. Anthony in New York were cheap and available in retail stores across the federal states. Dealers such as Anthony and Fredricks in New York published catalogs listing a hundred or more popular or well-known union generals. The Webster studio in Louisville, on the backs of some of its commercial *cartes*, listed the names of generals and colonels available for purchase.

The commercial popularity of a general's *carte* usually rested on his war record or even his death. Early in the war the *cartes* of popular or well-known major-generals like Ambrose Burnside, Irvin McDowell, George McClellan, Ormsby Mitchell, Don Carlos Buell, Quincy Gilmore, and Ben Butler sold in the thousands. Later in the war popular generals for *carte* buyers were Ulysses Grant, William T. Sherman, Dan Sickles, Joseph Hooker, Henry Halleck, and George Thomas. Due to the large number of *cartes* published of these generals they can be easily purchased at Civil War shows, on internet sites, or at traditional auction houses.

More obscure major generals are harder to find and usually bring higher prices. An example would be Major General John Reynolds, who was killed at Gettysburg. Apparently Reynolds sat for only one or two photographic views. Most *cartes* seen on the market of Reynolds show only a mid-chest view. Occasionally a full profile view is encountered. Another popular "Gettysburg" general is Joshua Chamberlain, whose *carte* sells for thousands of dollars.

Values of the *Cartes de visite*

The dollar value of a Civil War general *carte* is dependent upon a number of variables. Some generals may be purchased for $100, while others may cost up to $5,000. The variables that determine the price are:

Condition

The condition of a *carte* is very important, as it is a visual antique. The most frequent distraction to condition is the clipping of the corners for insertion into an album. The most serious problem in clipping is when the clip destroys part of the actual albumen paper photograph. A rough estimate is that substantial clipping and trimming can often cut the value of a *carte* by half.

Another condition issue is soiling from oily and greasy fingers. Often owners handled the cards, perhaps passing them around the parlor on a Sunday afternoon. Other *cartes* show moisture damage called "foxing", seriously reducing their monetary value. Period ink writing on a *carte* may or may not degrade the value; if on the back it is less a problem. An old ink inscription of the general's name is usually not a problem.

Another condition factor is the coloring and shading of the *carte*. Some are very light sepia toned, while others are much darker in tone and shade. In most cases collectors prefer the darker tones and shades. Some photographic studios, such as Alexander Gardner in Washington, seemed always to produce *cartes* that are light sepia toned.

A very difficult part of *carte* collecting is identifying the photographer that actually took the original negative. E.H. Anthony in New York published thousands of *cartes*, but perhaps took few original plates. Matthew Brady's studios in New York and Washington usually have a back mark identifying Brady as the photographer and Anthony as the distributor. Some studios, such as E.H. Anthony in New York, published catalogs showing *cartes* of hundreds of union and Confederate generals for sale.

The degree of resolution in the *carte* is sometimes a clue whether the name on the back mark is really the photographer. The author feels that glass plate negatives were often exchanged for commercial purposes from one photographic studio to another. Also, it appears the major photographic studios, despite copyright notices sometimes printed on the *cartes*, copied freely from other studios. The greater resolution or clarity in the *carte* demands a higher value. Perhaps the least desirable and cheapest *cartes* are taken from engravings printed in the same size as an albumen *carte*. Collectors should look very carefully at a *carte* before purchasing to make sure it is not from an engraving.

Rarity

The rarity of a *carte* of course is important, but not the single arbitrator of value. The *cartes* of many brigadier and major-generals are quite rare, but of marginal interest to collectors and therefore do not bring top prices. Other general's cartes are not particularly rare but bring extremely high prices. A good example is George Custer, an extremely desirable *carte* obtainable in many different poses. Most of the fully confirmed major-general *cartes* are not especially rare and valuable. Some of the exceptions to this are *cartes* of Francis Barlow, George Crook, John Gibbon, Benjamin Grierson, Francis Fessenden, Cadwallader Washburn, Edwin Morgan, Nelson Miles, John Reynolds, and Wager Swayne. Apparently, commercial photographic studios, for whatever reason, did not print large quantities of these generals' *cartes*, one possible reason being they were promoted late in the war or just did not gain much notoriety in the newspapers. Also, generals from more populous states might have more buyers.

Of very high interest to collectors are those *cartes* signed by the major-general. The value of these autographed *cartes* can be many times the value of an unsigned one. Collectors usually prefer to have the general's autograph on the front of the card. Almost all the generals signed their *cartes* using the army regulation signature format.

Perhaps among the rarest of *cartes* are those a major-general may have had made by a home town photographer to be given just to his family and friends. Sometimes these home town images were picked up and copied for commercial use, but often they were not.

Quality of the View (Pose)

Most civil war generals' *cartes* show one of three poses: full standing, full sitting, or from the chest up. Often the full standing and sitting poses show the general in a full field uniform with a sword. Occasionally, the general is shown in a fancy uniform with shoulder epaulets and dress sword. Even rarer are views that feature elaborate background props, such as chairs, tables, flags, and wooden pillars. Very rarely seen are outdoor views, or with other generals or personages. The more elaborate the uniform and studio setting the more attractive the *carte* is to collectors. *Cartes* showing a general with his staff are also desirable and bring a significant premium. Desirable to some collectors are *cartes* showing the general with his wife or family. The studio of Matthew Brady also published a number of montages of brigadier and major-generals. One often commented upon pose is one where a general has a hand stuck into his tunic imitating Napoleon Bonaparte.

The least desirable *carte* poses are head or chest up views. Even less desirable are poorly made second generation views. These *cartes* have been marginally copied by a photographer from another *carte* and not from the original glass plate. Copies sometimes show a reasonable amount of resolution, meaning the viewer can see details on the uniform buttons and stars on the shoulder straps. The buyer of a *carte* should usually look for a desirable view with good resolution, color tone, back mark, and absence of clipping to the mount.

Back Marks and Tax Stamps

On the back of many *cartes* of Civil War generals is a back mark identifying photographers or studios. Some back marks show elaborate designs, including flags and patriotic motifs. However, a majority of Civil War period *carte* back marks are rather plain. The value and desirability of a *carte* is enhanced by a back mark.

The back marks from the studios, such as Brady and Alexander Gardner, are valued by collectors and increase the value of a *carte*. The same can be said for photographer back marks locating the photographer in a field setting, such as at Vicksburg, Mississippi; Nashville, Tennessee; Corinth, Mississippi; New Orleans, Louisiana; or Louisville, Kentucky.

In 1864, the federal government imposed a tax on *cartes de visite* and other sundry goods to raise revenue to support the war. A two cent tax was levied on photographs selling for less than twenty-five cents, a three cent tax on those up to fifty cents, and five cents for those selling up to a dollar. The majority of *cartes* have a two or three cent revenue stamp. The stamps were supposed to be cancelled, but this often was not done by the photographer. The presence of a stamp indicates the *carte* was likely sold in either 1864 or 1865. The end of the war did not bring an end to publishing the *cartes* of Civil War generals, nor did it bring an end to the stamp tax.

Collecting Specialties

Civil War *carte* collectors often focus their collections on particular regiments, divisions, corps, army, or battle. A very strong field in union *carte* collecting focuses on the Battle of Gettysburg. A significant number of major-generals participated in the battle, but the more desirable *cartes* are those of brigadier generals commanding brigades and colonels leading key regiments.

Probably, collectors of generals' *cartes* either favor the eastern or western theaters of the war. Collectors living in eastern states seem to be most interested in the Army of the Potomac containing units mostly raised in New England, Pennsylvania, New York, and New Jersey. Many midwestern collectors are generally divided in their interest between the Army of the Tennessee, Army of the Cumberland, and Army of the Ohio. A smaller number of collectors specialize in *cartes* of generals fighting in the far western theater in Missouri, Kansas, and Indian Territory.

The collecting of *cartes* encourages many collectors to read widely in Civil War literature featuring the role the generals they hold in their collection played. A significant number of the major-generals are the subjects of biographies currently available from booksellers or online.

***Cates de Visite* in this Book**

All of the *cartes* contained in this book are in the author's personal collection. The first was purchased in 1992 at the Abraham Lincoln Bookstore in Chicago. The others have been acquired at Civil War shows or from dealers, auctions, or websites.

Lincoln's Major-Generals Their Military Careers and Lives

Armies are comprised of privates and generals. In the four years of the American Civil War more than several Federal generals rose from being privates to fully appointed and confirmed generals. Other generals came from West Point backgrounds, political positions, the professions, farming, and business. Americans both in the north and south could read about the generals in newspapers, and in some cases view them in newspaper woodcuts or engravings. However, the inexpensive carte de visite *provided a crystal clear image of the men leading their husbands, sons, relatives and friends in battle. The* carte de visite *additionally provided Americans with images of their national leaders in politics, theater, religion, and the arts.*

Augur, Christopher. *Carte de visite* by Brady, Washington. Author's Collection

AUGUR

Augur, Christopher. *Carte de visite* by Anthony, New York. Author's Collection

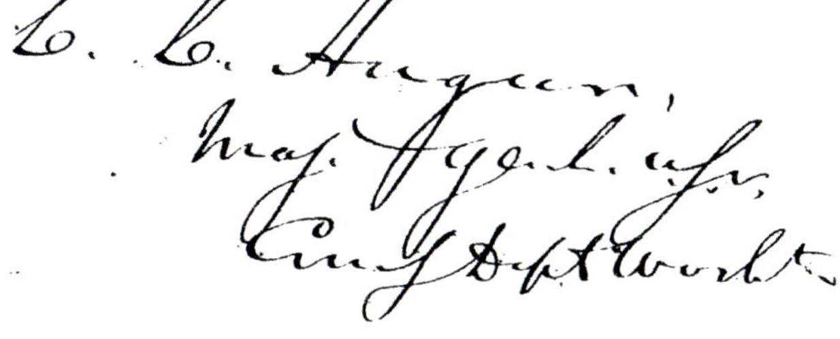

Augur, Christopher Columbus (1821-1898) Augur was born in New York but moved to Michigan with his widowed mother. He was appointed to the United States Military Academy in 1839 and graduated sixteenth of thirty-nine in the class of 1843. Thirteen of the graduates of his class became full generals: ten in the union army and three in the Confederate army. He was commissioned in the 2nd Infantry and served routine garrison duty until the commencement of the war with Mexico in 1846. He fought at the battles of Palo Alto and Resaca de la Palma and served as aide de camp to generals Hopping and Cushing. After the Mexican War, Auger was assigned in the 1850s to various frontier assignments in Oregon and Washington subduing hostile Indian tribes. In 1852, he received promotion to captain in the 4th Infantry, and in May 1861 to major in the 13th Infantry. In August 1861 he was appointed as Commandant of Cadets at the United Military States Academy. After leaving the Military Academy in December 1861 he received an appointment as a brigadier general of volunteers to command the 1st brigade in McDowell's division of General Nathaniel Bank's II Corps based along the Rappahannock line near Fredericksburg supporting McClellan's 1862 Virginia Peninsular Campaign. In August 1862, he was severely wounded in the rout of the federal army at the Battle of Cedar Mountain resulting from Bank's poor decision to attack General Stonewall Jackson. His gallantry and leadership at Cedar Mountain won him a brevet to colonel in the regular army and an appointment to major-general of volunteers. While recovering in Washington he served on a Military Court investigating the humiliating surrender of the Harpers Ferry garrison by Colonel Dixon Miles that had taken place during the Antietam Campaign. In November 1862, Augur was assigned as second in command of General Nathaniel Bank's Expedition to New Orleans. First in command of the District of Baton Rouge, he later commanded the left wing of Banks Army during the action at Port Hudson Plains and the later siege of Port Hudson. For his performance at Port Hudson in July 1863 he received a brevet to brigadier general in the regular army and promotion to Lieutenant Colonel of the 12th United States Infantry. In October 1863, Augur returned to Washington as President of Military Commissions, simultaneously commanding the XXII Corps and the Department of Washington. While serving in the Washington defenses, his command in conjunction with General Horatio Wright's VI Corps repulsed Confederate General Jubal Early's attack on the capital on July 11-12, 1864. He was appointed regimental Colonel of the 12th Infantry in March 1866 and brigadier general in the regular army in 1869. Augur served as department commander in the Department of the Platte from 1867 to 1871, and in the Department of Texas from 1872 to 1875. After the Civil War he was assigned to negotiate the Medicine Lodge Treaty in 1867 and the Fort Laramie Treaty in 1868. Augur, while a competent field general, was especially noted for his administrative abilities. He retired in 1885.

Augur, Christopher. *Carte de visite* by Brady, Washington. Author's Collection

BAKER

Baker, Edward. *Carte de visite by* Henszey, Philadelphia. A rare view of Baker in uniform. Author's collection.

Baker, Edward Dickinson (1811-1861) Born in London, England, he came to the United States as a child and spent his early years living in Illinois. He served in the Black Hawk War as a private and later moved to Springfield, studied law, and was admitted to the bar. While in Springfield he entered politics and became a close friend of fellow Whig Abraham Lincoln, whom he defeated in a contest for a Congressional seat. Baker was an orator of great skill, and perhaps just as politically ambitious as his friend Lincoln, who named his second son after Baker. He was a strong supporter of expansion and served in the Mexican War as colonel of the 4th Illinois. He received praise for leadership of his regiment at the Battle of Cerro Gordo. He returned to Illinois and held various political posts until 1852, when he moved at the request of the Republican Party to California and became a Republican force in the new state. However, he was unable to win political office due to the dominance of Democrats. In 1860 Baker moved to Oregon, which had just been admitted to the union in 1859. Shortly, with the support of Douglas Democrats, he became a U.S. Senator from that state. In the period before the outbreak of war Baker worked tirelessly to build support for the union cause in the Pacific states and stayed in constant contact with his friend Lincoln. Baker, from his Senate seat, advocated for the tenets of the Peace Convention and opposed the Crittenden Compromise. At the beginning of the war Baker declined a brigadier-general's appointment from his friend Lincoln, as he wished to remain in the Senate. However, under law he was allowed to serve as Colonel of the 71st Pennsylvania Volunteers, often referred to as the 1st California Volunteers. As colonel, he commanded a brigade in General Charles Stone's Division in the Army of the Potomac and was killed in the disastrous Battle of Ball's Bluff. Baker, perhaps thinking about a quick victory and political notoriety, crossed his troops over the Potomac on a planned demonstration movement that turned into a disaster when he placed his brigade in an exposed position atop Balls Bluff. Baker was quickly killed and his stricken troops were swept off the bluff, many drowning in the river below. Many bodies were later recovered downstream at the Washington docks. The day before the battle Lincoln and Baker had spent much of the day resting on the White House lawn. Lincoln was desolated by the death of his friend and posthumously appointed him a major-general. The appointment was not brought before the Senate for confirmation. The blame for Baker's fiasco was laid on General Stone, who was arbitrarily arrested and held without trial for six months. The illegal imprisonment of Stone was most likely a solitary action on the part of Secretary of War Edwin Stanton. Stone's patriotism was also questioned by the Congressional Committee on the Conduct of the War, which was unwilling to blame Ball's Bluff on their colleague Baker.

Baker, Edward. *Carte de visite* by Anthony, New York. Author's collection.

BANKS

Banks, Nathaniel. *Carte de visite* by Brady, Washington. Author's Collection

Banks, Nathaniel. *Carte de visite* by Fredricks, New York. Author's Collection

Banks, Nathaniel Prentice (1816-1894) Born in Waltham, Massachusetts, a cotton mill town, Banks as a teenager worked as a machinist in a mill superintended by his father. This work was the source of his political nickname, the "Bobbin Boy". He received a common education, became a newspaper editor, studied law, and was admitted to the bar. He was elected in 1849 to the legislature after three unsuccessful attempts. By 1851, he was speaker of the Massachusetts lower house. In 1853, he was elected as a Democrat to the United States Congress. Banks was to serve an additional nine terms under five different political party affiliations, including the Know-Nothings, Free-Soilers, and Democrats before joining the Republican party. In 1856, after 133 ballots, he was elected Speaker of the U.S. House of Representatives, then engaged in constant conflict over the institution of slavery and its expansion into new territories. Banks was a moderate in the sectional debates, and for whatever reason left Congress in 1858 to run and be elected Governor of Massachusetts, serving until 1860, when he became President of the Illinois Central Railroad. In 1861, newly elected Abraham Lincoln appointed him a major-general of volunteers, much to the consternation of many career Army officers. Among the first of the generals appointed for political rather than military reasons, Banks was influential in raising troops and political support from non-Republican New Englanders. However, his military acumen and expertise were sadly lacking, and General Stonewall Jackson nearly destroyed him in the summer of 1862. His forces that were assigned to guard the Shenandoah Valley were defeated and left behind a veritable horde of supplies for the Confederates. However Banks escaped capture, and with the remainder of his command joined General John Pope and the Army of Virginia. In another case of poor judgment he attacked General Stonewall Jackson, and in August 1862 was soundly defeated at the Battle of Cedar Mountain. Following the disaster at Cedar Mountain Banks was assigned to the defenses of Washington, but Lincoln soon appointed him to succeed another political general, Benjamin Butler, as commander of the Department of the Gulf, headquartered in New Orleans. Lincoln may have perceived Banks' New Orleans appointment to be as much political as military. Banks was able to restore some political peace in New Orleans left behind by Butler, but his campaign to capture Port Hudson resulted in heavy losses. However, once Grant captured Vicksburg on July 4, 1863, the Confederate garrison at Port Hudson surrendered in five days. Banks' military government in New Orleans was partially successful in initiating reconstruction efforts in Louisiana, but he was accused of spending a great amount of time and effort in searching for contraband cotton. In early1864, Banks sealed his military fate by bungling the ill-fated Red River Campaign. He was soundly defeated by Confederate General Richard Taylor with fewer forces at the Battle of at Sabine Cross-Road and the following Battle of Pleasant Hill. Despite having the assistance of a powerful Union naval force, Banks again demonstrated that he could not plan and execute a successful military campaign. The disaster on the Red River could have resulted in the total destruction of the cooperating Federal navy when the water level of the Red River above Alexandria suddenly fell, threatening to ground the fleet. Fortunately, Colonel Joseph Bailey was able to engineer an escape for the fleet, allowing it to descend down the Mississippi River along with Banks' battered army.

After the Red River Campaign Lincoln "shelved" Banks and replaced him with a career officer, General E.R.S. Canby, as Commander of the Department of the Gulf. Lincoln deemed it politically unwise to dismiss Banks, and instead gave him a minimal command in the Washington area. Banks resigned in August 1865. He then returned to his profession as an opportunistic politician and was immediately elected to Congress, where he served six terms, after which he returned to the Massachusetts legislature and served nine years as United States Marshall for Massachusetts. General Henry Halleck, Army Chief of Staff, once remarked that sending troops to battle under political generals like Banks and Butler was nothing less than murder. Lincoln was well aware of the military shortcomings of political generals like Nathaniel Banks, but he was also well aware of the battle on the home front to keep political support, supplies, money, and troops moving to the Union army.

BARLOW

Barlow, Francis. *Carte de visite* by Anthony, New York Author's Collection

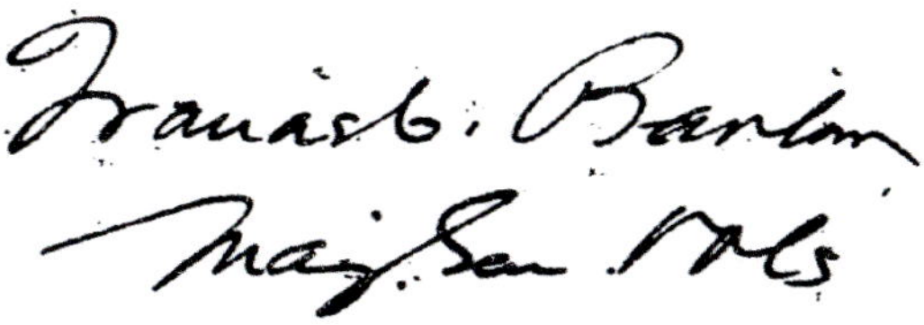

Barlow, Francis Channing (1834-1896) Although born in Brooklyn, New York, the son of a minister, he was raised in Brookline, Massachusetts. Barlow graduated from Harvard University and moved to New York, where he studied and practiced law in New York City. He frequently wrote for the *New York Tribune* till the beginning of the war. Barlow, unlike many others soon to be generals, had no military experience and enlisted in May 1861 as a private in the 12th New York Infantry, a ninety day unit. He reentered the Army with the 61st New York and quickly rose from lieutenant-colonel to colonel due to his performance during the 1862 Peninsula Campaign. His regiment fought well at the Battle of Antietam, where Barlow received a severe wound at "Bloody Lane" that required a long recovery. Two days after the Battle of Antietam he was appointed brigadier-general of volunteers. He returned to duty before the Battle of Chancellorsville, commanding a brigade in General Oliver O. Howard's XI Corps. Barlow's brigade was detached to the III Corps and was not routed along with the rest of Howard's troops during General Stonewall Jackson's devastating flank attack. At Gettysburg, Barlow's brigade fell back and fought effectively to a defensive position on Blocher's Knoll, now called Barlow's Knoll, but the forces of General Jubal Early overwhelmed the position and Barlow was seriously wounded and left for dead on the battlefield. However, being a general officer he was brought to the attention of Confederate General John B. Gordon. Believing Barlow to be mortally wounded, Gordon ordered that he be treated and moved to the rear. Gordon also gave permission for Barlow's wife, a union nurse, to pass through the lines to comfort her husband. Barlow and Arabella Griffith, ten years his senior, had been recently married, but seldom lived together, as their duties took them apart. She tragically died of typhus before the end of the war. It took Barlow almost a year to recover from his Gettysburg wounds, which included partial paralysis of his legs and arms. After being exchanged and recovered he rejoined the Army of the Potomac for General Ulysses Grant's 1864 Overland Campaign. Assigned as a division commander in General Winfield Scot Hancock's II Corps, Barlow found his military niche, as well as a compatible commanding officer. Hancock, supported by division commanders David Bell Birney, John Gibbon, and Barlow deftly used the II Corps as the main offensive weapon of the Army of the Potomac. At the Battle of Spotsylvania, Barlow and Birney's divisions formed the advance line and carried the assault on the "Mule Shoe" salient and fought all day at the "Bloody Angle," which resulted in victory for the Federals. Barlow's health deteriorated after the Battle of Cold Harbor and during the first phase of the Petersburg Campaign. He again went on sick leave, but returned in time for the Appomattox Campaign and the conclusion of the war. Promoted to major general of volunteers in 1865, Barlow left the Army and began a modestly successful political career. During the post-war years he was elected New York secretary of state, United States Marshall, and state Attorney General. He was a founder of the American Bar Association, prosecuted the "Tweed Ring," and investigated the disputed presidential election between Tilden and Hayes. He died in New York in 1896. Barlow was one of the very best "civilian" division commanders. Hard driving, a strict disciplinarian, and a bull dog in battle, his only serious failing was that of his health. Frail-looking and clean shaven, he always looked the part of the "boy general".

BERRY

Berry, Hiram. *Carte de visite* by Brady, Washington. Author's Collection.

Blair, Francis Preston, Jr. (1821-1875) was born in Lexington, Kentucky, February 19, 1821, to a prominent anti-slavery family. His father, Francis Preston Blair, owned a Washington newspaper, was an influential Washington political figure, and was one of the founders of the Republican Party. The elder Blair served Lincoln as an informal advisor, and upon Lincoln's request as an informal negotiator with the southern states. Francis Blair Jr. graduated from Princeton in 1841, and in 1843 began the practice of law in St. Louis, with his brother Montgomery later to be Postmaster General in the Lincoln administration. After serving as a private in the Mexican War and as New Mexico Territory Attorney General in 1847, he returned to St Louis and became involved in Missouri politics as a Free Soil Democrat, serving in the Missouri legislature from 1852-56. He was elected to Congress in 1856, but was defeated for reelection in 1858 and then founded the Union Party in Missouri, even though he personally owned slaves. Blair strongly supported Lincoln at the 1860 Chicago Convention and resisted the efforts of Missouri secessionists to take the state out of the union. His most notable act was leading St. Louis loyalists in forming a military organization of several thousand home guardsmen with the purpose of protecting the St. Louis Arsenal and its stand of 6,500 arms. Blair's group in 1861 captured Missouri state troops led by General Daniel Frost and effectively stopped secession efforts. He was elected to Congress in 1861 before resigning in August 1862 to accept a commission as a brigadier-general in the Missouri volunteers. Prior to leaving Congress he was a strong supporter of Lincoln and the early war efforts. Blair, unlike many border state politicians, advocated a strong all out federal effort to reunite the union. Returning to Missouri, he quickly raised seven volunteer regiments for federal service, and in 1862 was appointed a brigadier-general. He fought under his personal friend, General William T. Sherman, as a brigade commander at Chickasaw Bluffs and as a division commander at the siege of Vicksburg. Although he came from a civilian background and was notoriously sensitive, Blair was able to establish close relations with both Sherman and Grant. Both generals valued his military abilities and political influence. His leadership performance as a division commander at Lookout Mountain and Missionary Ridge verified their estimation of him as one of the best civilian generals. During Sherman's March to the Sea and the campaigns in South Carolina and North Carolina he served in command of both the XV and XVII Corps. He resigned from the Army in November 1865, and after a failed effort to regain his devastated personal finances managing a Mississippi plantation he returned to Missouri and re-entered politics. His lack of popularity with the Republican radicals holding rule in the Senate resulted in his being denied several federal positions offered by President Andrew Johnson. He ran in the vice presidential slot for Democrat Horatio Seymour's unsuccessful presidential attempt in 1870. Blair was appointed in 1871 to fill an unexpired term in the United States Senate. He returned to Washington but resigned in 1873 as his health failed, resulting in his death in 1875. At the time of his death he was Missouri State Superintendent of Insurance.

Blair, Frank. *Carte de visite* by Brady, Washington.

BLUNT

Blunt, James. *Carte de visite* by Addis and Noel, Leavenworth, Kansas. Author's Collection

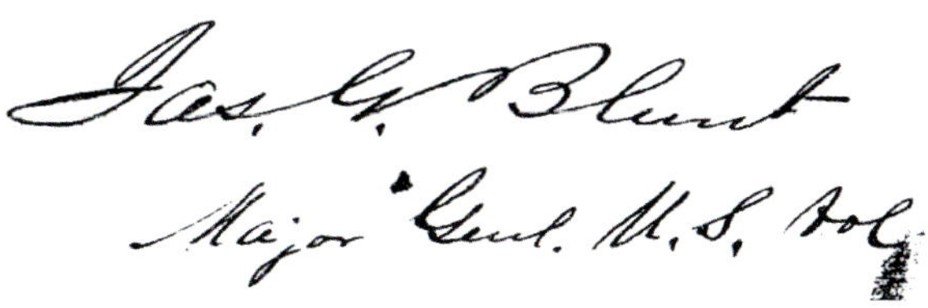

Blunt, James Gillpatrick (1826-1881) was born in Hancock County, Maine, and at the age of fifteen went to sea for five years, most likely serving in the whaling or fishing industry. Upon leaving the seafaring life Blunt studied medicine at Starling Medical College in Columbus, Ohio. After graduation he practiced medicine in several Ohio towns until moving in 1856 to Greely, Kansas, in Anderson County, a focus point of the "bleeding Kansas" troubles. Blunt became active as an abolitionist leader in the anti-slavery movement and allegedly became an ally of John Brown, and most certainly a political lieutenant of Senator James Lane. He was a member of the Kansas 1859 constitutional convention that preceded the state's entry to the union in January 1861. His military career began as second in command to Senator James Lane, the Colonel of the 3rd Kansas volunteers, sometimes referred to as the Kansas "Jayhawkers", and organized to retaliate for Missouri based pro-slavery force raids on Kansas. Many times the "Jayhawkers" committed the same atrocities as their Missouri guerilla counterparts. He entered federal service in April 1862 as a brigadier-general and commander of the Military Department of Kansas. Although having no formal military training, Blunt and his troops were able to route Confederate forces at Cane Hill and Old Fort Wayne. His forces were also victorious in several actions in the Indian Territories against Indians allied with the confederacy. In cooperation with General Francis Herron's forces in December 1862, Blunt defeated Confederate General Thomas Hindman's Army at Prairie Grove, stopping a Confederate attempt to march and occupy southern Missouri. Blunt was also able to capture and hold Van Buren, Arkansas. He was appointed a major-general in March 1863, with the appointment being dated to November 1862. Blunt suffered a significant defeat at the hands of Quantril's Raiders in October 1863 with eighty of his hundred man escort being killed while en route between Fort Scott and Fort Smith, Arkanas. In October 1864, this time in cooperation with General John Sanborn, he met and defeated the last attempt by Confederate General Sterling Price to invade Missouri. Blunt, although untrained in military tactics, understood the importance of mobility, and his campaigns usually accomplished most of their objectives. He also utilized Native American and black troops in his regiments. During the last year of the war he served as commander of federal forces in southern Kansas. Blunt left federal service in July 1865 and returned to the practice of medicine in Leavenworth, Kansas. Four years later he relocated to Washington and joined the ranks of many former senior officers as a claims agent representing former federal soldiers and civilians seeking claims against the government. He died in 1881 in a Washington D.C. area government hospital for the insane, reportedly from the effects of syphilis.

BROOKS

Brooks, William. *Carte de visite* by Brady, Washington. Author's collection.

Brooks, William Thomas Harbaugh (1821-1870) was born in Ohio, and at age sixteen was admitted in 1837 to the Military Academy, graduating forty-sixth in the class of 1841 that contained twenty future Civil War generals. He was commissioned in the 3rd Infantry and performed garrison duty until the Mexican War, where he was twice breveted for gallantry at the Battles of Monterey, Contreras, and Churubusco. Before the Civil War Brooks served on the staff of General David Twiggs between 1848 and 1851, and was stationed at various posts in New Mexico, where in 1858, while commanding Fort Defiance, he instigated a war with the Navahos after his black slave was killed by a Navaho. Brooks was a heavy drinker and acquired the nickname "Bully Brooks". At the onset of the Civil War Brooks was assigned to the defenses of Washington till appointed a brigadier-general of volunteers in September 1861. He then commanded a brigade of Vermont regiments in the Peninsula Campaign as part of General William F. Smith's division in the IV Corps. At the Battle of Savage's Station he received a serious wound, and was again wounded commanding his brigade at the Battle of Antietam. He returned to command a division in the VI Corps at the Battles of Fredericksburg and later at Chancellorsville. In the aftermath of the enormously bloody defeat of federal forces at Fredericksburg, Army of the Potomac commander General Ambrose Burnside attempted to remove a number of generals whom he felt were responsible for the defeat. Among the group was Brooks, who was accused by Burnside of using language that demoralized his troops and of constantly complaining about government policy, meaning Burnside's orders. Actually, Burnside thought Brooks to be a member of a disloyal group of Army of the Potomac generals that had gone over his head and complained directly to President Lincoln about his leadership at Fredericksburg. Brooks was not removed, but his career was irreparably damaged. One of the most vocal of Burnside's critics, General Joseph Hooker, was not removed, but succeeded Burnside as commander of the Army of the Potomac. For about a year after Chancellorsville Brooks commanded the Department of Monongahela and then returned to command a division in the XVIII Corps in the Army of the Potomac and the X Corps in the Army of the James. His last combat service was at Cold Harbor, Drewry's Bluff, and in the siege of Petersburg. He was appointed a major-general of volunteers in June 1863, but the appointment was revoked in April 1864, likely due to the political fall-out from Fredericksburg and his criticism of Burnside. Due to ill health he resigned from the army in July 1864 and purchased and operated a farm near Huntsville, Alabama.

BUELL

Buell, Don Carlos. *Carte de visite* by Frederick, New York. General Buell is shown in the uniform of a colonel. Author's Collection

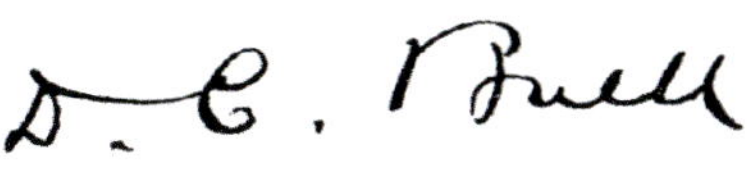

Buell, Don Carlos. *Carte de visite* by Brady, Washington. Author's Collection

Buell, Don Carlos (1818-1898) was born in Lowell, Ohio, admitted to West Point in 1837, and graduated thirty-second of fifty-two in the class of 1841, which saw twenty members serve as union and Confederate generals during the Civil War. In the Mexican War he received brevets to captain and major for gallantry in action. While in Mexico he was severely wounded at the Battle of Churubusco, causing a transfer from field to staff duties. Prior to the Civil War he served in various departments as an assistant adjutant general with the staff rank of lieutenant-colonel, achieving the reputation as one of the army's best administrative officers. With the commencement of Civil War hostilities in April 1861 Buell was stationed in San Francisco as assistant adjutant general. Before returning to Washington he was promoted from lieutenant-colonel in the regular army to brigadier-general of volunteers. Upon arriving in Washington, Buell was given a division command and assisted his friend General George McClellan in organizing and training the new expanded federal army. In November 1861 Buell was sent to Louisville, Kentucky, to replace General William T. Sherman as commander of the Department of the Cumberland, formerly the Department of Ohio. Buell's assignment was to take the Army of the Ohio from Louisville to Knoxville and push into Eastern Tennessee and free thousands of union loyalists from a heavy handed Confederate occupation. The relief of east Tennessee was a high priority for President Lincoln during most of the Civil War, as he anguished over the harsh conditions suffered by union loyalists. Buell immediately saw that no railroad extended into east Tennessee, nor did a good system of roads sufficient to support an army's elongated supply line. He proposed to Lincoln and Stanton an alternative plan to advance down the Tennessee and Cumberland Rivers and capture Nashville. Despite opposition from Lincoln, Buell launched his campaign to capture Nashville that culminated with a minimum of opposition perhaps attributable to the nearly simultaneous battles of Forts Donaldson and Henry won by federal forces under General Ulysses Grant. Buell's success at Nashville, achieved without serious damage to the Army of the Ohio, enabled it to quickly prepare and move from Nashville to Pittsburg Landing on the western bank of the Tennessee in time to support Grant and Sherman at the Battle of Shiloh. His arrival during the last hours of fighting on the first day provided the necessary reinforcements Grant needed to regain ground lost and mount attacks on the second day, forcing a Confederate retreat to Corinth, Mississippi. General Grant, in his memoirs, lauded Buell for providing critical assistance at Shiloh. He and the Army of the Ohio then participated in the subsequent Corinth campaign under the direction of General Henry Halleck. In March 1862 he was promoted to major-general of volunteers and was ordered to take four divisions and advance toward Chattanooga, repairing railroads between Corinth and central Tennessee. The Confederates were able to destroy Buell's line of supply from Louisville, causing him to give up the move on Chattanooga. In hopes of bringing Kentucky into the confederacy, Confederate Generals Braxton Bragg and Kirby Smith launched a swift movement toward Louisville in September 1862. Buell and the Army of the Ohio won a race with Bragg to Louisville and fought an indecisive battle at Perryville. Buell did not actually take part in the Battle of Perryville during the first day of the battle, even though he was only several miles away with more than half of the Army of the Ohio. In the aftermath of the tactical victory that stopped the Confederate invasion of Kentucky, Buell committed a cardinal sin in the eyes of the Lincoln Administration by not pursuing Bragg's retreating forces with his superior numbers. This brought on a Commission of Inquiry that issued no recommendation as to whether Buell was guilty or not guilty of incompetence. On October 30, 1862, Buell was relieved of his command by General William Rosecrans. He awaited new orders for nearly a year, and in June 1864 resigned his commission both in the volunteers and regular army, even though General Grant had offered him a command. Buell was arguably one of the finest officers in the pre-Civil War army, but due to his uninspiring personality and reluctance to employ his army he lost the support of Lincoln and the public. His long friendship with General George McClellan did not help his reputation in Washington. Buell was perhaps misplaced as a field commander and might have succeeded in a role in the Quartermaster Corps or as Adjutant General. After leaving federal service he was engaged in mining activities in Kentucky.

BUFORD

Buford, John. *Carte de visite* by Brady, Washington. Author's Collection

Buford, John (1826-1863) was born in Woodford County, Kentucky, but moved to Rock Island, Illinois, from where he was admitted to West Point, graduating sixteenth in the class of 1848. Commissioned in the 1st Dragoons, he served garrison duty at Jefferson Barracks near St. Louis, and frontier assignments in Kansas, Texas, and New Mexico until transferred in 1849 to the 2nd Dragoons. In the early 1850s he again served in frontier assignments, including participation in the Sioux Expedition of 1855, the Kansas slavery conflicts in 1856-7, and the Utah Expedition in 1857-8. Buford was promoted to captain in the 2nd dragoons in 1859 and continued on frontier duty in Oregon and Utah. At the onset of the Civil War he and the 2nd Dragoons marched from Utah to Kansas and then on to Washington. Upon arriving in the capital he was assigned as a staff major and assistant Inspector-General within the defenses of Washington until General John Pope, Commander of the Army of Virginia, requested that he be appointed a brigadier-general of volunteers. He received his general's star with rank dated from July 27, 1862, and was immediately assigned command of the cavalry reserve brigade in the Army of Virginia. In the federal disaster at Second Bull Run Buford ably demonstrated why many would later consider him one of the best federal cavalrymen. He was seriously wounded in the knee at the Battle of Second Bull Run after reporting the approach of General James Longstreet moving through Thoroughfare Gap toward Pope's forces. In the Antietam campaign he served as chief of cavalry for the Army of the Potomac, a nominal staff position, under General George McClellan, and in the same role during the Fredericksburg campaign under General Ambrose Burnside. In January 1863, General Joseph Hooker took command of the Army of the Potomac and immediately began a series of reforms, including a reorganization of the cavalry. Hooker directed his Chief of Cavalry, George Stoneman, to consolidate all cavalry, numbering about 10,000 troops, to fight as a single offensive force. Then, unwisely, Hooker sent most of his mounted force on an ill-conceived effort to seize Richmond and free union prisoners of war. The original intent of this mounted movement was for a quick strike south, but rain and high water in rivers caused delays that alerted Confederate forces. The delay also resulted in Hooker not having the use of most of his cavalry at the Battle of Chancellorsville, where it might have detected General Stonewall Jackson's flank movement. At Chancellorsville, Buford ably commanded the Reserve Brigade of regular cavalry in the 1st Division. After Hooker's removal after the Battle of Chancellorsville, General Alfred Pleasonton replaced Stoneman and Buford was given a division and fought with it at the Battle of Brandy Station. In the Battle of Gettysburg he demonstrated an astute sense of tactical high ground, and that a division of cavalry armed with breech loading weapons and fighting dismounted could successfully engage infantry. Buford, on July 1, 1863, engaged the advance of General A.P. Hill's Corps on the Cashtown road and sufficiently halted them until General John Reynolds could deploy the lead elements of the federal I Corps. His division then was unwittingly sent by Pleasonton to resupply at Emmitsburg, Maryland, dangerously exposing the federal left flank. His defense on the first day at Gettysburg was one of the highlights of the war for the federal cavalry. Following Gettysburg he participated in cavalry skirmishes, pursuing the enemy across the Rapidan, but was once forced to "cut" his way back through Confederate forces to federal lines. His division was engaged in the combat at Bristoe, Virginia, in October 1863, and shortly after this engagement he was forced to return to Washington sick with typhoid fever. General Buford died on December 16, 1863, shortly after learning President Abraham Lincoln had signed his appointment to major-general. If he had survived, it is likely that he may have commanded the Army of the Potomac cavalry or the federal cavalry in the western theater. Buford possessed superb battlefield leadership with an understanding of logistics and the use of cavalry as a battlefield force.

Buford, John. *Carte de visite* by Brady, Washington. Author's Collection

BURNSIDE

Burnside, Ambrose. *Carte de visite* by Brady, Washington. Author's Collection

Burnside, Ambrose. *Carte de vsite* by unidentified photographer. Author's Collection.

Burnside, Ambrose Everett (1824-1881) wads born in Liberty, Indiana, in a family of modest means. He received a common education and was apprenticed to a tailor. At the age of nineteen he was appointed to the Military Academy, graduating eighteenth in the class of 1847. He was commissioned a second lieutenant in the 2nd Artillery, serving in the Mexico City garrison. In late 1847 he was transferred to the 3rd Artillery serving in New Mexico, where he was wounded in a fight with Apaches. He was promoted to first lieutenant in 1851 and resigned in 1853 to manufacture firearms in Bristol, Rhode Island. His primary invention, patented in 1856, was the "Burnside Breech-Loading Rifle", a durable and somewhat suitable weapon for cavalry in its carbine version. Unfortunately, the demand for breech loading weapons was not strong enough in the late 1850s to prevent Burnside's company from failing, and he was forced to assign his patents to others. During the Civil War, thousands of Burnside carbines were used by the federal army. Burnside possessed a very affable personality, and some of his friends claimed that he viewed life in a very casual fashion. His engaging personality and military background helped him in gaining an appointment as a major-general in the Rhode Island militia, a nomination to Congress, and most importantly a job with his friend, George McClellan, vice president of the Illinois Central Railroad. At the outbreak of war he organized the 1st Rhode Island Infantry Regiment and quickly marched it to Washington, being one of the first units to arrive after Fort Sumter. He quickly became a friend of Lincoln, and the two likely talked a great deal about firearms inventions, in which Lincoln was passionately interested in. Burnside led his brigade without distinction at the Battle of Bull Run and was soon appointed a brigadier-general of volunteers. Lincoln, holding a high opinion of Burnside's abilities, assigned him command of a small three brigade expedition to the coast of North Carolina, and fortunately for Burnside it turned out to be one of the first successes of the war for Lincoln. Appointed to major-general, he returned to the Army of the Potomac at the head of the IX Corps in time for the Battle of Second Bull Run. Some authorities report that Burnside turned down the command of the Army of the Potomac after McClellan's Peninsular Campaign, and again after the shelving of John Pope following the Battle of Second Bull Run. At the Battle of Antietam Burnside commanded his IX Corps and Hooker's I Corps, and made a series of questionable if not poor battlefield decisions, including the slow action at "Burnsides Bridge" that provided time for General A.P. Hill's corps to arrive on the field to prevent a serious defeat for the Confederates. A partial blame for Burnside's lapses are attributed to General McClellan placing Burnsides' two corps on opposite ends of the line of battle, making communication difficult if not impossible. However, Burnside clearly demonstrated at Antietam that he was not an adequate candidate to command the Army of the Potomac. General McClellan failed to follow up his hard won advantage at Antietam, further displeasing President Lincoln and his cabinet, and on November 10, 1862, he ordered Burnside to command the Army of the Potomac. Trying to satisfy Lincoln's constant wish for the Army of the Potomac to always be moving forward toward Richmond, Burnside developed a plan to move through Fredericksburg on the way to the Confederate capital. On December 13, 1863, Burnside launched the Battle of Fredericksburg, which quickly turned into a bloodbath for federal troops attacking the Confederate fortifications on Mayre's Heights. The element of surprise had been lost when pontoon boats arrived ten days late and Confederate forces had been allowed to converge and fortify. Burnside ordered frontal charges that had little chance to succeed. In an almost frantic state of mind he told his generals that he would personally lead a final charge on the last day of the battle. After Fredericksburg, the Army of the Potomac went into winter quarters until Burnside ordered the infamous "Mud March" in January 1863, resulting in a number of his disgruntled generals going directly to President Lincoln and requesting his removal from command. Lincoln was infuriated by their action, but realized that Burnside could no longer be an effective leader of the Army of the Potomac. The president was faced with few good choices and replaced Burnside with Joseph Hooker, one of the seven disgruntled generals. Burnside was then sent to command the Department of Ohio, and soon became embroiled in a controversy over jailing Copperhead congressman Clement Vallandigham, who was later released and sent south behind Confederate lines. He also had to deal with the raids of John Hunt Morgan into Ohio and Indiana. The IX Corps, in late fall 1864 and with Burnside in command, was ordered south to Knoxville, occupied the city in November, and then suddenly came under siege by Confederate General James Longstreet. General Grant, ordered by Union Army Commander Halleck and President Lincoln, dispatched General William T. Sherman with his forces after the Battle of Missionary Ridge to relieve the Knoxville garrison. Sherman marched his exhausted troops in the dead of winter to Knoxville to find the claims of Burnside to be inflated. Inexplicably, Burnside received the thanks of Congress for the "siege" of Knoxville. The IX Corps left Knoxville and was sent back to the Army of the Potomac for the 1864 Overland Campaign. As Army of the Potomac commander, George Meade was junior in rank to Burnside; the IX corps reported directly to General-in-Chief Grant, and operated in tandem with the Army of the Potomac. Burnside and the IX Corps were minimally effective during the 1864 Overland Campaign, and members of Grant's staff felt that Burnside had a problem in being able to make firm decisions in committing troops to battle. During the siege of Petersburg Burnside showed poor judgment in supervising the mine explosion at the Battle of the Crater. General Grant requested that he be relieved and President Lincoln concurred. Burnside resigned from the Army in April 1865. In post war years he was elected three times governor of Rhode Island and to the United States Senate. Burnside perhaps was a classic example of a general who was a high ranking general because everyone liked him and forgave him for his lack of ability. Even General McClellan, writing to his wife a few hours after being relieved of the command of the Army of the Potomac by Burnside, showed no animosity toward his friend. In an earlier letter to his wife he bluntly stated that he had little confidence in "Burn's ability but had no intention of relieving him of command". Perhaps Burnside was the most reluctant major-general in the union army, unable to convince his superiors of his limitations.

BUTLER

Butler, Benjamin. *Carte de visite* by Brady, Washington. Author's Collection

Butler, Benjamin and Generals of Departments. *Carte de visite* by Anthony, New York showing Union Army Departmental Commanders in about 1861-1862. Author's Collection.

Butler, Benjamin Franklin (1818-1893) was born in New Hampshire, but moved to Lowell, Massachusetts, as a youth. He graduated from Colby College and later became a lawyer in Lowell specializing in criminal law. In 1853, Butler ran and was elected as a Democrat to the Massachusetts House of Representatives, followed later in 1859 with an election to the Senate. A strong Democrat, Butler served as a delegate to the 1860 Democratic Convention that split apart the Democratic Party, resulting in the election of Republican Abraham Lincoln. Before the war Butler had been appointed as a brigadier-general in the Massachusetts Militia, and in that capacity led the 8th Massachusetts Militia to the relief of Washington DC within a week after the attack on Fort Sumter. Butler, in going to the relief of the capital, bypassed Baltimore, where the 6th Massachusetts had been violently attacked by citizens in the streets. Butler, without specific orders, then began repairing railroad tracks around Baltimore and carried out negotiations with Maryland Governor Thomas Hicks. President Lincoln, to reward Butler and send a message to Democrats, appointed him over the objections of General Winfield Scott, the first volunteer major-general, with the date of rank being May 16, 1861. His first assignment was to subdue secessionist efforts in Maryland, especially Baltimore, which he did with but 900 men. Butler's efforts played a significant part in keeping Maryland in the union. He was then reassigned to command the Department of Virginia, and while in command of this department his forces were soundly defeated in the Battle of Big Bethel but retained control of Fortress Monroe. At this time Butler declared escaped slaves within his lines to be captured "contraband of war" and refused to return them to their owners. This legal twist, devised by the brilliant lawyer, allowed "captured" slaves to remain and be employed by Federal forces. This action by Butler was to have a profound effect on later emancipation debates. In August 1861, Butler led a successful combined army and naval force to the Hatteras Inlet in North Carolina. Afterwards he was reassigned to New England to recruit and organize another amphibious force, this time to seize New Orleans. The Navy force, commanded by Admiral David Farragut, was able to pass Fort Jackson and take the surrender of New Orleans without the assistance of Butler's forces. Butler then began his controversial rule of New Orleans and its ever hostile public. In the eyes of southerners, Butler was probably the most despised of Federal generals. This reputation was enhanced by false claims that he seized the silverware of New Orleans families. The term "Beast" was added to his sobriquet of "Spoons" when he issued an infamous order against New Orleans women making desultory remarks and taking insulting actions against Federal officers. Butler was also accused of being involved in corrupt cotton selling activities, but these charges probably should have been made against his brother, who was engaged in many questionable New Orleans business activities. His actions in New Orleans resulted in Confederate President Jefferson Davis issuing a proclamation declaring Butler an "outlaw". Butler's administration of New Orleans was brought to an end by heated arguments with numerous European consulates over cotton sales and import and export regulations. Most authorities agree that Butler's administration of New Orleans was effective, but at the same time there is little doubt that his family and friends lined their pockets with graft and favored treatment. Lincoln shelved Butler for nearly a year, during which he was a frequent visitor to the capitol, engaged in developing political goodwill with Republican congressmen and senators. In 1863, Lincoln returned Butler to command two corps to be called the Army of James and to work in concert with now-Lieutenant-General Ulysses Grant's 1864 Overland Campaign. Butler's forces were transported below Richmond and were to pressure Richmond from the south, while Grant's army pressured the city from the north. Butler blundered into getting the Army of the James bottled up at the Bermuda Hundreds. This effectively took the Army of the James out of support range for Grant's movement on Richmond. Butler's last military effort was the capture of Fort Fisher, again working in cooperation with the Navy. The effort ended in a fiasco, and Butler was relieved and sent home to await orders that never came. He resigned in November 1865 and was elected to Congress in 1866 as a Radical Republican, and was a leader in the attempt to impeach President Andrew Johnson. He served five terms in Congress and one as Governor of Massachusetts. In 1884 he ran for President on the Greenback Party ticket. Butler was a shrewd, aggressive, and ambitious politician with some vision and a never ending ambition to gain military fame. Lincoln probably made one of his worst appointments when he made Butler the commander of the Army of the James. If the Army of the James had been led competently the war may have been brought to a close many months before Appomattox.

BUTTERFIELD

Butterfield, Daniel. *Carte de visite* by Brady, Washington. Author's Collection.

Butterfield, Daniel (1831-1901) was born in Utica, New York. His father, John Butterfield, was the owner of the Overland Mail Company. He attended Union College, and later studied law before becoming superintendent of the eastern branch of the American Express Company based in New York City. Prior to the Civil War Butterfield was active in New York militia units, and a month after the firing on Fort Sumter was Colonel of the 12th New York Militia, a ninety day regiment. Butterfield, through political preference, was later transferred to the newly formed 12th U.S. Infantry as Lieutenant-Colonel. By September 1861, he was appointed a brigadier-general of volunteers and assigned a brigade in General George Morell's Division of the V Corps. In the 1862 Virginia Peninsula Campaign, Butterfield and his brigade were conspicuous in the battles of Hanover Court House, Mechanicsville, and Gaines Mill, where he was wounded in a charge while personally carrying the flag of the 3rd Pennsylvania. Thirty years later he was awarded the Medal of Honor for this feat. In September 1862 Butterfield was appointed major-general of volunteers, and in November was made Colonel of the U.S. 5th Infantry. These two promotions were seen by many to be the result more of political influence than military ability. Butterfield replaced George Morell as Division Commander on October 30, 1862, and assumed command of the V Corps when General Fitz John Porter was removed after the Battle of Second Bull Run. He credibly led the V Corps at the Battle of Fredericksburg. Upon Burnside's removal as commander of the Army of the Potomac, the new commander, General Joseph Hooker, selected Butterfield to be his chief of staff, with responsibility to restructure the army. Hooker and Butterfield succeeded in regrouping and upgrading the army, but this came to naught at the Battle of Chancellorsville, where Hooker was incapacitated and the federals were routed. One of Butterfield's reforms was the creation of corps badges, flags, and insignia so that officers and troops could identify their respective commands. After Hooker's removal Butterfield stayed due to General George Meade's reluctance to take on a new chief of staff in the middle of a campaign. On the third day of the Battle of Gettysburg Butterfield was wounded by a spent shell and Meade was spared having to formally relieve him. At a later date Meade and Butterfield became embroiled in a conflict over whether Meade had issued a "retreat order" at Gettysburg. Butterfield rejoined General Hooker, now in the western army, as his chief of staff and participated in the battles of Missionary Ridge and Lookout Mountain. Later, during the Atlanta Campaign, he returned to field command, leading a division of the XX Corps before being furloughed due to illness. It was during the Atlanta campaign that Butterfield wrote the famous "Taps". Upon regaining his health he was given a brief assignment in Vicksburg, and after the war a recruiting assignment in New York in his rank of a full regular army colonel. At conclusion of the war Butterfield received brevets both as a brigadier-general and major-general in the regular army. He resigned from the Army in 1870 and was involved in various business interests, principally the American Express Company. He was a strong supporter of the GAR and a frequent speaker at veterans' banquets. He died in 1901 and is buried at West Point, even though he never attended the Military Academy. In some respects Butterfield was a Civil War enigma, as he was greatly disliked by fellow officers for being untrustworthy and possessing low moral standards. However, he gained quick promotions without any apparent close relationships with the Lincoln administration.

CADWALADER

Cadwalader, George. *Carte de visite* by Brady, New York. Author's Collection

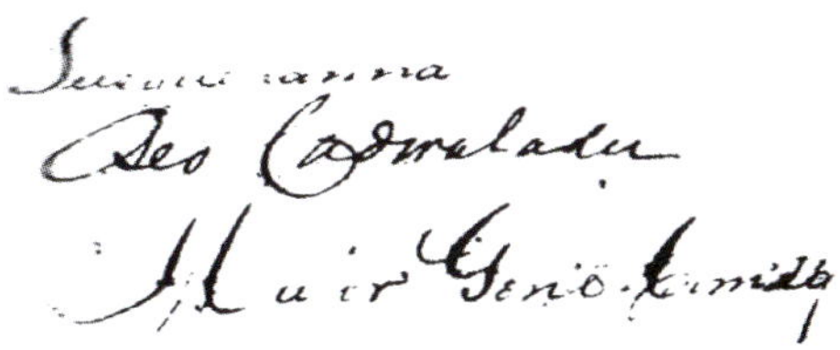

Cadwalader, George (1806-1879) Son of General Thomas Cadwalader, a War of 1812 hero and Philadelphia patrician. Cadwalader studied law and engaged in business interests, as well as being active in the Pennsylvania militia. In 1844, as a militia brigadier-general, he forcefully put down "anti-foreign" riots inspired by the Know-Nothing Party, causing some Philadelphia anti-catholics to hang him in effigy. He fought in the Mexican War as a brigadier-general of volunteers and was breveted as a major-general of volunteers for his role in the Battle of Chapultepec. Governor Andrew Curtin of Pennsylvania ordered General Cadwalader to Baltimore at the beginning of the war in April 1861 to quell anti-union riots and govern the city until federal units could relieve him. While commanding in Baltimore he had John Merryman arrested without a warrant for recruiting troops for the Confederate army. United States Supreme Court Chief Justice Roger Taney issued a *writ of habeas corpus* to release Merryman that Cadwalader ignored by claiming that he had been ordered by President Lincoln to suspend *habeas corpus*. The issue of whether *habeas corpus* could be suspended during a time of war or emergency later resulted in the historic Supreme Court case of *Ex parte Merryman*. His next assignment was to accompany as a division commander General Robert Patterson on the ill-fated Winchester expedition that failed to promptly support federal forces engaged at the Battle of Bull Run. In April 1862 he was appointed and confirmed as a major-general of volunteers and received numerous administrative assignments during the remainder of the war years. One significant assignment was as a member of the board to revise army regulations. From 1863 until the end of the war he commanded significant army activities, especially recruiting in the Philadelphia area and throughout the Department of Pennsylvania. At times he served as a Lincoln advisor on matters both civil and military. After the war he returned to private interests and died in 1879.

CANBY

Canby, E.R.S. Canby. *Carte de visite* by Fredricks, New York. Author's Collection

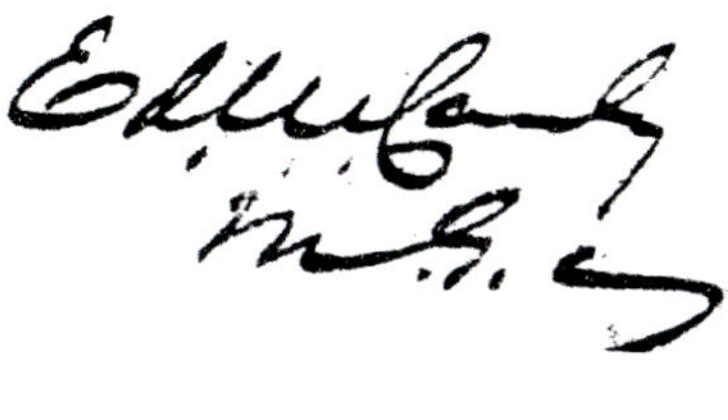

Canby, E.R.S. Canby, *Carte de visite* by Brady, New York. Author's Collection

Canby, Edward Richard Sprigg (1817-1873) was born in Kentucky, and attended Wabash College in Indiana before being admitted to the Military Academy in the class of 1839. He graduated thirty of thirty-one and was commissioned in the 2nd Infantry, serving in the Florida Indian Wars before being assigned to relocate Indian tribes to Arkansas. He was then engaged in recruiting and garrison duty in Detroit before being promoted to first lieutenant. Canby served in the Mexican War as chief of staff to General Bennett Riley at Vera Cruz, Cerro Gordo, Contreras, Churubusco, and the capture of Mexico City. He received brevets to captain, major, and lieutenant-colonel while serving in Riley's brigade. At the end of hostilities, Canby was assigned to duties in the Adjutant Generals Office in Washington. Promoted to major in 1855 in the 10th Infantry, Canby conducted numerous inspections of army posts across the nation and served in the Utah Expedition in 1856. In 1860, he was assigned first to Fort Garland, New Mexico, and led the Navaho Expedition of 1860-1861, in which he and his subordinate, Major Henry Sibley, saw very few Navahos. The beginning of the Civil War found him operating from Fort Defiance, Arizona, where he was promoted to Colonel of the 19th Infantry in May 1861. This promotion also put him in command of the Department of New Mexico. Canby was successful in repulsing the Confederate invasion of New Mexico led by General Henry Sibley and his Texas army. Sibley's objective was to conquer all territory west of Texas, including California and its important gold mines. Canby was able to organize a small army from scattered federal units and New Mexican volunteers. This force, supported by quick marching Colorado militia units, turned back the Confederates by cutting their overextended supply lines at the Battle of Glorieta Pass. This seldom mentioned battle is sometimes referred to as the "Gettysburg of the West". Canby soon left New Mexico after being appointed a brigadier-general. He spent nearly two years in the Adjutant General's Office in a role similar to Assistant Secretary of the Army. During the New York Draft Riots in 1863 he took command of troops in New York City, quelling riots and restarting the draft. He was appointed major-general of volunteers May 7, 1864, commanding the Division of West Mississippi, where he was severely wounded by guerrillas while making an inspection near White River, Arkansas. In November 1864 Canby took control of General Nathaniel Banks' troops just retreating from their ill-fated Red River campaign. At Lincoln's order Canby organized an effort to capture Mobile, Alabama. This joint campaign of army and naval forces led by Admiral David Farragut and General Gordon Granger was successful. Canby received official thanks from President Lincoln for securing Mobile Bay, and further thanks from Congress for the subsequent surrender of the city of Mobile. Canby was among the very few Federal generals that were successful in all their campaigns. He received the surrender of all the Confederate forces west of the Mississippi in May 1865, and continued in his command until called back to the Adjutant General's Office, remaining there on Reconstruction duties until assigned to the west coast in 1870. He served as commander of the Department of the Columbia until 1873, then becoming commander of the Division of the Pacific. He was assassinated in 1873 by the Modoc Indians in Southern Oregon during peace and treaty negotiations. His death led to an all-out war on the small group of Modocs by the army, which suffered numerous casualties in the lava bed battles. Canby was a superb army administrator, but as a person lacked some social amenities, and often appeared to be a stern disciplinarian. General Grant did not consider him a top rate field general, but felt he was irreplaceable in the Adjutant Generals Department.

CASEY

Casey, Silas. *Carte de visite* with no back mark but likely by Brady. Author's Collection

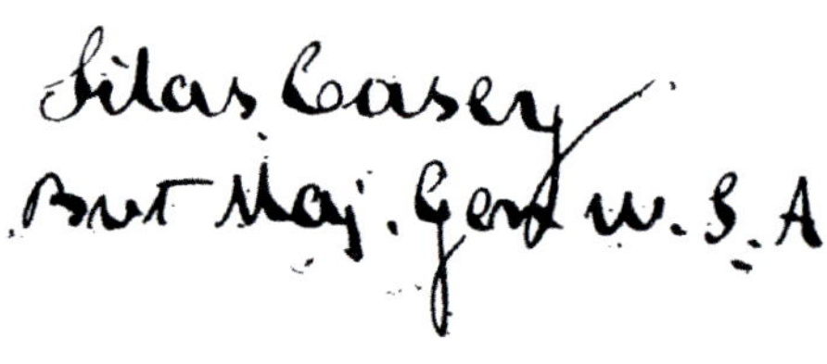

Casey, Silas. *Carte de visite* with no back mark but likely by Brady. Author's Collection

Casey, Silas (1807-1882) was born in East Greenwich, Rhode Island. Casey entered the Military Academy in 1822 and graduated thirty-ninth of forty-one in the class of 1826. He was commissioned a second lieutenant in the 2nd Infantry and served in numerous frontier posts and army garrisons. Promoted to captain in 1839, he served meritoriously in the Mexican War, including making a "forlorn" assault in the storming of Chapultepec, where he was seriously wounded. Casey received brevets to major and lieutenant-colonel for his Mexican War service. After Mexico he mainly served in California, Oregon, and Washington garrisons until 1855, when he was appointed lieutenant-colonel of the reconstituted 9th Infantry. Prior to the Civil War, troops under Casey's command in the Pacific Northwest were engaged in numerous skirmishes and several small scale Indian wars in the Puget

Sound area. His subordinate, Captain George Pickett, created an international incident with the British over contested occupation of an island in the Puget Sound area. Pickett defied British forces in what was called the "Pig War". Casey was a military scholar and published *Casey's Infantry Tactics*, which was adopted in 1862 and became mandatory reading for volunteer officers during the Civil War. The previous "tactics" manual used by the Army had been written by General William Hardee of the Confederate army. Casey returned to Washington from the Pacific Coast, and in August 1861 was appointed brigadier-general of volunteers and assigned to training troops within the Washington defenses. In General McClellan's 1862 Peninsula campaign, Casey commanded a division in General Erasmus Keyes' IV Corps that was roughly handled and over run at the Battle of Fair Oaks. Despite this battlefield setback, Casey was breveted a brigadier-general in the regular Army, most likely to clear the way for his removal from field command. For the remainder of the war he commanded a provisional brigade and division in the Washington defenses and served on boards, including those charged with examining white officers desiring to serve in black units. While stationed in Washington Casey revised his *Infantry Tactics*, the new title being *Infantry Tactics for Colored Troops*. He also served on the controversial court-martial board that tried General Fitz-John Porter for his actions at the Battle of Second Bull Run. The board was handpicked by Secretary of War Edwin Stanton and soon reached a guilty verdict that resulted in Porter being dismissed from the army and disqualified from other federal government service. After the war Casey served several more years in garrison assignments, finally resigning in 1868 after forty years of continuous service.

CLAY

Clay, Cassius. *Carte de visite* by Brady, Washington. Author's Collection

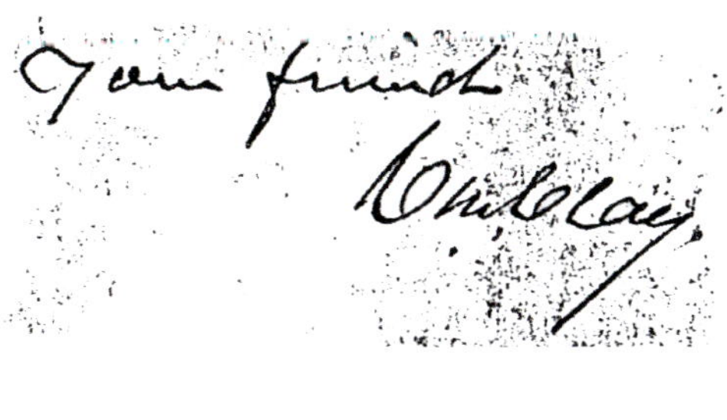

Clay, Cassius Marcellus (1810-1903) was born in Kentucky to a distinguished and wealthy family. He graduated from Yale University in 1832. He was elected to the Kentucky legislature in 1835 and immediately made known his opposition to slavery. In 1845 he opened a newspaper called the *True American* in Lexington that was virulently against slavery. A mob attacked the newspaper and Clay came close to being made a martyr in the abolitionist movement. He took part in the Mexican War and was taken prisoner while serving as a captain with the 1st Kentucky Cavalry. Following the war he continued his efforts to emancipate slaves, even though his family held large numbers of slaves. Clay, forever marching to his own drummer, was not always supported by abolitionist groups, as he felt the main reason for emancipation of slaves was to eliminate the institutions' debilitating effect on the non-slave holding white population. Clay became an early and important border state Republican and was always a strong Lincoln supporter. Some authorities believe that many Republican leaders considered Clay for the vice presidency. After the election Lincoln seriously considered him for several cabinet posts, but finally offered him a diplomatic post as Minister to Russia. Before leaving for Russia in late March 1861, Clay organized an irregular militia force called the "Clay Guards" immediately after the firing on Fort Sumter. This brief irregular unit was to protect the capital until regular and state forces could reach the city. He returned from Russia in the middle of 1862 to accept a major-general's appointment from Lincoln that was later confirmed by the Senate. It is questionable whether Lincoln ever considered giving Clay a field command. This was soon a moot question, as Clay refused to serve as a general while slavery was permitted and protected in the occupied southern states. In later years, Clay claimed credit for Lincoln's emancipation declaration. While he was a fully commissioned major-general of volunteers from April 1862 until March 1865, Clay spent the remainder of the war in his post at St. Petersburg. Returning to the United States in 1869, he began an erratic career in national politics, changing back and forth between the Democratic and Republican parties. Always manifesting volatile behavior, he fought a number of bloody duels, usually with a bowie knife. His last years were spent almost completely paranoid, and for years he had a mounted cannon in the doorway of his "Whitehall" mansion in Kentucky. He was legally declared insane and died in 1903.

COUCH

Couch, Darius. *Carte de visite* with no back mark, but likely by Whitehurst, Washington. Author's Collection

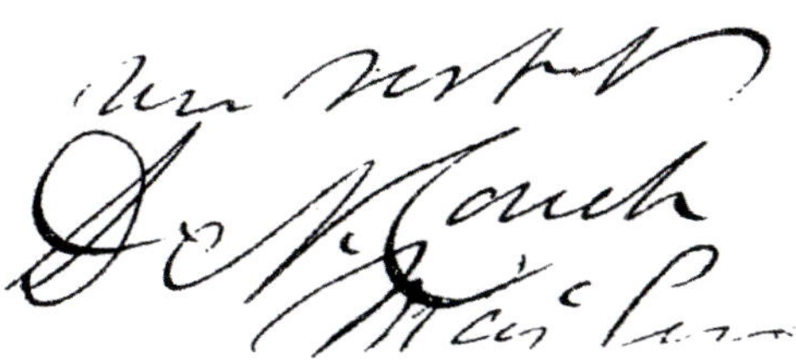

Couch, Darius. *Carte de visite*. Brady, Washington. Author's collection.

Couch, Darius Nash (1822-1897) was born in New York, entered the Military Academy at age 20, and graduated thirteenth of fifty-nine in the class of 1846 with classmates George McClellan, Thomas (Stonewall) Jackson, and sixteen other future Civil War generals. Couch was commissioned in the 4th Artillery and sent to Mexico, where he received a brevet to first lieutenant for bravery at the Battle of Buena Vista. Following the Mexican War, he fought against Indians in Florida and served in various artillery garrisons. An interesting time in Couch's pre-Civil War career was a leave of absence in 1853 when he served as a naturalist on a Smithsonian expedition to Mexico. He resigned his commission in 1855 and engaged in mercantile interests in New York City until 1858, when he accepted a management position in Norton, Massachusetts, manufacturing copper sheathing. Couch entered the Civil War commanding the 7th Massachusetts Volunteers, and at the request of his West Point classmate General George McClellan was appointed a brigadier-general of volunteers. In 1861 he served in the Washington defenses training troops and was not involved in the Battle of Bull Run. Couch commanded a division in General Erasmus Keyes' IV Corps during the McClellan led Peninsula Campaign and was highly praised by his superiors for his spirited fighting at the Battle of Seven Pines. Always of frail health, Couch became incapacitated with dysentery during the Peninsula campaign that would bother him for the rest of his life. He attempted to resign while on sick leave, but McClellan refused to forward his papers to Lincoln, instead convincing Couch to remain with his command. He was appointed a major-general of volunteers in July 1862 and fought with his division at Maryland Heights, Second Bull Run, and Fredericksburg, where as commander of the II Corps he led his troops on a futile assault to capture Mayre's Hill. At Chancellorsville, Couch was second in command to General Joseph Hooker, commander of the Army of the Potomac. He personally disliked Hooker and mistrusted his ability to lead the army. Following a discussion with Lincoln after the Chancellorsville defeat, he requested to be relieved from serving under Hooker. He was subsequently assigned to command the Department of the Susquehanna and was responsible for organizing and ably commanding the Pennsylvania militia during the Gettysburg campaign. Couch and Pennsylvania Governor Andrew Curtin worked closely together on a difficult task of quickly organizing citizens to oppose Lee's forces. Couch's reserves prevented the Confederates from crossing the Susquehanna River and were able to provide General George Meade with intelligence and some flank protection. After another period of illness, Couch assumed command of the XXII Corps, which played a key role in the decisive Battle of Nashville fought in December 1864. He finished the Civil War commanding the XXII Corps in the North Carolina campaign and resigned from the volunteers and regular Army on May 26, 1865. Couch was a very accomplished professional soldier, but often lacked tact and patience, and has been undervalued as a Federal division and corps commander. After the war and still plagued by bouts of chronic dysentery, he held various federal and state appointments.

Cox

Cox, Jacob. *Carte de visite* by unidentified photographer. Author's collection.

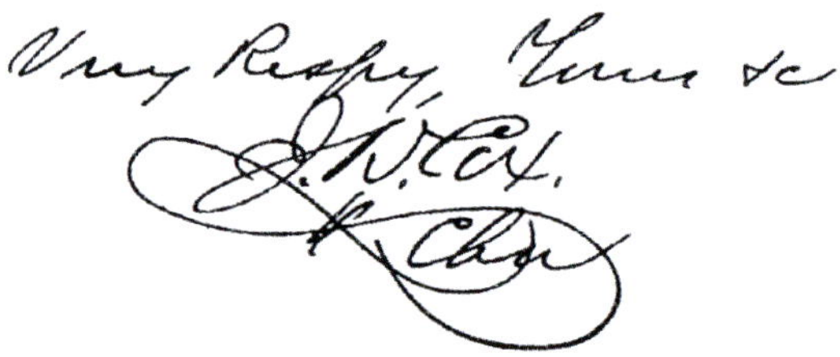

Cox, Jacob Dolson (1828-1900) One of many Ohio Civil War generals, Cox was born in Canada, but returned at an early age to Ohio. He graduated from Oberlin College in 1851, served several years as a school superintendent in Warren, Ohio, and entered legal practice in 1853. True to the principles of Oberlin, Cox was a strong abolitionist and a founder of the Ohio Republican Party. He was elected to the Ohio State Senate in 1858 and soon developed close ties with his senate colleague James Garfield, Governor Salmon Chase, and Ohio Governor-elect William Dennison. At the beginning of the war Cox was appointed as a brigadier-general in the Ohio militia and was active in raising and organizing troops. In May 1861 he was appointed a brigadier-general of volunteers and led the Ohio Kanawha Brigade in the West Virginia campaign commanded by General George McClellan. At the conclusion of the campaign he was assigned command of the Kanawha Mountain Department until given command in 1862 of a division in the Army of Virginia under General John Pope. His arrival in Virginia was not in time to support Pope at the federal disaster at the Battle of Second Bull Run. Cox's division led the Army of the Potomac movement at the Battle of South Mountain, where he assumed command of the IX Corps when its commander, General Jesse Reno, was killed. Before the Battle of Antietam Cox requested General Ambrose Burnside to return him to division command, but Burnside refused and the IX Corps performed poorly at "Burnside's Bridge", a key part of the battlefield. He was appointed major-general in March 1863, but the appointment was rescinded, as according to law there was at that time an excess of major-generals. He returned to Ohio and served as commander of the Department of Ohio until returning to field duty in 1864 as a division commander in the XXIII Corps during General William T. Sherman's Atlanta campaign. He displayed astute tactical ability at the Battle of Kennesaw Mountain, where his flanking movement denied the Confederates a position that seemed impervious to assault. Cox did not accompany Sherman on the March to the Sea, but played a key role in the repulse of General John B. Hood's Confederate troops at the bloody Battle of Franklin in middle Tennessee. At the Battle of Nashville in December 1864 his division, on the right wing, rolled back Confederate attacks and participated in the pursuit of Hood's defeated army. He was confirmed as a major-general of volunteers in December 1864 before fighting with the XXIII Corps in the North Carolina campaign that ended with the surrender of General Joseph Johnston's army. In post war years he was elected Governor of Ohio in 1866, but was not re-nominated by his party due to his support of President Andrew Johnson's reconstruction policies. Later he served as Grant's Secretary of the Interior and supported civil service reform in opposition to other members of Grant's administration. He resigned in 1870 and returned to Ohio and a law practice in Cincinnati. After serving a term in Congress he became dean of the Cincinnati Law School and later the president of the University of Cincinnati. Cox was an extensive writer on Civil War battles and campaigns, some of which were controversial. Jacob Cox wrote in his *Military Reminiscences* that civilians possessing the right personal qualities and obtaining proper training and experience could be the equals of officers and generals receiving an education at the Military Academy. Cox was certainly one of the better civilian generals.

CRITTENDEN

Crittenden, Thomas. *Carte de visite* by Brady, Washington. Author's collection.

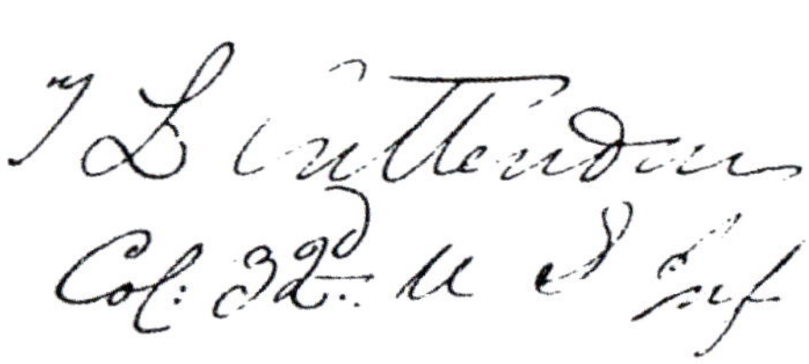

Crittenden, Thomas Leonidas (1819-1883) was born in Kentucky, the son of U.S. Senator John Crittenden. He practiced law before the Mexican War, where he served as an aide to General Zachary Taylor and as Lieutenant-Colonel of the 3rd Kentucky. After the war he briefly served in a diplomatic post and participated in a mercantile firm in Louisville. Like his father he was a strong opponent of secession, and in 1861 commanded loyal Kentucky state militia forces after General Simon Buckner and his supporters joined the southern cause. Among those joining the south was his brother George, who later became a Confederate general. Crittenden was mustered into federal service as a brigadier-general of volunteers in September 1961 with a division command in the Army of the Ohio commanded by General Don Carlos Buell. He credibly led the 5th division at the battles of Shiloh and Stone River. He was cited for gallantry at the Battle of Shiloh and for making an important defensive stand at Stone River. He was soon thereafter appointed a major-general of volunteers and named to command the XXI Corps. At the Battle of Chickamauga, Crittenden's XXI Corps was routed along with two thirds of the federal army, including its commander, General William Rosecrans. Only a resourceful and fierce resistance by General George Thomas saved the Army of the Cumberland from being annihilated by Confederate General Braxton Bragg's forces. Crittenden, along with General James Negley and General Alexander McCook, were made scapegoats by Rosecrans for the debacle at Chickamauga. Later courts-of-inquiry absolved them of malfeasance, but their military careers were forever tarnished and none of the three held prominent commands during the remainder of the war. In 1864, he was given a division command in Burnsides IX Corps attached to the Army of the Potomac, but served only briefly and resigned in December 1864, claiming the assignment called for rank less than that of a major-general. However, General Meade considered him a poor division commander and quickly approved his request to resign. After the war he was breveted a brigadier-general in the regular army for gallantry at Stone River. President Johnson, in 1865, appointed him Colonel of the 32nd U.S. Infantry, and he served with his regiment in the Arizona territory until 1869, when he was transferred to the 17th Infantry. He was retired for age in 1881. Crittenden's only son John, serving in the 20th Infantry, was detailed to the 7th Cavalry and killed at the Battle of the Little Big Horn in 1876. When asked as to where to send his son's remains, Crittenden's answer was that a soldier should be buried where he fell. With the exception of the Battle of Chickamauga he was a very capable commander at the brigade level, but lacked sufficient military training and experience to command at a division and corps level.

Crittenden, Thomas. *Carte de visite* by Webster, Louisville. Author's collection..

CROOK

Crook, George. *Carte de visite* by Anthony, New York. Author's collection.

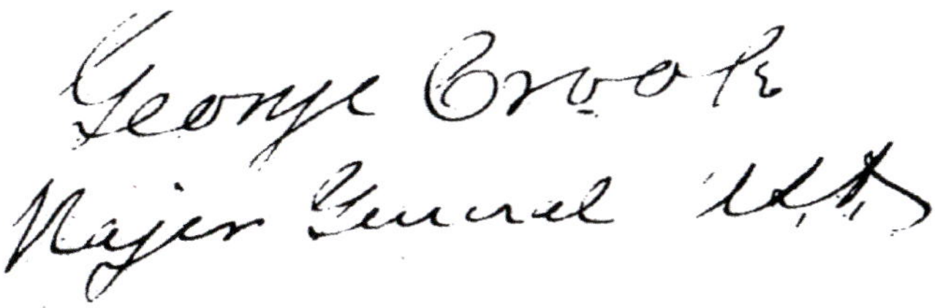

Crook, George, W. (1828-1890) was born in Ohio. He entered the Military Academy in 1848 with the class of 1854, in which he finished thirty-eighth of forty-three. Commissioned into the 4th Infantry, Crook served at various posts in California and Washington subduing Indian outbreaks. In a skirmish during the Pitt River War in 1857 he was wounded by an arrow. Crook participated in the Yakima War of 1858 and spent the remaining three years before the Civil War in California posts. He was promoted in May 1861 to captain in the 4th U.S. Infantry, and soon after as colonel of the 36th Ohio Volunteers stationed in western Virginia. Crook was seriously wounded in May 1862 at the Battle of Lewisburg and received a brevet to major in the regular army. In August 1862, he received an appointment as brigadier-general of volunteers and fought at the Battle of South Mountain and the Battle of Antietam, from which he received a brevet to lieutenant-colonel in the regular army. Transferred to the Army of the Cumberland, he commanded the 2nd Cavalry Division and was distinguished at the Battle of Chickamauga by his pursuit and defeat of General Joseph Wheeler's cavalry at Farmington, Tennessee. He returned in February 1864 to West Virginia in command of the Kanawha District and was engaged in numerous raids and won the hard fought Battle of Cloyd's Mountain. In 1864, he received command of the Department of Western Virginia and the VIII Corps in the Army of the Shenandoah commanded by General Philip Sheridan. After the Battle of Cedar Creek he returned to his departmental command with headquarters located in Cumberland, Maryland. He was appointed major-general in October 1864, and on February 21, 1865, Crook and General Benjamin Kelley were captured in the early morning hours while in their hotel rooms by a band of sixty partisan rangers led by Captain Jesse McNeill. This daring event occurred in the midst of 10,000 federal troops and certainly was not the high point of Crook's career. The only positive aspect of the capture was Crook's later marriage to a sister of one of the rangers. Crook and Kelley were sent to Richmond, but were exchanged in time for Crook to lead a cavalry division in the Army of the Potomac in the last battles of the Civil War at Dinwiddie Courthouse, Fisher's Hill, Jaylor's Creek, Farmville, and Appomattox. On March 13, 1865, Crook received brevets as a brigadier-general and major-general in the regular army. He mustered out of volunteer service on January 15, 1866, and was assigned Lieutenant-Colonel of the 23rd Infantry. His first assignment was in the Pacific Northwest, where he defeated a group of Paiute and Modoc Indians at the battle of Infernal Caverns. In 1867 he led forces that finally brought to a close the Snake Indian War that had started in 1864. His next campaign was against the Apache in Arizona Territory, where he utilized Apache scouts to fight against their own people. In May 1876 Crook, in charge of the Bighorn and Yellowstone Expedition, met and fought the Sioux at the Battle of the Rosebud. The outcome of the battle was a tactical victory for Crook, but stopped his movement to eventually join with General Terry in command of the Little Big Horn Expedition. Till his death in 1890 he was almost in continuous service against Indian tribes in the Southwest and on the Great Plains. He held various department commands and was a keen student of Indian cultures. In his later years he was a strong advocate of Indian rights. Crook was an innovative Indian fighter and a more than competent cavalry and infantry leader in the Civil War.

CURTIS

Curtis, Samuel. *Carte de visite* by Hoelke, St. Louis. Author's collection.

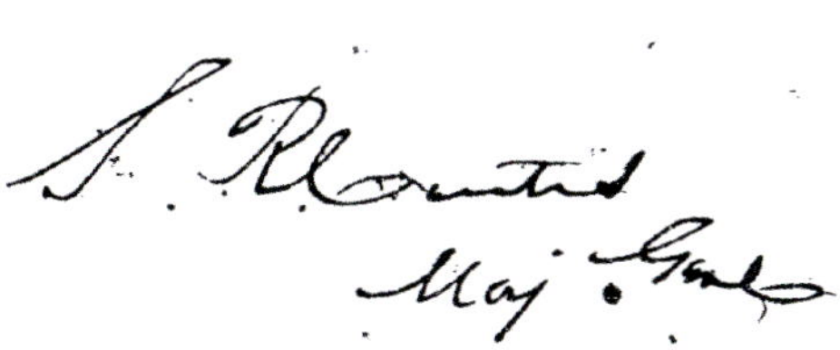

Curtis, Samuel Ryan (1805-1866) was born in New York. Curtis' family moved to Ohio, from which he was appointed to the Military Academy in the class of 1831, graduating twenty-seventh. He was commissioned in the 7th Infantry and first stationed at Fort Gibson, Indian Territory. He resigned after only a year of service and became a civil engineer, later serving in the Ohio militia as a colonel. At the beginning of the Mexican War he was appointed adjutant general of the Ohio Militia, responsible for recruiting the state's quota of troops. He was later made colonel of the 2nd Ohio Volunteers, but mainly held staff and administrative positions, including that of aide to General John Wool during his campaign in Mexico. As a field commander he defeated an attempt by Mexican General Urrea to capture the military depot at Camargo. Returning to the states, he continued his career in engineering, including major river and harbor projects in St. Louis and Des Moines. He left engineering in 1855 and entered the field of law, and was elected to the U.S. House of Representatives from Iowa in 1857, serving until the outbreak of the Civil War. While in Congress he was a member of the Committee on Military Affairs. His first Civil War position was as colonel of 2d Regiment of Iowa Volunteers mustered into federal service in June 1861. Curtis did not actually serve in the regiment, as he had been appointed a brigadier-general of volunteers in May 1861 and given assignments at Jefferson Barrack and in the Southwestern District of Missouri. In February 1862 he received command of the Army of the Southwest and engaged in various skirmishes with Confederate forces before defeating Confederate General Sterling Price at the critical battle of Pea Ridge, Arkansas. After Pea Ridge, Curtis marched his Army of the Southwest a thousand miles through Missouri and Arkansas, expelling Confederate forces. Appointed to major-general of volunteers in March 1862, he was given command of the Department of Missouri. He soon clashed with Missouri Governor Hamilton Gamble, who did not share his abolitionist views. President Lincoln was forced to transfer Curtis to command the Department of Kansas, which was later merged into the Department of the Northwest. In February 1865 he led a successful expedition against hostile Indians on the Upper Arkansas and Platte rivers. His last Civil War assignment was pursuing General Price in his retreat after the last Confederate attempt to invade Missouri. Curtis, in July 1865, was appointed United States Commissioner to negotiate treaties with the Sioux and other Indian tribes. He was mustered out of the volunteer service April 30, 1866, and died on December 26, 1866, at Council Bluffs, Iowa. Even having commanded a federal army in a very important federal victory at Pea Ridge, Curtis is seldom mentioned to any extent in works describing the Civil War in the west.

CUSTER

Custer, George. *Carte de visite* by Brady, Washington. Author's collection.

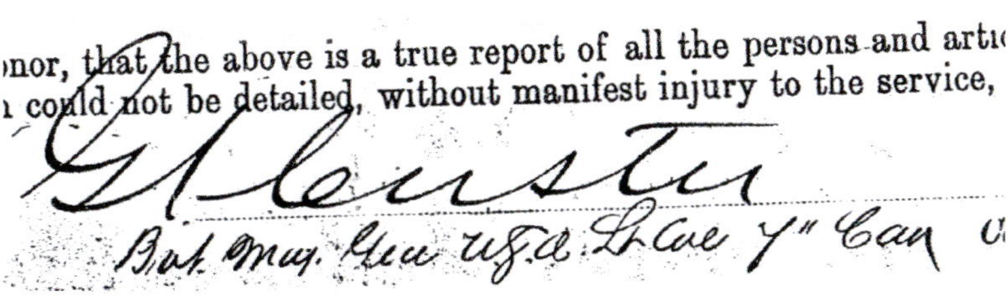

nor, that the above is a true report of all the persons and arti
could not be detailed, without manifest injury to the service,

Custer, George, *Carte de visite* by Brady, Washington. Author's collection.

Custer, George Armstrong (1839-1876) was born in New Rumley, Ohio, but often resided in Monroe, Michigan. Custer taught school briefly before being admitted to the Military Academy in 1857, finishing last in the class of 1861. He was commissioned in the 2d Cavalry on June 24, 1861, and three days later participated in the Battle of Bull Run carrying dispatches from General Winfield Scott to General Irvin McDowell on the battlefield at Centerville. By July 1861 he was a first lieutenant in the 5th Cavalry, serving as an additional aide-de-camp to General George McClellan in the 1862 Peninsula Campaign. He continued to serve on McClellan's staff as an aide-de-camp during the Antietam Campaign. On numerous occasions Custer demonstrated bold, daring and sometimes questionable behavior that included a balloon flight to observe Confederate lines. In September 1862 Custer became aide-de-camp to General Alfred Pleasanton, chief of cavalry for the Army of the Potomac. In June 1863, upon the recommendation of Pleasanton, Custer jumped rank from captain to brigadier-general of volunteers, commanding a brigade of Michigan cavalry in General Judson Kilpatrick's cavalry division. At the Battle of Aldie and the Battle of Gettysburg, Custer demonstrated remarkable ability to lead mounted forces. After the Gettysburg campaign, he received a brevet to major in the regular army for gallantry in action. Custer, unlike many fellow cavalry commanders, possessed a remarkable degree of luck, as he was never seriously wounded or ill enough to prevent him being involved in all of the cavalry battles fought by the Army of the Potomac, beginning at Aldie and ending at Appomattox. His performance at the Battle of Yellow Tavern, where Confederate General Jeb Stuart was mortally wounded, was noted both in army dispatches and by the national press. While commanding a cavalry division in General Philip Sheridan's Virginia campaigns he was awarded a brevet to lieutenant-colonel in the regular army for his gallantry at the Battle of Winchester that took place in September 1864. He was also appointed to major-general of volunteers after the defeats of Confederate General Jubal Early at the Battle Waynesboro and the Battle of Fisher's Hill. In the 1865 Appomattox campaign, Custer demonstrated leadership and gallantry at the Battles of Dinwiddie Court House, Five Forks, Saylors Creek and Appomattox Station. In his volunteer rank of major-general he was assigned to division command in the Department of the Gulf Coast directly after the surrender. In November 1865 he was appointed chief of cavalry for the Department of Texas, where he enforced unpopular military government upon civilians and exacted harsh discipline on his volunteer soldiers desiring to go home. In 1866, he received the lieutenant-colonel's position in the newly formed 7th Cavalry. He participated in General Winfield Hancock's unsuccessful campaign against the Cheyenne in 1867-68. In November 1868 Custer, under orders from General Sheridan, engaged the Sioux and Cheyenne in a freezing winter campaign, and in a surprise attack brought the campaign to a conclusion when he defeated the Cheyenne at the Battle of Washita. Custer's actions at the battle have been questioned by some authorities as being poorly conceived and actually destroying a village that was not hostile. His leaving Major Joel Elliot and a number of troops behind to their deaths at the hands of Cheyenne reinforcements created a bitter split in the 7th Cavalry between pro and anti-Custer factions. This dissension persisted for years, and perhaps affected the regiment's later performance. Prior to the Battle of Washita, Custer was court-martialed for an unauthorized leave of absence to visit his wife. At the same time some of his officers also filed charges against him for ordering illegal punishment and unnecessary firing on deserters. He was found guilty of the charges of an unauthorized absence and was suspended from duty for a year. General Philip Sheridan had Custer returned to duty in time to lead his regiment in the Washita campaign. After reconstruction duty in the South, Custer and the 7th Cavalry participated in General David Stanley's Yellowstone Expedition in 1873. Custer and Stanley detested each other, and Custer was nearly court-martialed for disobedience. He led an expedition into the Black Hills in 1874, setting off a gold rush that clearly violated Sioux treaty rights. From Fort Abraham Lincoln in June 1876 Custer set off to join the Big Horn Expedition under the command of General Alfred Terry. On June 25, 1876, Custer and 226 men of the 7th Cavalry were killed by the combined forces of Sioux and Cheyenne in southeast Montana. The famed "Custer's Luck" which followed him through the Civil War deserted him at the Little Big Horn. Custer was a vain, impetuous, unscrupulous, and fiercely ambitious officer seldom concerned about the welfare of his men. However, in spite of these negatives he was a highly effective cavalry commander in the Civil War, where boldness and daring were needed to fully utilize mounted forces.

Custer, George. *Carte de visite* by Brady, Washington. Author's collection.

DANA

Dana, Napoleon. *Carte de visite* by Brady, Washington. Author's collection.

Dana, Napoleon Jackson Tecumseh (1822-1905) was born into a military family at Fort Sullivan, Maine. Dana entered the Military Academy in 1838 and graduated twenty-ninth in the class of 1842. He was commissioned into the 7th Infantry and served in garrison duty until the military occupation of Texas in 1845. He served in the Mexican War, fighting in the Battles of Brownsville, Monterey, Vera Cruz, and Cerro Gordo, where he was seriously wounded and left for dead on the battleground. He later received a brevet to captain for his gallant and meritorious conduct storming Telegraph Hill during the Battle of Cerro Gordo. His post war assignments were supervising recruiting efforts and acting as an assistant quartermaster at Fort Snelling, Minnesota. Dana resigned from the army in 1855 and engaged in the banking business in St. Paul, Minnesota. He remained active in military affairs by serving as a brigadier-general in the Minnesota militia. After the firing on Fort Sumter, he was commissioned as colonel of the 1st Minnesota, which became one of the finest regiments in the federal army. Dana and the 1st Minnesota saw action in the Ball's Bluff disaster that resulted in the death of Lincoln's close friend, Oregon Senator Edward Baker. He was appointed a brigadier-general of volunteers in February 1823, and commanded a brigade in General John Sedgwick's division of the II Corps during the battles of the Virginia Peninsula campaign. He was severely wounded at the Battle of Antietam and later received an appointment to major-general. He did not return to duty until July 1863, when he was briefly assigned to head the Department of Philadelphia. He was then assigned to command various operations on the Texas Coast. In 1864 he commanded the XVI Corps and Districts of West Tennessee and Vicksburg. Dana was in charge of the Department of Mississippi with headquarters at Vicksburg when the steamboat *Sultana*, being used as a troop ship, was allowed to be in poor repair and overcrowded as it set up the Mississippi to take union troops and former prisoners of war to St. Louis. It blew up due to faulty boilers south of Memphis and nearly 1,800 lives were lost. As it occurred on May 26, 1865, just days after Lincoln's assassination, the tragedy did not receive full national attention. General Dana and none of his subordinates were ever held accountable for the tragedy. He resigned from the Army on May 27, 1865, and became a representative and agent of the American-Russian Commercial Company. In the 1870s he held various positions in railroad companies and served as deputy commissioner of United States government pensions.

DAVIES

Davies, Henry. *Carte de visite* by Brady, Washington. Author's collection.

Davies, Henry Eugene (1836-1894) was born in New York City and educated at Harvard, Williams and Columbia colleges. Davies entered the legal profession in New York City until the commencement of the Civil War, when he entered the army in 1861 as a captain in the 5th New York Infantry. The regiment fought in the Federal defeat at Big Bethel, and Davies was appointed a major in the 2nd New York (Harris) Cavalry in August 1861. His unit was part of General Irvin McDowell's forces holding the Rappahannock line during the Virginia Peninsula campaign led by General George McClellan. He took part in the Battle of Fredericksburg and accompanied Stonemans' Raid during the Chancellorsville Campaign. After the Second Battle of Bull Run, Davies was promoted to lieutenant-colonel in December 1862 and to Colonel of the 2d New York Cavalry in June 1863. He did not take part in the cavalry actions at the Battle of Gettysburg, as his regiment was being refitted after taking heavy losses at the cavalry battles of Aldie and Beverly Ford. In September 1863 he was appointed brigadier-general of volunteers. In late 1863 he was assigned to command the 1st Brigade in the 3rd Division of the Army of the Potomac Cavalry Corps and ably led his brigade in the battles of Bristoe Station and Mine Run. In the spring of 1864 he was elevated to division command and participated in nearly all of the cavalry actions of the Army of the Potomac until the surrender at Appomattox. He was distinguished in both General Judson Kilpatrick's and General Philip Sheridan's raids on Richmond and was wounded at the Battle of Hatcher's Run. Davies received a brevet to major-general of volunteers during the siege of Petersburg and was appointed to the full rank of major-general of volunteers on May 4, 1865. He was soon assigned as commander of the Middle District of Alabama, and not intending a military career, resigned from the Army on January 1, 1866. He returned to New York City and served as a city administrator and district attorney until 1872, when he returned to his law practice. He was a noted author, writing a biography of General Philip Sheridan. He was also an enthusiastic hunter, and wrote of his adventures hunting buffalo on the plains with General Sheridan and Buffalo Bill Cody. Although surrounded in the Army of the Potomac Cavalry Corps by West Point trained officers, Davies' thorough intelligence and courage demonstrated that civilians could be adequate if not good leaders of cavalry.

DIX

Dix, John. *Carte de visite* by Brady, New York. Author's collection.

Dix, John Adams (1798-1879) was born in New Hampshire and served in the War of 1812. He entered the army as a cadet in the 14th U.S. Infantry, commanded by his father, Colonel Timothy Adams Dix. He was later promoted to ensign and served on the Canadian frontier, fighting at the Battle of Lundy Lane as an aide to General Jacob Brown. His father died during the war, but Dix remained in the army until 1828. During his years in the army he had studied law and gained admission to the bar in the District of Columbia. He entered the legal profession in Cooperstown, New York, and for the next several decades served as superintendent of public schools, adjutant general, and secretary of state for New York. He also owned a newspaper and wrote editorials favoring the Jackson Democrats. By 1845 he was selected as a Free Soil Democrat to fill an unexpired term as U.S. Senator from New York. He supported James Buchanan for President in 1856 and opposed the election of Abraham Lincoln in 1860. In the last months of Buchanan's presidency Dix accepted the position of Secretary of the Treasury. It was while in this office that he sent his famous message to federal officials in New Orleans, "If anyone attempts to haul down the American flag, shoot him on the spot". During the early days of the Civil War Dix served as president of the Union Defense League, and through his leadership brought New York solidly into the war. When Lincoln made his first call for troops, Governor Edwin Morgan of New York appointed Dix a major-general in the New York Militia. After raising seventeen regiments and being appointed a major-general of volunteers in federal service Dix was ordered by General Winfield Scott to take command of federal forces stationed in Arlington and Alexandria, Virginia. This was seen by many congressional leaders as being ill advised, and President Lincoln then reassigned him to the Department of Maryland, where he was able to adroitly prevent secession efforts in Baltimore that threatened to take the state out of the union. In May 1862 General Dix was put in command of federal forces at Fortress Monroe and ordered to make a movement up the York River to White House. In doing so he was successful in cutting the line of communication between the Army of Northern Virginia and Richmond. This movement also resulted in the federals controlling the area between the Pamunkey and Rappahannock rivers. When almost in sight of Richmond General Dix's forces were recalled back to the defense of Washington, which was thought by President Lincoln and Secretary of War Stanton to be threatened by General Robert E. Lee's army. He superseded General John Wool in New York City during the Draft Riots and quelled the disturbances. Dix, while in New York, was also able to quickly return confidence to the financial markets that were vital to financing the war. He was mustered out of federal service in November 1865 and became Minister to France. Later he was elected Governor of New York and died in 1879. Although Dix may have been considered too old for field service, he rendered good military service to the union.

Dix, John. *Carte de visite* by Anthony, New York. Author's collection.

DODGE

Dodge, Grenville. *Carte de visite* by Brady, Washington. Author's collection.

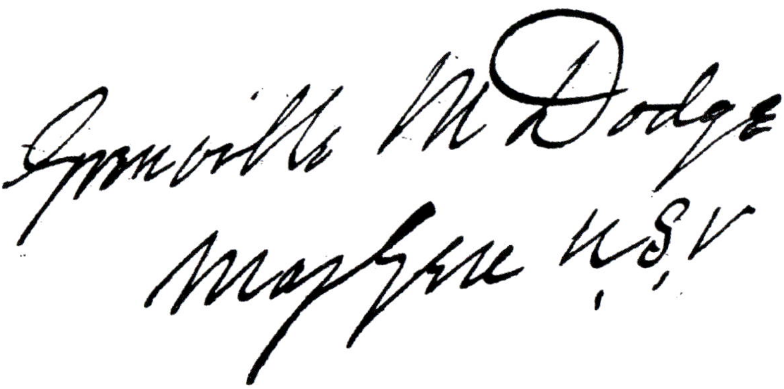

Dodge, Grenville Mellen (1831-1916) was born in Danvers, Massachusetts. He completed a diploma in 1850 in civil and military engineering at Norwich Academy, the second leading institution in providing officers to the Federal army. In 1851 he moved to Illinois and then to Iowa, engaging in surveying and railroad construction until the beginning of the Civil War. As with many other future Federal generals, he first was active in raising state troops that were later mustered into federal service. Dodge not only raised Iowa troops, but also made a trip to Washington to acquire arms and equipment for the state. Several months later he was mustered into the federal army as colonel of the 4th Iowa Infantry and served in Missouri with General John C. Fremont before being relieved of command. Dodge assumed command of a brigade in 1862 in the Army of the Southwest and was successful in capturing Springfield in the first phase of General Samuel Curtis' campaign to secure Arkansas and Missouri. He fought at the important Battle of Pea Ridge, where he was seriously wounded. For gallantry and meritorious conduct he was appointed to brigadier-general of volunteers dated to March 12, 1861. Appointed commander of the district of Mississippi in June 1862, Dodge had his first opportunity to demonstrate his previous civilian expertise in railroad construction. He repaired the Mississippi and Ohio railroad, providing a vital supply line to General Ulysses Grant's Vicksburg campaign, and at the same time he won several limited engagements against Confederate forces at the Hatchie River and Island 10. In the autumn of 1862 he was put in command of the 2nd Division of the Army of the Tennessee, and during the Vicksburg campaign operated an essentially independent command based at Corinth, Mississippi, protecting rail supply lines and mounting frequent raids. Dodge left Corinth in 1864, and on his way to join Grant at Chattanooga repaired or rebuilt the Memphis-Charleston railroad, a critical supply source for Grant's army, which would soon be fighting the Battles of Lookout Mountain and Missionary Ridge. In the Georgia campaign he fought well at the Battle Resaca and received appointment to major-general of volunteers dated to June 1864. During the Atlanta Campaign he led the XV Corps of General William T. Sherman's Army and was severely wounded in the head. He replaced General William Rosecrans in the Department of Missouri in December 1864 and remained several months before being transferred to the Department of Kansas to quell Indian hostilities and subdue bands of guerrillas. Dodge effectively punished both Indians and guerillas in a ruthless manner. He resigned from the army in 1866 to become chief engineer of the Union Pacific railroad and worked closely with Generals Sherman and Grant in extending the Union Pacific tracks through hostile Indian country. The three generals saw the railroad as a primary weapon against the tribes, as it moved settlers on to the great plains. It also facilitated commercial buffalo hunting that killed millions of buffalo, eliminating the primary food source and livelihood of plains tribes, such as the Sioux, Cheynenne, and Kiowa. Dodge, always interested in politics, was elected to Congress in 1867, but declined re-nomination and accepted the position of chief engineer of the Texas Pacific railroad, which he held between 1871 and 1881. In his career he built thousands of miles of road and was an effective lobbyist for railways. In his later years he was active in Civil War veterans' organizations and wrote several books on his experiences in the Civil War.

Dodge, Grenville. *Carte de visite* by Brady, Washington. Author's collection.

DOUBLEDAY

Doubleday, Abner. *Carte de visite* by Brady, Washington. Author's collection.

Doubleday, Abner. *Carte de visite* by Brady, Washington. Author's collection.

Doubleday, Abner (1819-1893) was born in upstate New York, and he was a practicing surveyor before entering the Military Academy in the class of 1842 and finishing twenty-fourth of forty-eight. He was commissioned in the 3rd Artillery and served in artillery garrisons until the Mexican War, where he was engaged in the battles at Monterey, Rinconda Pass, and Buena Vista. Unlike most of his contemporary junior officers, he did not receive any brevets in the war. After the Mexican War he returned to garrison duties, with the exception of fighting against the Seminole Indians in Florida in 1855 and 1856. Promoted to captain in the 1st Artillery in 1855, Doubleday was assigned duty at Fort Moultrie, South Carolina. In 1860, after a year's leave he returned to Charleston and was posted in the defense of Fort Sumter, located in Charleston Harbor. He reputedly aimed or fired the first artillery round in response to Confederate batteries on April 12, 1861. Doubleday has been cited by some historians as having been very opposed to surrendering Fort Sumter. On May 14, 1861, he was promoted to major in the 17th Infantry and served with General John Patterson in the Shenandoah Valley. Beginning with the Northern Virginia campaign in May 1862, Doubleday, as a brigadier-general of volunteers in brigade command in the III Corps, was involved in a series of battles and campaigns, including Second Bull Run, Antietam, Fredericksburg, and Chancellorsville. He often led his division, as General Rufus King and General John Hatch were both wounded or too ill to command. He was appointed major-general of volunteers November 29, 1862. When General John Reynolds became commander of a wing of the Army of the Potomac a few days before the Battle of Gettysburg, Doubleday was the senior division commander in the I Corps. At Gettysburg, the I Corps supported Buford's cavalry and engaged the leading units of the Army of Northern Virginia. Doubleday took command of the field when Reynolds was killed until relieved by General O.O. Howard. Doubleday's outnumbered I Corps fought hard for five hours before, along with Howard's XI Corps, they were driven through the town of Gettysburg to Cemetery Hill. After the first day the I Corps was almost decimated. On July 3rd, the second day of the battle, General George Meade, now in charge of the Army of the Potomac, relieved Doubleday as I Corps commander in favor of General John Newton. The reason for the relief was due to his reputation as being extremely slow to act. Doubleday then returned to division command and never forgot or forgave Meade's obvious lack of confidence in his leadership. Doubleday spent the remainder of the war mostly in Washington assignments. He reportedly, in trying to justify his actions at Gettysburg, wrote the longest battle report of any general taking part in the battle. He was breveted major-general in the regular army in 1865. Remaining in the army, he assumed several duty assignments in Texas and in other reconstruction states. He retired in 1873, and later wrote several works on his army experiences. Whether or not he invented baseball is open to question.

Doubleday, Abner. *Carte de visite* by Brady, Washington, showing General Doubleday with his wife. Author's collection.

EMORY

Emory, William. *Carte de visite* by Anthony, New York. Author's collection.

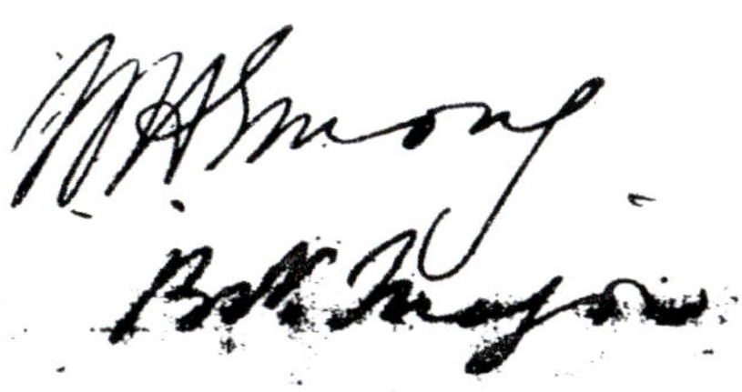

Emory, William Hemsley (1811-1887) was born in Queen Anne's County, Maryland He entered the Military Academy in 1827, graduating fourteenth in the class of 1831. Emory was commissioned in the 4th Artillery, where he served until resigning in 1836 to become a civil engineer. He returned to the army in 1838 as a first lieutenant in the Topographical Engineers, where he would compile a distinguished record. In 1844 Emory served on an expedition from Texas to California and compiled *Notes of a Military Reconnaissance from Fort Leavenworth in Missouri to San Diego California*. He received brevets to captain and major in the Mexican War for gallantry and meritorious conduct at the Battles of San Pasqual, San Gabriel, and Plains of Mesa. All of these engagements were with General Stephen Watts Kearney's expedition from New Mexico to California. Emory also received commendation for his work in establishing the boundary between the United States and Mexico in accordance with the Treaty of Guadalupe Hildago. Until the Civil War he was engaged in various surveying projects, compiling maps and writing scientific publications on the West. His frontier duty included the Utah Expedition in 1858, and at Fort Arbuckle, Indian Territory, during the Kansas disturbances. He was on an inspection tour of Pacific military installations in 1860-61, and while there was promoted to Lieutenant-olonel of the 1st Cavalry on January, 31, 1861. In field command of the 1st Cavalry companies stationed at Forts Cobb, Smith, Washita, and Arbuckle, he was able to assemble his meager forces and make a successful march to Fort Leavenworth. On the march he captured en route, without a loss of man in his command, a small group of rebel Texas troops. He resigned from the 1st Cavalry in May 1861 and was reappointed later in the same month as Lieutenant-Colonel of the 6th Cavalry. Emory was appointed a brigadier-general of volunteer forces in March 1862, and took part in the Virginia Peninsula Campaign engagements at Yorktown, Williamsburg, and Hanover Court House. He was especially lauded for leading a heroic cavalry charge at the Battle of Hanover Court House.

In late 1862 he was charged with organizing an infantry division that became part of General Nathaniel Bank's New Orleans Expedition and was engaged in the attack on Port Hudson while commanding a division of the XIX Corps. In Bank's ill-fated Red River Expedition in 1864 Emory won commendation for his leadership at the battles of Sabine Crossroads, Pleasant Hill and Cane River. In May 1864 he assumed command of the XIX Corps and was breveted major-general of volunteers in July 1864. Emory and the XIX Corps left New Orleans and returned to the defenses of Washington in time to participate in the repulse of General Jubal Early's raid on the capital. He commanded the XIX Corps in the 1864 Shenandoah Campaign and was engaged in the Battles of Opequan, Fishers' Hill, and Cedar Creek. He received a brevet to major-general in the regular army for gallant service at Cedar Creek, and five months after the surrender at Appomattox was appointed major-general of volunteers. His post war assignments included the Departments of West Virginia, Washington, the Gulf, and Republican (Platte). He also was a member of a number of army boards, and retired in 1876 as a brigadier general. Emory's role in the Civil War was similar to some other union officers coming from slave states or border-states with leanings toward the Confederacy. His promotions lagged behind his contemporaries, and he ranked fifth from last of those being appointed to be major generals of volunteers.

FESSENDEN

Fessenden, Francis. *Carte de visite* by Brady, Washington. Author's collection.

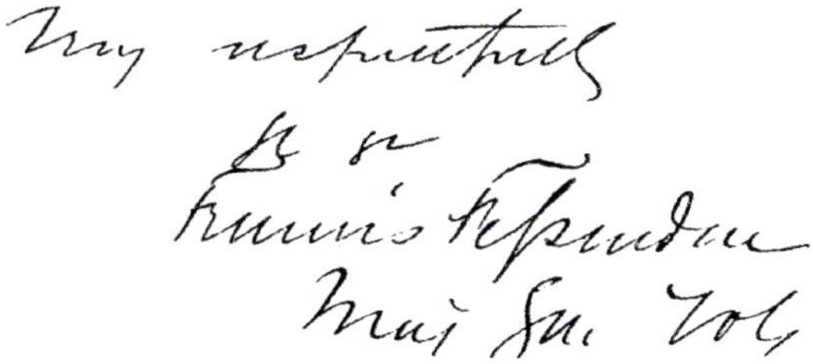

Fessenden, Francis (1839-1906) was born in Maine. He graduated from Bowdoin College in 1858 before studying law at Harvard. Being the son of United States Senator William Pitt Fessenden, later to be Lincoln's Secretary of the Treasury, probably accounts for him being appointed a captain in the 19th U.S. Infantry in May 1861. He was wounded leading his company in the second day of the Battle of Shiloh. After returning to duty he was appointed colonel of the 25th Maine Volunteers in September 1862, and was stationed in the defenses of Washington until appointed Colonel of the 30th Maine and taking part in General Nathaniel Banks' ill-fated 1864 Red River Expedition, where he led a brigade in the XIX Crops. Fessenden fought at Sabine Cross-roads, Pleasant Hill, and Monett's Bluff, where he received commendation and lost a leg. In July 1864 he was awarded brevets of major and lieutenant in the regular army and an appointment as a brigadier-general of volunteers. After recovering from his wound he was assigned a brigade in the Department of West Virginia. When appointed a major-general of volunteers in November 1865 he commanded the 1st Infantry Division in the same department. In late 1865 and early 1866 he served on the Wirz Military Commission that rendered a death verdict for the former commandant of Andersonville Prison. He also served as assistant commissioner of the Bureau of Freedmen and Abandoned Lands before retiring as a brigadier general in the regular army in November 1866. While performing credibly, the only explanation for his rapid rise to general rank was the political prominence of his father. His older brother, James Fessenden, also achieved a brigadier-general's star.

FOSTER

Foster, John. *Carte de visite* by Brady, New York. Author's collection.

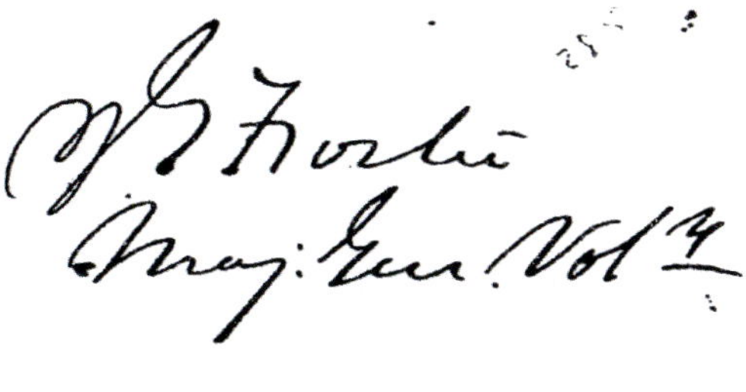

Foster, John. *Carte de visite* by Brady, Washington. Author's collection.

FREMONT

Fremont, John C. *Carte de visite* by Brady, Washington. Author's collection.

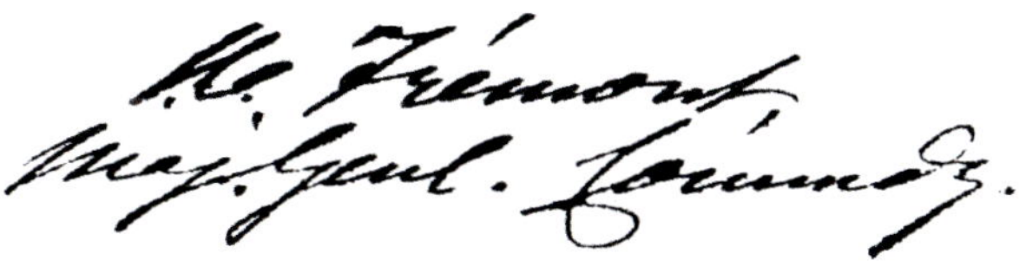

Fremont, John Charles (1813-1890) was born in Savannah, Georgia, and did not receive a formal military education. He attended Charleston College in South Carolina for several years, was expelled, and then briefly taught mathematics aboard a U.S. Navy vessel. Two years later he qualified as a professor of mathematics in the Navy, not to be confused with the U.S. Naval Academy. With political support from John Poinsett, a strong supporter of President Andrew Jackson in South Carolina, Fremont received an appointment in 1838 as a second lieutenant in the U.S. Army Topographical Engineers. On an expedition to Minnesota with distinguished scientist J.N. Nicollet he met Senator Thomas Hart Benton, later to be his father-in-law and a strong supporter of his explorations in the western United States. His first of many well publicized exploring expeditions was in 1842 to the Rocky Mountains. His second exploration in 1843 extended from St. Louis to the Great Salt Lake and into the Columbia River country. In making the return, Fremont's company met with extreme winter weather and returned west to the Sierra Nevada and Sutter's Fort, near present day Sacramento. His 1844 return trip took a southern route, and Fremont was back in St. Louis by late July 1844. Garnering political support and permission from the Army, Fremont returned to California in 1845, but soon was forced by Mexican authorities to move north to Oregon, where he received instructions from Washington to march back to Northern California. He assembled local forces and secured the area from Mexican authority and received promotion to lieutenant-colonel. The California settlers elected Fremont territorial governor on July 4, 1846. In the summer of 1847, the Navy's Pacific squadron captured Monterey and Commodore Robert Stockton was appointed by President John Polk to establish American power in all of California. Stockton appointed Fremont military commandant and governor, thereby ending the Bear Flag Revolution. A few months later General Stephen Watts Kearney, marching from Santa Fe, arrived in California with orders to establish a government. A dispute over authority arose between Kearney and Stockton, with Fremont electing to side with Commander Stockton. General Kearney brought court-martial charges against Fremont, and in a highly publicized court-martial Fremont, in 1847, was found guilty of mutiny, disobedience to orders, and conduct prejudiced to the good order of the service. President Polk approved the mutiny and disobedience charges, but did not impose the sentence of the court, thus allowing Fremont to resign. After his resignation from the Army he mounted another westward exploration in 1848 that resulted in near death for his party. After another expedition Fremont was elected to the U.S. Senate from California for a short time in 1850-51. Also, he and his wife acquired extensive property interests in California and became wealthy in the gold rush years. By 1856, due to his many explorations and newspaper coverage, Fremont was a household name, and the fledgling Republican Party selected him to run against Democrat James Buchanan. Fremont, long identified with abolitionists, lost the election by 174 to 114 electoral votes. Lincoln, shortly after his election, considered Fremont for several appointments, but after the firing on Fort Sumter offered Fremont a major-general's appointment in the regular Army. Fremont, at the time of the appointment, was in Europe, but returned to meet with Lincoln, receiving a broad set of orders to take command of military efforts in the Western Department. His department was confronted with civil insurrections in Missouri, and Confederate movements in Arkansas and up the Mississippi threatening Illinois and northern Kentucky. Soon after the Battle of Wilson's Creek in August 1861 he proclaimed martial law, arrested secessionists, assumed control of Missouri state government, and to the great consternation of President Lincoln ordered the freeing of slaves owned by individuals in rebellion against the United States. Lincoln instructed him to rescind the order, but he refused and Lincoln annulled it by presidential order. This, together with repeated and numerous charges of inept administration and corruption, led to his removal from command November 2, 1861. Due to political pressure originating in the radical wing of the Republican Party, Lincoln was forced to give Fremont another command. In March 1862 he was placed in command of the Mountain Department in Virginia. Fremont's only significant military action was the pursuit of General Stonewall

Fremont, John C. *Carte de visite* by Brady, Washington. Author's collection.

Jackson and an unsuccessful engagement at Cross Keys that allowed Jackson to make an escape with his army. Fremont resigned in June 1862 when General John Pope was placed in command of the Army of Virginia and the Mountain Department ceased to exist as an independent command. Fremont left Virginia for New York City, where he remained for the duration of the war awaiting orders. After the war Fremont was engaged in unprofitable railroad ventures and was Governor of the Arizona Territory between 1878 and 1881. He and his wife Jesse lived in near poverty in California for many years preceding his death in 1890. Fremont possessed charisma, but was an unstable personality ill-suited to lead large and important military operations.

Fremont, Jesse Hart Benton. *Carte de visite* by Anthony, New York. Jesse Fremont was very much a partner in General Fremont's military and political affairs. Author's collection.

French

French, William. *Carte de visite* by Brady, Washington. Author's collection.

French, William. *Carte de visite* by Brady, Washington. Author's collection.

French, William H. (1815-1881) was born in Baltimore. He entered the Military Academy in 1833, graduating twenty-second in the class of 1837. He was commissioned in the 1st Artillery and fought in the Florida Indian Wars. He also participated in the Cherokee removal that resulted in the *Trail of Tears* and the deaths of many Cherokees before reaching the Indian Territory in present day Oklahoma. He primarily served in staff positions during the Mexican War, but did receive brevets to captain and major for gallantry in the assault and capture of Mexico City. Promoted to captain in the 1st Artillery in 1848, he served in various artillery posts and on boards until the outbreak of the Civil War, at which time he was stationed at Fort Duncan, Texas. Appointed a brigadier- general of volunteers in September 1861, French led a brigade in the II Corps without particular distinction, and was breveted to lieutenant-colonel in the regular army for service at the Battle of Fair Oaks during the Peninsula Campaign. He led the 3rd division of the II Corps at the Battle of Antietam and was appointed to major-general of volunteers in November 1862, just before the Battle of Fredericksburg. After the Battle of Chancellorsville, French was assigned command of the District of Harper's Ferry, protecting the lines of communication to the Army of the Potomac. When General Dan Sickles, commander of the III Corps, was seriously wounded at Gettysburg, French, as senior division commander, became the III Corps commander on July 7, 1863. He led the III Corps during the campaigns following Gettysburg, but was charged after the Battle of Mine Run by General George Meade with slowness in action that allowed General Lee to escape from the slow pursuit of the Army of the Potomac. Until the Battle of Mine Run French had apparently enjoyed the confidence of General Meade, who was continually under pressure from Lincoln, Stanton, and the Committee on the Conduct of the War to rapidly follow-up on the victory at Gettysburg. In the spring of 1864 the III Corps was eliminated, meaning French was without a command. With his military reputation ruined he was mustered out of the volunteers on May 6, 1864, and served in staff assignments and as a lieutenant- colonel in the 2rd Artillery until the conclusion of the war. Post-war assignments included boards, inspections, and garrison duty. Some sources indicate that French's fall from grace with General Meade was over his excessive drinking and probable alcoholism.

GARFIELD

Garfield, James. *Carte de visite* by unidentified photographer. Author's collection.

Garfield, James. *Carte de visite* of the future President by Brady, Washington. Author's collection.

Garfield, James Abram (1831-1881) was born in Ohio. He graduated from Williams College in 1856, taught school, and was elected to the Ohio State Senate in 1859. In the first days of the Civil War he was successful in recruiting the 42nd Ohio Volunteers, in which without any military experience he was selected lieutenant-colonel. In December 1861, he was promoted to be Colonel of the 42nd Ohio Volunteers, comprised largely of students from Hiram College. Partially due to his scholarly abilities in reading and learning military science concerning the preparation of troops he was given command of the 18th Brigade in the Army of the Ohio. In insignificant actions at Middle Creek and Pound Gap Garfield was fortunate in opposing the hapless Confederate General Humphrey Marshall. These battles, being early in the war, brought a degree of fame to Garfield as the "Hero of Sandy Valley". He was appointed brigadier-general of volunteers in January 1862 and accompanied General Buell in the reinforcement of General Grant at the Battle of Shiloh, where he credibly commanded his brigade in the second day of the battle. After the siege at Corinth, Garfield became seriously ill and returned to Ohio to recuperate. When recovered he was ordered to Washington to sit on the court-martial of General Fitz John Porter, where he supported the verdict to dismiss Porter from the army. Probably for his cooperation with Secretary Stanton and General Henry Halleck on the Porter court-martial, he was offered a field command that he declined. However, he did accept a position as chief of staff to General William Rosecrans commanding the Army of the Cumberland. Garfield accompanied General Rosecrans in the Tullahoma Campaign and in the capture of Chattanooga. At the Battle of Chickamauga, Garfield was responsible for writing all of Rosecrans' orders except the one ordering the movement of General Thomas Wood's division to a position creating a gap in the federal lines soon exploited by General James Longstreet. General Rosecrans then began a frenzied retreat towards Chattanooga, with Garfield remaining on the field to discover where federal resistance still remained. He discovered General George Thomas still fighting on Muleshoe Ridge and stayed to assist in the defense. This action resulted in Garfield not being associated with the fleeing Rosecrans, and he was appointed major-general of volunteers in September 1863. Garfield's reputation in the army was always questionable, as he was obviously disloyal to Rosecrans while serving him as chief of staff. He was elected to Congress and scheduled to take his seat on December 7, 1863. At the request of President Lincoln he declined his September appointment as a major-general of volunteers. He served on the Military Affairs Committee as a strong supporter of the administration's policies, including those on the draft and bounties for reenlisting veterans. He was elected president in 1880 and was assassinated in 1881.

GIBBON

Gibbon, John. *Carte de visite* by Brady, Washington. Author's collection.

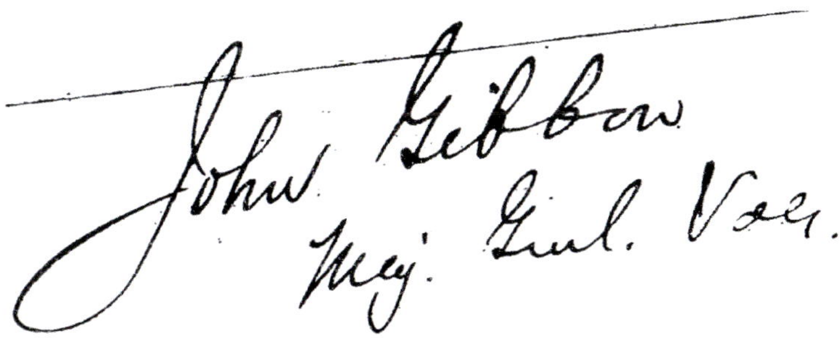

Gibbon, John (1827-1896) was born in Pennsylvania, but was raised in North Carolina. He entered the Military Academy in 1842, graduating twentieth in the class of 1847. Commissioned in the 3rd Artillery, Gibbon served briefly in the Mexican War and in actions against the Florida Indians. Gibbon was transferred to the Military Academy in 1855 and served as an artillery instructor until 1859, when he was sent to the Utah Territory. In 1859 he authored *The Artillerist's Manual*, a scientific treatment on gunnery that was used by both federal and Confederate artillerists. The outbreak of Civil War forced Gibbon's unit to march overland from Fort Crittenden, Utah, to Fort Leavenworth, Kansas. His first war assignment was as chief of artillery in General Irvin McDowell's division at the Battle of Bull Run. In late 1861 he also served as Chief of Artillery for the I Corps in the Army of the Potomac. Appointed to brigadier-general of volunteers and brigade command in the 3rd Division of the I Corps, he commanded the "Black Hat" brigade through all the battles of the Northern Virginia, Maryland, Rappahannock, and Pennsylvania Campaigns. After a hard fought battle with General Stonewall Jackson's troops at the Second Battle of Bull Run, Gibbon's brigade became known as the "Iron Brigade" and was the only western brigade in the Army of the Potomac. Gibbon was seriously wounded at the Battle of Fredericksburg and awarded a brevet as lieutenant-colonel in the regular Army. Disabled till shortly before the battle of Gettysburg, Gibbon and the "Iron Brigade" fought valiantly on Cemetery Ridge. At Gettysburg, after the wounding of General Winfield Hancock, he commanded the II Corps before again being wounded on the third day of the battle. He returned to his command for the Overland Campaign to Richmond and fought in all of its battles until the siege of Richmond. In 1864 the II Corps was unquestioningly the hardest fighting corps in the Army of the Potomac, but by Petersburg was essentially "fought out". Gibbon was promoted to major-general of volunteers to date from June 7, 1864, and given command of the XXIV Corps in the Army of the James. In the last few weeks of the war Gibbon participated in several actions, including the capture of Petersburg. He was one of the general officers acting as commissioners receiving the surrender of the Army of Northern Virginia. Mustered out of the volunteers January 15, 1866, Gibbon assumed command of the U.S. 36th Infantry as colonel before moving to the 7th U.S. Infantry in 1869. He served many years on frontier duty in various posts across the West. In 1876, he commanded a part of the "Little Bighorn" Yellowstone Expedition and had no role in, nor did he receive any blame for the Custer Massacre. Gibbon's troops arrived after the Battle of the Little Big Horn to rescue survivors and bury Custer's dead troops and provide transportation for the wounded. In 1877 Gibbon led his regiment against the Nez Perce and was seriously wounded at the Battle of Big Hole Pass. He later commanded the Departments of the Columbia and the Pacific. He was promoted to brigadier-general in the regular army in 1885 and retired in 1891.Gibbon was a hard fighting soldier, but many times lacked the personal tact necessary for success in the military hierarchy.

Gibbon, John. *Carte de visite* by Broadbent and Phillips, Philadelphia. This photograph most likely taken just after the end of the civil war. Author's collection.

GILLEM

Gillem, Alvan. *Carte de visite* by Anthony, New York. Author's collection.

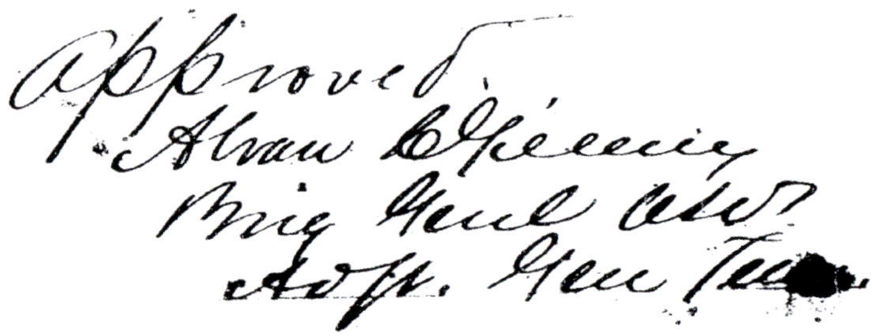

Gillem, Alvan Cullem (1830-1875) was born in Tennessee. He was admitted to the Military Academy in 1847, graduating eleventh in the class of 1851. He was commissioned in the 1st Artillery and began his career participating in fighting against Florida Indians and serving in frontier posts in Texas. His first Civil War assignment was acting as quartermaster for General George Thomas at the Battle of Mill Springs. In the 1862 Shiloh Campaign he was promoted captain and chief quartermaster of the Army of the Ohio. After the Battle of Shiloh he supervised the siege artillery of General Buell's forces in the advance on Corinth. In May 1862, Gillem became colonel of the 10th Tennessee Volunteers and fought in the battles of Lavergne and Harpeth River, as well as guarding important railroad lines in middle Tennessee. In June 1863, at the recommendation of Senator Andrew Johnson of Tennessee, then serving as military governor, Gillem was made Adjutant General of the state. He had previously been Provost Marshall of Nashville from August 1862 to December 1862. In August 1863 he was appointed a major-general of volunteers, and from this time until the end of the war the Tennessee born Gillem served in some capacity in that state, largely due to the efforts of future vice president Andrew Johnson. While in Nashville he received command of a cavalry division in the Army of the Cumberland, which did not accompany General William T. Sherman on the Atlanta Campaign. In November 1864 he led an expedition into East Tennessee, and at Greenville surprised and killed Confederate General John Hunt Morgan. In December 1864 he was in command of the Tennessee Cavalry on the unsuccessful raid into Southwest Virginia led by General George Stoneman. Upon the reorganization of the Tennessee state government in 1865, Gillem was elected to the legislature and received numerous reconstruction assignments, while at the same time serving as Colonel of the 24th U.S. Infantry. Gillem carried out his reconstruction duties with leniency and conciliation that soon brought him into disfavor with Radical Republicans in the congress. After Johnson's term of office, Gillem was transferred to the 11th Infantry and served at Galveston and Fort Concho, Texas. From Benicia Barracks, California, he commanded troops engaged in the Modoc Campaign, fighting the battle of the Lava Beds in 1873. In 1875, Gillem became seriously ill and died near Nashville on December 2, 1875.

GILMORE

Gilmore, Quincy. *Carte de visite* by Brady, Washington. Author's collection.

Gilmore, Quincy. *Carte de visite* by Brady, Washington. Author's collection.

Gilmore, Quincy Adams (1825-1888) was born in Ohio. He taught school three years before being admitted to the Military Academy in 1845 in the class of 1849, in which he finished first. He was commissioned in the Corps of Engineers and served in several construction projects before returning to West Point in 1852 in various capacities, including that of instructor in engineering and quartermaster. He was promoted to first-lieutenant in 1856 and served up to the Civil War in administration and supervising the construction of the New York Harbor fortifications. His first Civil War assignment was as chief of engineers in General Ambrose Burnside's Port Royal Expedition in 1861. He built the fortifications on Hilton Head Island that did much to solidify the federal control of that part of the North Carolina coast. Gilmore, in May 1862, organized the bombardment of Fort Pulaski, which was a strong defensive fortification protecting the water approach to Savannah, Georgia. His creative use of massed mortar batteries and rifled guns placed on Tybee Island insured the reduction and capture of the brick masonry constructed fort. His actions at Fort Pulaski brought him newspaper notoriety and brevets as lieutenant-colonel in the regular army and as brigadier-general of volunteers. In September 1863 Gilmore was placed in command of a division of Kentucky forces and defeated a Confederate force at the Battle of Somerset on March 30, 1863. In June 1863 he returned south and assumed command of the Department of the South and the X Corps, leading it in the capture of Fort Wagner and Battery Gregg in the operations against Charleston, South Carolina. Gilmore, utilizing a mammoth battery dubbed the "Swamp Angel", created a new age for long range gunnery. For his efforts he was appointed to major-general of volunteers and a brevet colonel in the regular army. Transferred in 1864 to command the X Corps in the Army of the James, he was engaged in the landing at Bermuda Hundreds, the action at Swift Creek, and the capture of the line in front of Drewry's Bluff. Gilmore may or may not have recommended to Butler to entrench and bottle up his army in the Bermuda Hundreds. However, Butler blamed Gilmore, who was only partially to blame for Butler's own ineptitude at Bermuda Hundred. Gilmore soon left Butler's Army of the James and was placed in command of the XIX Corps, based in the Washington defenses. In July 1864 Gilmore and elements of the XIX Corps defended the capital from Confederate General Jubal Early's raid. In pursuing Early he was seriously injured when his horse fell on his leg. In 1865 he returned to command the Department of the South until near the end of the war. Gilmore resigned from the volunteer forces in December 1865, reverting back to his regular rank of major of engineers, even though he had been breveted as brigadier and major-general in the regular army. He resumed his engineering duties and remained in the army till his death in 1888. Gilmore was one of the most capable, creative, and effective engineers in the army, and by his use of rifled cannon and mortars rendered masonry fortifications to be obsolete.

GRANGER

Granger, Gordon. *Carte de visite* by Anthony, New York. Author's collection.

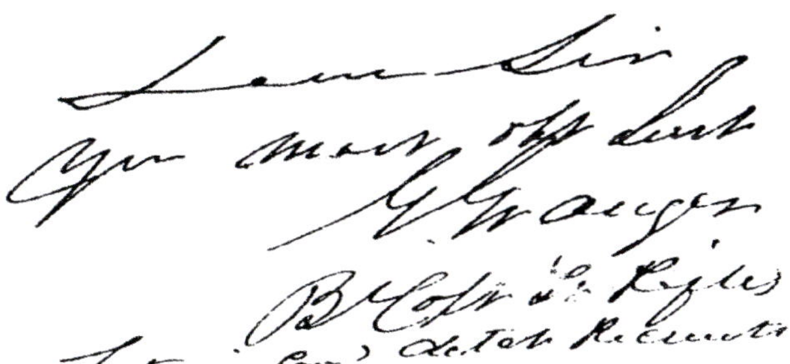

Granger, Gordon (1822-1846) was born in New York. He entered the Military Academy in 1841 as a member of the class of 1845, in which he finished thirty-fifth. He was commissioned in the 2d Infantry, but soon transferred to the Mounted Rifles and participated in most of the battles of the Mexican War, receiving brevets for gallantry in action at the battles of Contreras, Churubusco, and Chapultepec. After Mexico Granger remained in the Mounted Rifles and served in numerous duty stations in Texas, New Mexico, Oregon, and Washington, mainly on patrols and skirmishes with Indian tribes. On leave of absence in 1860-61, Granger's first Civil War assignment was on the staff of General George McClellan in Cincinnati. In June through August 1861 he accompanied General Samuel Sturgis' command as assistant adjutant general at the Missouri battles of Dug Spring and Wilson's Creek. He was appointed colonel of the newly mustered 2d Michigan Cavalry in September 1861 and commanded the St. Louis Arsenal until late December 1861. From this point on Granger was involved in nearly continuous combat with the western armies. Commanding a brigade in the Army of the Mississippi, he was engaged in the movement on New Madrid, Missouri, and the capture of Island No. 10. Following the advance and siege of Corinth, Granger received appointment as a brigadier-general of volunteers and assignment as chief of cavalry of the Army of the Mississippi. In July 1862 Granger was placed in command of the Army of Kentucky and the District of Central Kentucky, and stopped Nathan Bedford Forrest's raid into the interior of Tennessee and Van Dorn's raid across the Duck River. One of the few federal generals to distinguish himself at Chickamauga, he marched his reserve corps to the "sound" of the guns to reinforce General George Thomas, and possibly saved the federal army from an even more horrendous defeat. At Chickamauga his division suffered forty-four percent casualties in less than two hours, illustrating the ferocity of Thomas' battle to hold Horseshoe Ridge. In October 1863, Granger assumed command of the IV Corps and played a prominent role in the federal victory at the Battle of Missionary Ridge. He then accompanied General William T. Sherman's winter weather march to relieve the Confederate General James Longstreet's siege of federal General Ambrose Burnside at Knoxville. After being granted a leave of absence he was given command of a division in the Military Division of West Mississippi and won a victory at Fort Gaines, Florida. He was then put in command of the XIII Corps and ably led it at the capture of Mobile, Alabama, near the end of the war. He was breveted a major-general in the regular army in 1865 and made colonel of the 25th Infantry. Granger commanded the District of Memphis several times during reconstruction and died while in command of the District of New Mexico in January 1876. Granger was a hard drinking, profane, strict disciplinarian. A hard fighting general not always appreciated by his superiors, but usually placed by them in the thick of battle. In a written note to General Rosecrans he fairly well described himself, "The battle is neither to the swift nor to the strong but to him that holds on to the end". General Ulysses Grant would probably have agreed with Granger.

GRANT

Grant, U.S. *Carte de visite* by Brady, Washington. Author's collection.

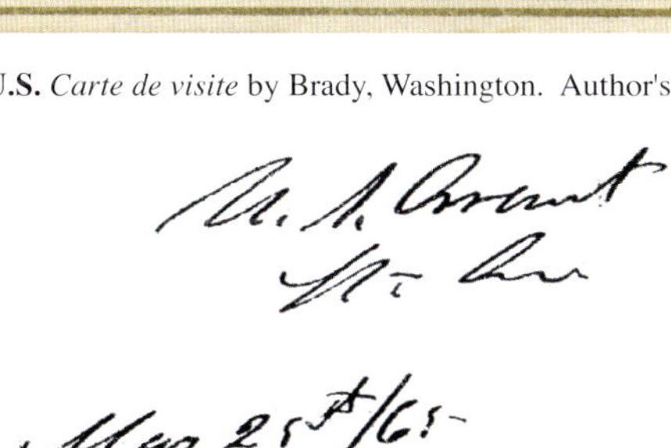

Grant, Ulysses Simpson (1822-1885) was born in Ohio. He was appointed to the Military Academy in 1839, graduating twenty-first of thirty-nine in the class of 1843. He was commissioned into the 4th U.S. Infantry and served on frontier duty until the Mexican War. Grant took part in numerous battles of that war and was breveted to first-lieutenant and captain for gallantry at the battles of Molino del Ray and Chapultepec. He was promoted to first-lieutenant in 1847 and appointed quartermaster of the 4th Infantry. Returning to the United States, Grant served in garrison duty at Fort Wayne, Michigan, and at Sacket's Harbor, Maine, before being posted to Benicia Barracks, California. He served in other isolated western duty stations far away from his family that eventually led to his resignation from the army in July 1854. Following his resignation, he was engaged in a number of pursuits in Missouri and Illinois that were financially unsuccessful. Upon the firing on Fort Sumter Grant had difficulty in obtaining a command, and it wasn't until June 1861 that Governor Richard Yates of Illinois appointed him Colonel of the 21st Illinois Volunteers. Grant's regiment was ordered to Missouri August 7, 1861, after his appointment to brigadier-general of volunteers with the rank dated May 17, 1861. His appointment was one of four brigadier generalships given to the state of Illinois, and Grant's appointment was probably the result of the political influence of Congressman Elihu Washburne, a fellow citizen of Grants' in Galena, Illinois. Washburne continued to support Grant for the rest of the war, and was an important intermediary with the Lincoln administration when Grant became general-in-chief of the federal army. Grant received command of federal forces stationed at Cairo, Illinois, in September 1861, and soon ordered the seizure of Paducah, Kentucky. In November 1861 he suffered a near defeat at the Battle of Belmont with his partially trained troops. On February 2, 1862, Grant's forces, containing three divisions and accompanied by the ships of Admiral Andrew Foote, captured Fort Henry, and on February 13th captured Fort Donelson, along with thousands of Confederate prisoners. In receiving the surrender of Fort Donelson, Grant stipulated that it be unconditional, and from this time Grant would be referred to in the press as "Unconditional Surrender" Grant. President Lincoln was pleased to finally find a "fighting general", and appointed Grant a major-general of volunteers with date of rank being February 17, 1862. After the fall of Fort Donelson Grant became commander of the District of West Tennessee and moved up the Tennessee River to support efforts of General Don Carlos Buell to take Nashville. On April 6, 1862, Grant's forces at Pittsburg landing, several miles upriver from Savannah, Tennessee, were attacked by General Albert Sidney Johnston. In two days of bloody fighting Grant was able to force the Confederate army to retreat back toward its supply base at Corinth, Mississippi. The Battle of Shiloh was a pivotal action in the Civil War, as it proved that both Grant and Sherman, even though surprised by Johnston, could "fight" a large army in the midst of blood, chaos, and confusion. Fortunately, the Army of the Ohio, led by General Don Carlos, arrived to reinforce Grant at the end of the first day of battle. Grant's superior General Henry Halleck, thinking that Grant had been derelict in being surprised at Shiloh, took personal command of the federal army and marched it at a snail's pace toward Corinth, throwing up entrenchments each night. Designated second in command, Grant was ignored until Halleck was ordered back to Washington to become Lincoln's general-in-chief. Grant then personally commanded the army at the victories of Iuka, Hatchie, and Corinth before making his first attempt to capture Vicksburg. The first movement toward Vicksburg failed when his base of supplies at Holly Springs,

Grant, U.S. *Carte de visite* by Brady, Washington. Grant is wearing a mourning band after President Lincoln's assassination. Author's collection.

Mississippi, was captured in a raid by Confederate General Earl Van Doren. His second attempt in 1863 was successful, as the federal army marched down the west bank of the Mississippi River below Vicksburg and then crossed back. Before putting Vicksburg under siege Grant's army defeated Confederate forces led by General John Pemberton at the battles of Champion Hill, Raymond, and the Big Black. The Mississippi state capital of Jackson was also captured. Suffering repeated defeats, Pemberton was forced to pull his remaining forces into the strong fortifications surrounding the city.

The investment of Vicksburg was eventually successful, with Pemberton surrendering on July 4, 1863. After his victory at Vicksburg that effectively cut the confederacy in half, Grant was promoted to major-general in the regular army. After the federal defeat at the Battle of Chickamauga, General William Rosecrans withdrew the Army of the Cumberland into the defenses of Chattanooga, where he was relieved by General George Thomas. Grant, now in charge of all federal forces in the West, through use of railroads and opening wagon roads was able to move sufficient supplies on the "Cracker Line" to sustain Thomas at Chattanooga. With reinforcements from the Army of the Tennessee, the battles of Lookout Mountain and Missionary Ridge were fought in September 1863, forcing General Braxton Bragg to retreat south into Georgia. Grant soundly trounced Bragg in one of the worst defeats for the Confederate army in the war. President Lincoln then appointed Grant in January 1864 to be a lieutenant-general in the regular army and General-in-Chief of all federal armies. Grant and Lincoln developed a strategic plan involving a coordinated movement involving all union forces. Understanding that sources of manpower for Confederate armies was dwindling, Grant reasoned that coordinated movements by federal armies in all theaters of the war would eventually break the back of southern resistance. One part of this strategy included General George Meade and the Army of the Potomac driving south toward Richmond and occupying the full attention of General Robert E. Lee's Army of Northern Virginia. At the same time General Benjamin Butler and the Army of the James was to be transported south of Richmond to cut Lee's communications and put pressure on Richmond from the south. General William Sherman, with the Army of the Tennessee and the Army of Cumberland, was to move south and capture Atlanta. General Nathaniel Banks, in the Department of the Gulf, was to put pressure on the Confederates with an expedition up the Red River. Two other federal forces were to move down the Shenandoah Valley towards Richmond. Grant, wishing not to be caught up in Washington politics, coordinated the federal forces from his headquarters attached to the Army of the Potomac. The 1864 Overland Campaign began with the Battle of the Wilderness in May 1864, and continued until April 1865, when Lee's army was driven to Appomattox and a final surrender. Grant continued as General-in-Chief of the Army after the end of hostilities and the assassination of President Lincoln. In the political turmoil of Andrew Johnson's administration Grant became embroiled in conflicts between Radical Republicans, Secretary of War Edwin Stanton, and President Johnson. He became General of the Army in August 1867, Secretary of War *ad interim* for a period in 1867, and was elected President of the United States in 1868, serving two terms until 1876. His two terms of office are often portrayed as being full of corruption and cronyism. Grant himself was honest, but lacked good judgment in selecting cabinet officers and making political appointments. After leaving office Grant traveled abroad for several years and returned to become a businessman in New York. Unfortunately, Grant was a better general than businessman, and in the early 1880s Grant's

Grant, U.S. *Carte de visite* by Brady, Washington. General Grant is wearing the uniform of a Lieutenant-General. Author's collection.

brokerage business went into bankruptcy. Fortunately, admirers provided him a trust fund and his political supporters were able to get his name returned to the Army list, carrying a lifelong pension. His last years were characterized by illness, and in 1885 he died before the publication of his *Personal Memoirs of U.S. Grant* would earn $450,000 for his wife and family.

Grant, U.S. *Carte de visite* by unidentified photographer. General Grant is shown with Julia Grant and their children. Author's collection.

Grant, U.S. *Carte de visite* by Anthony, New York. General Grant is shown with generals serving in the Army of the Potomac in 1864 and 1865. Author's collection.

GRIERSON

Grierson, Benjamin. *Carte de visite* by Alexander Gardner, Washington. Author's collection.

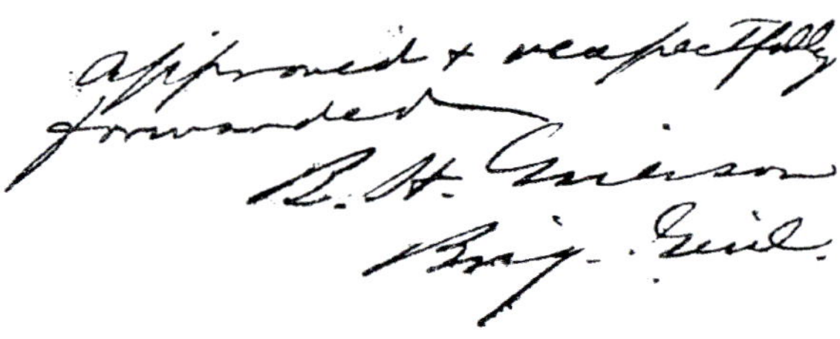

Grierson, Benjamin Henry (1826-1911) was born in Pennsylvania but raised in Illinois. He became a music teacher in Jacksonville and later operated a store in Meredosia, on the Illinois River. At the beginning of the Civil War Grierson enlisted as a private, then became a captain and a volunteer aide-de-camp to Illinois Brigadier-General Benjamin Prentice. In October 1861 he was commissioned as a major in the 6th Illinois Cavalry, later becoming colonel in April 1862. Grierson and the 6th Illinois, divided into squadrons posted at three different locations, participated in numerous skirmishes in western Tennessee and Mississippi. After Van Dorn's destruction of Grant's supply depot at Holly Springs Grierson was sent in pursuit. In April 1863, under orders from Grant, Grierson embarked on one of the most significant and successful cavalry raids of the war. With three regiments of cavalry, Grierson left the federal garrison at LaGrange, Tennessee, and marched seventeen days through Mississippi, destroying railroads and property before reaching Baton Rouge, Louisiana. This raid resulted in Confederate troops being redeployed away from Grant's line of march toward Vicksburg. Grierson's raid also demonstrated to Confederate leaders that federal troops could successfully operate without supply lines deep in southern territory. He was appointed brigadier-general of volunteers and participated in Sherman's Meridian Campaign, and in actions against Nathan Bedford Forrest at Brice's Cross Roads and at Tupelo, Mississippi, where Forrest was soundly defeated by General A.J. Smith's Division of the Army of the Tennessee. He was engaged in the Mobile campaign and was appointed major-general of volunteers dated May 1865. Mustered out of volunteer service in April 1866, he received an appointment as Colonel of the 10th U.S. Cavalry, a newly raised black regiment. For the next twenty years Grierson commanded the 10th Cavalry buffalo soldiers in frontier duty, mostly in Texas and Oklahoma. He had a less than friendly relationship with General Philip Sheridan and did not receive promotion to brigadier-general until 1890, several years after Sheridan's death. He retired in late 1890 and became a rancher. Grierson certainly proved himself an able leader of cavalry, but for whatever reasons never was given important commands during or after the Civil War by either Sherman, Grant, or Sheridan.

GRIFFIN

Griffin, Charles. *Carte de visite* by Brady, Washington. Author's collection.

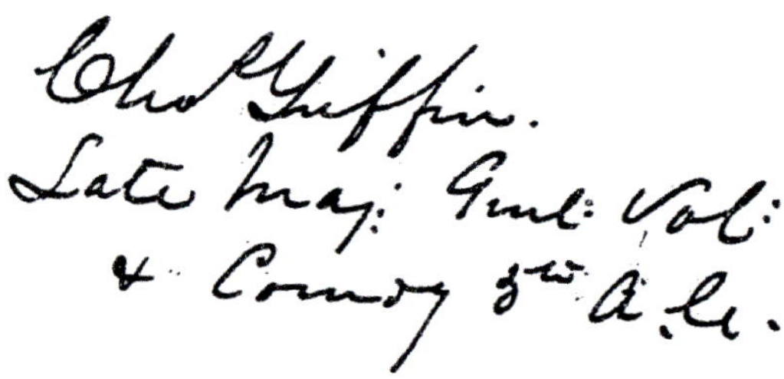

Hamilton, Charles Smith (1822-1891) was born in New York and schooled at Aurora Academy before entering the Military Academy in 1839. He graduated thirty-sixth of thirty-nine in the class of 1843. Hamiliton was commissioned in the 2d Infantry and served in garrison duty until the Mexican War, in which he received a brevet to captain for gallantry at the battles of Contrereas and Churubusco. Hamilton was seriously wounded at the Battle of Molino del Rey. In 1848, he was promoted to first-lieutenant and transferred to the 5th Infantry, serving as quartermaster in frontier duty stations in Texas and the Indian Territory. He resigned from the army in April 30, 1853, and engaged in farming and manufacturing flour in Fond du Lac, Wisconsin. Hamilton returned to military service in the first weeks of the Civil War as colonel of the 3rd Wisconsin Volunteers and a brigadier-general of volunteers with rank dated May 17, 1861. He commanded the 1st Division of General Nathaniel Banks' failed attempt in late 1862 to stop the advance of General Stonewall Jackson up the Shenandoah Valley. In the Virginia Peninsula Campaign he was transferred to the Army of the Potomac, commanding a division in General Samuel Heintzelman's III Corps. After the siege of Yorktown he was removed from his command by General George McClellan for alleged incompetence and was replaced by General Philip Kearny. With political influence, Hamilton was transferred to a division command in the Army of the Mississippi led by General William Rosecrans. He fought in the Battles of Iuka and Corinth and received appointment to major-general of volunteers dated September 19, 1862. Hamilton led the left wing of Grant's Army of the Tennessee in actions at Oxford, Mississippi, and commanded the District of Corinth until being appointed temporarily to command the XVI Corps and the District of West Tennessee. Hamilton was an ambitious officer, often using political influence to gain assignments and to blunt criticism for his failings in the field. This was obvious when he boldly attempted to use political pressure to secure command of the XVII Corps from General James McPherson. For this underhanded effort General Grant withdrew support for Hamilton and requested his removal from the Army of the Tennessee. Grant, at the time of the removal recommendation, was not aware that Hamilton had privately told Senator James Doolittle of Wisconsin that Grant was a drunkard. This, along with Hamilton's previous conflict with General McClellan, resulted in his forced resignation in April 1863. He returned to Wisconsin and engaged in private business after becoming a member of the University of Wisconsin Board of Regents. Strangely, Grant appointed him a U.S. Marshall in 1869.

HAMILTON, SCHUYLER

Hamilton, Schuyler. *Carte de visite* by Brady, Washington. Author's collection.

Hamilton, Schuyler (1822-1903) was born in New York City. A grandson of Alexander Hamilton, he entered the Military Academy in 1837 and graduated twenty-fourth in the class of 1841. At the age of nineteen he was commissioned in the 1st Infantry and served on frontier duty till the Mexican War. He was engaged at the Battle of Monterey and the skirmish of Mil Flores, where he was seriously wounded by a musket ball in the abdomen and by a lance that penetrated his chest and pierced a lung. He resigned from the army in 1855 after having served as an aide to General Winfield Scott for seven years. At the outbreak of the Civil War he returned to serve on Scott's staff as military secretary, holding the staff rank of colonel. Upon Scott's retirement, Hamilton became assistant chief of staff and commander of the Department of St. Louis under General Henry Halleck, commanding the Department of Missouri. Halleck was probably instrumental in gaining an appointment to brigadier-general dated to November 12, 1861, for his brother-in-law. Hamilton was given division command in General John Pope's Army of the Mississippi and participated in the Battles of New Madrid and Island No. 10. With Pope he endured Halleck's slow advance on Corinth, commanding the left wing of the Army of the Mississippi. He received the appointment of major-general of volunteers in September 17, 1862, and shortly after fell ill with a severe case of malaria. His long illness not only made his resignation from the army necessary, but it also caused his appointment to major-general of volunteers not to be sent to the Senate for confirmation. He resigned from the army on February 27, 1863, and in later years tried often to be reinstated. Hamilton was a competent and brave officer, but had health problems serious enough to disqualify him from commands in the field. It is unknown whether his attempts to stay in the army were directed toward field or staff assignments.

HANCOCK

Hancock, Winfield Scott. *Carte de visite* by Brady, Washington. Author's collection.

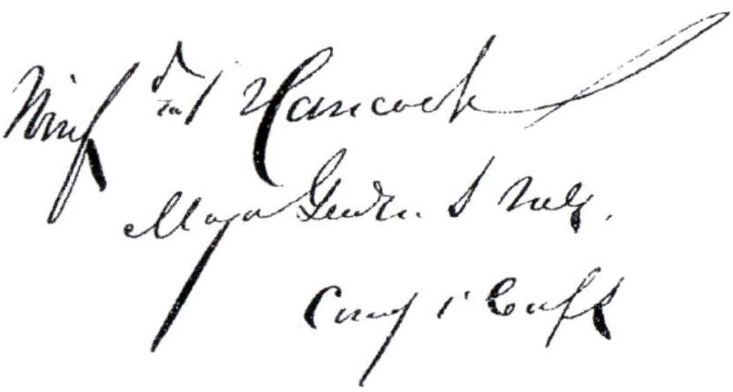

Hancock, Winfield Scott (1824-1826) was born in Pennsylvania, and at the age of sixteen was admitted to the Military Academy, graduating eighteenth of twenty-five in the class of 1844. This famous class contained a plethora of union Civil War generals, including Ulysses Grant, George McClellan, William Franklin, William F. Smith, Joseph Reynolds, William Rosecrans, and Nathaniel Lyon. Among his classmates serving in the Confederate army were Stonewall Jackson, George Pickett, Kirby Smith, Simon Buckner, and James Longstreet. Hancock was commissioned in the 6th Infantry, and for two years was posted on frontier duty in the Indian Territory. In 1846 he was stationed with his company near the Mexican border till ordered into Mexico. He saw his first battle action at the National Bridge, leading a storming party and capturing the bridge. For this and other actions in Mexico he was breveted a first-lieutenant. Hancock returned from Mexico as his regiment's quartermaster stationed at Jefferson Barracks, near St. Louis, and then at Fort Snelling, Minnesota. In 1855 he was promoted to captain and was ordered to accompany General William Harney's forces in the seemingly never ending wars against the Seminoles in Florida. He was next ordered to Kansas with General William Harney to suppress the disturbances between anti-slavery and pro-slavery groups. In 1858, he accompanied the 6th Infantry on General Harney's expedition from Fort Bridger, Utah, to California. He remained in California as chief quartermaster of the Southern District of California until the outbreak of the Civil War. Hancock was appointed as a brigadier-general of volunteers in September 1861, commanding a brigade in the IV Corps. His brigade saw hard action during the Virginia Peninsula Campaign, and he was mentioned in dispatches from General McClellan, saying that his leadership was superb. For the rest of the war he was mentioned in the press and elsewhere as "Hancock the Superb". He commanded a division in the II Corps during the battles of South Mountain and Antietam, where he was particularly praised for actions in the second day of that battle. After taking command of the II Corps following the death of General Israel Richardson in November 1862 he received appointment to major-general of volunteers. He led his division at the Battle of Fredericksburg, making a fearless assault on Marye's Heights against what may have been the most severe fire of the war. After the federal defeat at the Battle of Chancellorsville Hancock's II Corps covered the retreat of the Army of the Potomac from heavy Confederate attacks as it crossed back over the Rappahannock. In the Gettysburg Campaign Hancock commanded the II Corps, and arrived on the field several hours after the death of General John Reynolds. He promptly carried out orders given him by General Meade and took command of the I Corps and XI Corps after they retreated through the town of Gettysburg to Cemetery Hill. He organized the federal forces on Cemetery Ridge that were able to prevent the Confederates from rolling up the left of the federal line. In the second day, Hancock was ordered by General Meade to reinforce the overextended lines of General Dan Sickles' III Corps from being overwhelmed by General James Longstreet's flanking attacks in the Peach Orchard, Devils Den, and on the Round Tops. On the third day of the battle Hancock's II Corps turned back the celebrated Confederate charge of General George Pickett's command. In this action he was seriously wounded when a bullet hit his saddle and drove nails and bits of leather into his leg and groin. He commanded the II Corps during the 1864 Richmond Campaign, but was continuously hampered by his Gettysburg wound. The II Corps usually served as the spearhead of the Army of the Potomac in the battles of the Wilderness, Spotsylvania, Cold Harbor, and Petersburg. With high casualties and a lack of replacements it eventually became a shadow of its former self. The same could be said of Hancock, as he fought his last good battle at Spotsylvania. He received promotion to brigadier-general in the regular army in August 1864, and by November 1864 was forced to go on sick leave. While still incapacitated, Hancock agreed to raise a Veteran Reserve Corps comprised of veterans already having served three years. This effort was not successful, and he served the remainder of the war in an administrative assignment. In 1866, he was made a major-general in the regular army and commanded an expedition against tribes of plains Indians in 1866-67. Hancock was nominated by the Democratic National Convention in 1880 as their presidential candidate, and ran against and narrowly lost to James A. Garfield, another former Civil War general. He continued in the Army and died in 1886 while in command of the Department of the East. Grant always spoke of Hancock as being the finest general in the war who never exercised a high independent command.

Hancock, Winfield Scott. *Carte de visite* by Rockwood, New York. This photograph was taken several years after the war. Author's collection.

HARTSUFF

Hartsuff, George. *Carte de visite* by Brady, Washington. Author's collection.

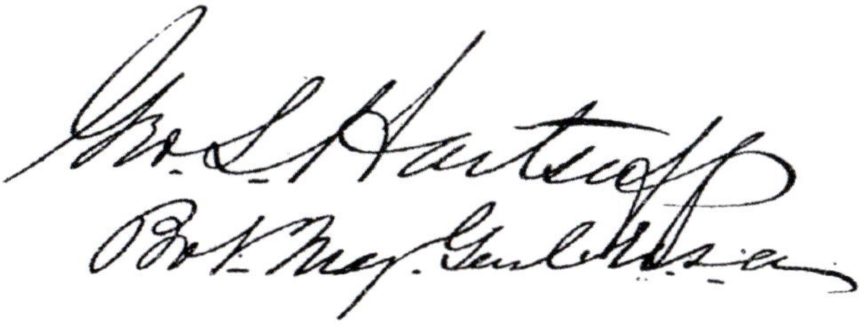

Hartsuff, George Lucas (1830-1874) was born in New York, but raised in Michigan. Hartsuff was admitted to the Military Academy in 1848 and graduated nineteenth in the class of 1852. Commissioned in the 2d Artillery, he served in frontier posts and was severely wounded twice fighting the Seminole Indians in Florida. These wounds, which eventually resulted in his death, incapacitated him for months. He finally returned to duty in September 1856 at West Point as assistant instructor of artillery tactics. In September 1860 Hartsuff survived the wreck of a steamship in Lake Michigan. His participation in the Civil War began with being assigned as a brevet captain in the Adjutant General's Office, and he was sent on the secret expedition to reinforce Fort Pickens, Florida. He returned to Washington and became chief of staff to General William Rosecrans, commanding the Department of West Virginia. In April 1862 Hartsuff was appointed brigadier-general of volunteers and placed in command of a brigade in General Irvin McDowell's Corps. He fought well at the Battle of Second Bull Run, receiving a promotion to major in the regular army. At the Battle of Antietam Hartsuff was again severely wounded and was incapacitated for a number of months, but still received an appointment to major-general of volunteers. In April 1863 he was placed in command of the XXIII Corps in Kentucky and led its efforts to contain Confederate John Hunt Morgan. Again incapacitated, he briefly was assigned to command fortification works in the siege of Petersburg, and at the end of the war was reassigned to the Adjutant General's Office. Until his retirement in 1871 he served in various departments as adjutant general. He died from the effects of his wounds in 1874.

HAZEN

Hazen, William. *Carte de visite* by Webster, Louisville, Kentucky. Author's collection.

Hazen, William Babcock (1830-1887) was born in Vermont, but moved at an early age to Ohio. Hazen was admitted to the Military Academy in 1851, graduating twenty-eighth in the class of 1855. He was commissioned in the 8th U.S. Infantry, and before the outbreak of the Civil War served in various frontier assignments in Oregon and Texas. In 1859 he was seriously wounded in a battle with Comanche Indians on the Yano River in Texas and spent nearly two years on sick leave. He was a captain in the 8th Infantry when assigned to the Military Academy in February 1861 as an instructor in tactics. In October 1861 he became colonel of the 41st Ohio through the assistance of Lieutenant-Colonel James Garfield, a boyhood friend and an upcoming Ohio politician. Soon elevated to brigade command in General Don Carlos Buell's Army of the Ohio, Hazen, in the second day at the Battle at Shiloh, commanded a charge that protected the right wing of General William Nelson's division. After Shiloh he received an appointment as brigadier-general of volunteers in November 1862. At the Battle of Stone's River Hazen's reputation was enhanced by repulsing numerous Confederate assaults, although he lost nearly a third of his brigade. Later he personally had erected on the battleground a memorial honoring the dead. This was to be the first of many Civil War monuments erected by states and veteran organizations. Unlike many of General William Rosecran's generals, Hazen performed credibly at the Battle of Chickamauga in September 1863. His movement during the Chattanooga campaign at Brown's Ferry, laying fifty-two pontoons for bridging the Tennessee River and seizing Lookout Valley, opened the federal supply line called the "cracker line" to the Army of the Cumberland. At the Battle of Missionary Ridge Hazen's troops were among the first to the top of the ridge and captured eighteen Confederate field pieces. He was given command of the 2rd division in the XV Corps during the Atlanta Campaign and on General William Sherman's March to the Sea. At the end of the March to the Sea he was assigned to move on Fort McAllister, which he successfully stormed, thereby opening the Ogeechee River and securing a coastal base for Sherman's army. He was appointed major-general of volunteers in December 1864. After the Battle of Bentonville, North Carolina, on April 15, 1865, he was given command of the XV Corps and led it in the grand review in Washington. Mustered out of the volunteers in 1866 after receiving brevets to brigadier-general and major-general in the regular army, he became colonel of the 38th Infantry and later the 6th Infantry. He fought in numerous Indian campaigns until finally appointed a brigadier-general in 1880 as the army's chief signal officer. He also spent a year as an observer during the Franco-Prussian War. Hazen at times was contentious and engaged in long term conflicts over Indian policy with General George Custer and General Philip Sheridan. He also helped expose the illegal and corrupt workings of the spoils system in post trading contracts on Indian reservations. This led to the impeachment of Secretary of War William Belknap and to the displeasure of President Grant. Hazen also ran afoul of Secretary of War Robert Lincoln and damaged his chances for promotion and transfer from isolated posts such as Fort Buford, Montana.

HEINTZELMAN

Heintzelman, Samuel. *Carte de visite* by Brady, Washington. Author's collection.

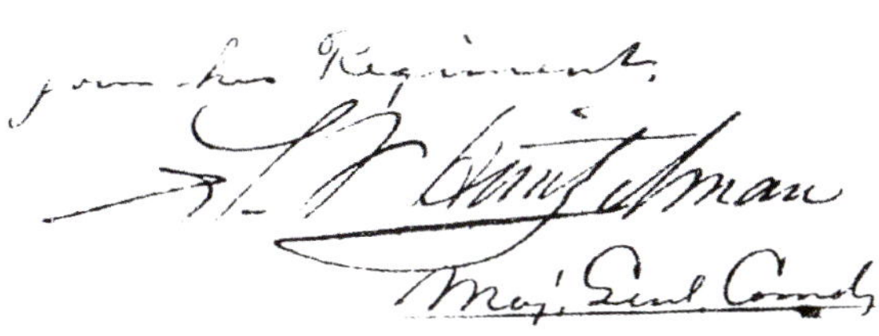

Heintzelman, Samuel. *Carte de visite* by Brady, Washington. Author's collection.

Heintzelman, Samuel Peter (1805-1880) was born in Pennsylvania. He was appointed to the Military Academy in 1822 and graduated seventeenth in the class of 1826. Heintzelman was commissioned in the 3rd Infantry, and was to spend the next forty-three years in service. Prior to the Mexican War he served mainly garrison duties in various posts, both in the south and on the frontier. In the War with Mexico he was breveted to major for gallantry at the Battle of Huamantla. In 1848 Heintzelman was transferred to frontier duty at San Diego, California, and in 1850 constructed Fort Yuma, Arizona, until relieved in 1852. At this isolated post he participated in several skirmishes with the Yuma Indians. He commanded the Department of Southern California until 1854. Heintzelman was promoted to major in the 1st Infantry in 1855, and until the outbreak of the Civil War was stationed on frontier duty in Texas. In 1859 he commanded the forces sent to capture Cortina's Mexican marauders after their attack on Brownsville. At the start of the Civil War he was on recruiting duty and was ordered to Washington, being made colonel of the 17th Infantry and brigadier-general of volunteers. His first combat was leading a successful attack and capture of Alexandria, Virginia, on May 24, 1861. He then commanded the 3rd Division of McDowell's army at the Battle of Bull Run and was slightly wounded. Heintzelman then served in the Washington defenses until the commencement of General George McClellan's Virginia Peninsula Campaign in March 1862. He commanded the III Corps of the Army of the Potomac at the siege of Yorktown, Malvern Hill, Oak Grove, and Savage Station. He was then appointed major-general of volunteers and awarded a brevet to brigadier-general in the regular army for the Battles of Williamsburg and Seven Pines. The aging Heintzelman's overall performance in the Peninsula Campaign was mediocre at best, and he was fortunate in having aggressive and competent subordinates, such as Philip Kearny and Joseph Hooker, leading divisions. The III Corps was ordered from Harrison's Landing to join General John Pope's Army of Virginia just before its defeat at the Second Battle of Bull Run. The III Corps at Second Bull Run was repelled at Groveton in their attack on Stonewall Jackson's forces. After the Battle of Second Bull Run, Heintzelman commanded the XXIII Corps and the southern part of the Washington defenses until relieved in October 1863. He was, in effect, shelved for the remainder of the war, commanding the Department of the North, including Ohio, Indiana, Michigan, and Illinois. Mustered out of volunteer service in August 1865, Heintzelman returned to the 17th Infantry then stationed in Texas. He retired from active duty in 1869 after forty-seven years of service.

HERRON

Herron, Francis. *Carte de visite* by Brown, St. Louis. Author's collection.

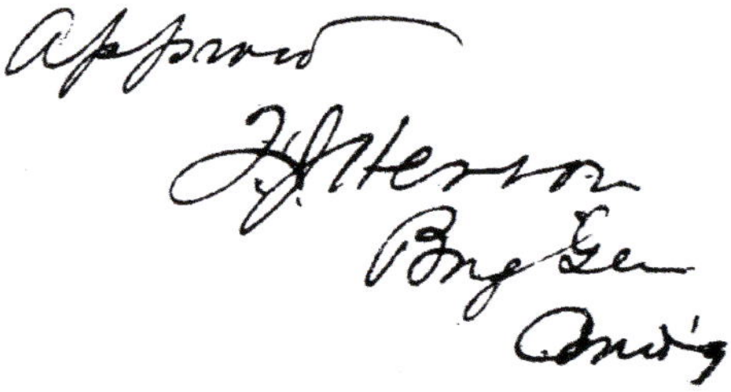

Herron, Jay Francis (1837-1902) was born in Pennsylvania. He attended Pittsburgh University, and with his brothers in 1855 established a bank in Dubuque, Iowa. Active in the militia and a strong supporter of Abraham Lincoln, he was among the first to join the war effort in Iowa. Herron was mustered in as captain of the 1st Iowa Infantry and fought in General Nathaniel Lyon's ill-fated Battle of Wilson's Creek. In September 1861 he was appointed Lieutenant Colonel of the 9th Iowa and fought valiantly at the Battle of Pea Ridge, for which he was appointed a brigadier-general of volunteers commanding the 3rd Division in the Army of the Frontier. At Wilson's Creek Herron was both wounded and captured, but was repatriated in time to lead two divisions in the Army of the Frontier on a spectacular forced march of a hundred and fourteen miles in three days from Wilson's Creek to join General James Blunt's forces at Prairie Grove. Herron's heroic march reached Blunt before they together successfully engaged the slower moving army of Confederate General Thomas Hindman. There is little doubt that Herron saved Blunt's small force from being overwhelmed by Hindman's much larger force. For his relief of Blunt he was appointed major-general of volunteers, being the youngest major-general in either the Federal army or the Confederate army at time of appointment. After the Battle of Prairie Grove Herron captured Van Buren, Arkansas, and in March 1863 joined General Ulysses Grant's army at Vicksburg, serving as commander of a division in the Army of the Tennessee. He led the left wing and later effected the investment and capture of Yazoo City. Herron was aboard the gunboat *De Kalb* with navy captain John G. Walker when it was destroyed by a torpedo. After the Vicksburg Campaign Herron moved through a number of commands, including the XIII Corps. In 1864 he was sent to the Gulf Coast with the XIII Corps to prevent cotton smuggling, and to quietly coordinate with President Benito Juarez of Mexico to prevent French troops from establishing posts on the border. He was transferred in 1865 to command the Department of Northern Louisiana and cooperated with General E.R.S. Canby in capturing Mobile. Herron also engaged Confederate General Richard Taylor before taking the final surrender of the Trans-Mississippi army. In 1865, he was appointed a commissioner to negotiate treaties with Indian tribes, and on June 7 1865 resigned from the army and began a carpet bag career in Louisiana reconstruction politics. As a New Orleans lawyer, he managed to be selected U.S. Marshall for the district of Louisiana and won election as Secretary of State in 1872. He moved to New York in 1876 and was associated with manufacturing interests, often participating in meetings and reunions of the Grand Army of the Republic and the Loyal Legion. According to his death certificate he died a pauper in 1902.

HITCHCOCK

Hitchcock, Ethan Allen. *Carte de visite by* Black and Case, Boston. Author's collection.

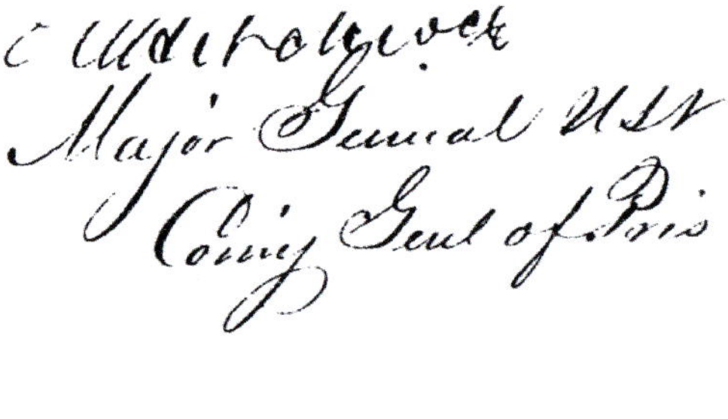

Hitchcock, Ethan Allen. *Carte de visite* by Appleton, New York. Author's collection.

Hitchcock, Ethan Allen (1798-1870) was born in Vermont. He entered the Military Academy in 1814 and graduated in 1817. Hitchcock was commissioned a third lieutenant in the Corps of Artillery, and in 1818 was promoted to second-lieutenant. In 1818 he was promoted again to both second-lieutenant and first-lieutenant in the 8th Infantry. He saw action in the Florida Indian Wars periodically from 1829 to 1843 as a captain in the 1st Infantry, major in the 8th Infantry, and lieutenant-colonel of the 3rd Infantry. Hitchcock also served in the 1830s as an instructor at the Military Academy and in the Canadian Border Disturbances. During the Mexican War Hitchcock received a brevet to brigadier-general for his conduct and gallantry at the battles of Contreras, Churbusco, and Molino Del Rey. In 1847 General Winfield Scott appointed him the army's inspector general during the march to capture Mexico City. He returned from Mexico City as colonel of the 2nd Infantry, but was forced to take a year's sick leave before assuming command of the Pacific Division from 1851 to 1854. He was in garrison duty at Carlisle Barracks in 1855, and resigned from the army when Secretary of War Jefferson Davis refused his request for extension of a sick leave. Prior to the Civil War Hitchcock resided in St. Louis and wrote extensively on esoteric philosophical topics and studied literature. At the outbreak of the war General Winfield Scott requested his services, and in February 1862 he received a commission as major-general of volunteers and was ordered to Washington, where to his shock Secretary of War Stanton offered him command of the Army of the Potomac and all other Federal forces. Hitchcock was able to convince Stanton that he was much too old for field duty and suffered from ill health. Instead, he assumed the role of an adviser to Stanton and later Lincoln. Perhaps his most important contribution was as head of the War Board. This seldom mentioned group consisted of key military and government leaders advising the President on a regular basis. Later Hitchcock became not only a trusted Lincoln advisor, but also a personal friend of the president. He also competently served in the important position as commissioner of prisoners and exchange. In November 1865 President Johnson appointed him Commissary General of Prisoners to manage the consideration and judgment of claims against the government during the Civil War. One of the great soldier-scholars, Hitchcock was a brilliant administrator and perhaps rendered his friend Abraham Lincoln his best service by refusing field command.

HOOKER

Hooker, Joseph. *Carte de visite* by Fredricks, New York. Author's collection.

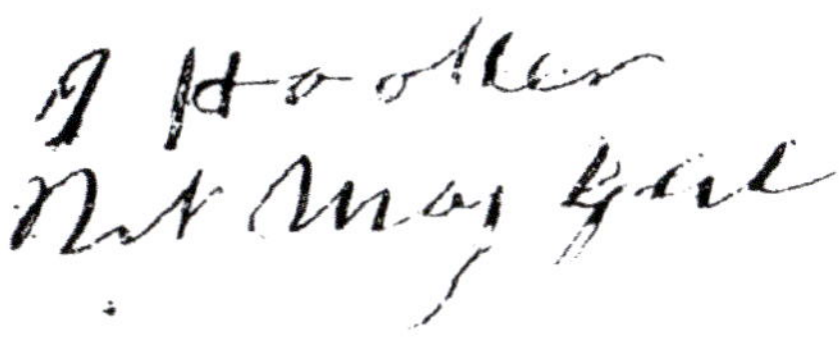

Hooker, Joseph (1814-1879) was born in Massachusetts. He was admitted to the Military Academy in 1833, graduating twenty-ninth in the class of 1837. Hooker was commissioned in the 1st Artillery, serving in the Florida War from 1837-38 and later in the Canadian Border Disturbances. He served as the regimental adjutant stationed at the 1st Artillery headquarters from 1841 to 1846. During the Mexican War Hooker served on the staffs of Generals Persifor Smith, Thomas Hamar, William Butler, and Gideon Pillow. As a staff officer he was engaged in numerous battles, and was awarded brevets up to lieutenant-colonel, a feat no other lieutenant accomplished during the war. He was assigned to the Pacific Division in 1849 and remained there until a leave of absence that was extended from 1851 to 1853, at which time he resigned from the army. Residing in California, he farmed and was superintendent of a company building military roads in western Oregon. From 1859-61 he was a colonel in the California Militia. At the end of the Mexican War Hooker had testified against the conduct of General Winfield Scott, and this likely prevented him from being initially accepted for service at the onset of the Civil War. Upon a personal appeal to President Lincoln, Hooker was appointed a brigadier general of volunteers and assigned in August 1861 to the defenses of Washington, with the responsibility of guarding the lower Potomac River.

In the 1862 Virginia Peninsula Campaign, Hooker commanded the 2d Division of the III Corps in all the battles in the campaign leading up to the evacuation from Harrison's Landing. Hooker's division was one of General Heintzelman's III Corps divisions sent to reinforce General John Pope and the Army of the Virginia at the Battle of Second Bull Run. He was appointed a major-general of volunteers for service in the Peninsula Campaign, where he earned his sobriquet "Fighting Joe Hooker" from a press telegram saying that "Hooker was still fighting". Placed in command of the I Corps, Hooker capably commanded it at the Battle of Chantilly and the Battle of Antietam, where he was seriously wounded in the foot. Upon returning from sick leave Hooker commanded the V Corps at the Battle of Fredericksburg, where he bitterly criticized Army of the Potomac commander General Ambrose Burnside. For his intemperate action he was among several generals Burnside demanded be cashiered from the Army. Instead, Burnside was removed and Hooker became commander of the Army of the Potomac. Lincoln, desperate for an aggressive and fighting general, selected Hooker, who had the strong backing of Secretary of the Treasury Salmon Chase and radical Republicans. Over the winter of 1862-63, Hooker reorganized and greatly improved the condition of the army. His spring campaign against the Army of Northern Virginia began with an adroit movement of his 135,000 troops across the Rapidan and Rapphannock Rivers, but at Chancellorsville Court House Hooker's XI Corps, under their new leader, General O.O. Howard, was surprised and routed by Stonewall Jackson's famous flank attack. In the battle Hooker received a head injury and was knocked unconscious for a period of time. At a council of his corps commanders Hooker made the decision to fall back across the Rapphannock River, and then skillfully deployed his forces to protect Baltimore and Washington. Once Hooker had his army over the Rapphannock he requested reinforcements be sent to him from the Harper's Ferry garrison. Army general-in-chief Henry Halleck refused and Hooker asked to be relieved of command. Halleck, who had been engaged with Hooker in a long running feud, accepted the request. Hooker probably felt that Halleck and President Lincoln would refuse his request for relief at such a perilous time for the Army of the Potomac, as Lee was invading Maryland. However, Lincoln likely

Hooker, Joseph. *Carte de visite by* Brady, Washington. Author's collection.

felt that Hooker was either unfit or could not overcome dissension with his corps and division commanders. He was immediately replaced by General George Meade just three days before the battle of Gettysburg. After General William Rosecrans' severe defeat at the battle of Chickamauga Hooker was assigned to jointly command the XI and XII Corps, and moved his troops by rail to Chattanooga, Tennessee. His two corps were later consolidated into the XX Corps to fight the famous Battle of Lookout Mountain, sometimes referred to as the Battle in the Clouds. The action on Lookout Mountain was viewed by Grant as a minor action and the clouds as being merely mist. When General James McPherson was killed in front of Atlanta, Hooker, being the senior corps commander, expected General William T. Sherman to appoint him commander of the Army of the Tennessee. Despite showing solid corps leadership in the Atlanta Campaign, Sherman chose General O.O. Howard, Hooker's subordinate and junior. In protest Hooker asked to be relieved from an army that did not honor seniority of rank. This brought an end to Hooker's Civil War field service. He was assigned several Department commands till 1869, when he was placed on the retired list due to injuries. Hooker, while a good fighting general, lacked moral fiber. and probably was affected by his hard bouts of drinking.

HOWARD

Howard, Oliver Otis. *Carte de visite* by Gardner, Washington. Author's collection.

Howard, Oliver Otis (1830-1909) was born in Maine, and graduated from Bowdoin College before being admitted to the Military Academy in 1850, graduating fourth in the class of 1854. He was commissioned in the Ordnance Department, which received relatively few West Point graduates. Howard served in several garrisons before becoming chief ordnance officer for General William Harney on his expedition against the Seminole Indians. He was assigned in 1858 as assistant professor of mathematics at the Military Academy and remained there until the outbreak of the Civil War. He resigned from the Army effective June 7, 1861, to lead a regiment of Maine volunteers on a march to reinforce the few federal forces guarding Washington. As a colonel, he commanded the 3rd brigade of General Samuel Heintzelman's 3rd division of General Irvin McDowell's army in the Federal defeat at the Battle of Bull Run. He received appointment to brigadier-general of volunteers in September 1861, and commanded a brigade in the 1862 Peninsula Campaign, losing his right arm at the Battle of Seven Pines. After recuperation he rejoined the army, being placed by General Edwin Sumner in charge of the II Corps rear guard, which after the Second Battle of Bull Run successfully fought off Confederate forces, allowing the Army of Virginia to retreat back to the Washington defenses. When General John Sedgwick was wounded at Antietam, Howard took command of the 2nd Division of the II Corps. He continued to lead the division at the Battle of Fredericksburg. When appointed to major-general of volunteers Howard was placed in command of the XI Corps after the removal of General Franz Sigel. Howard's corps formed the federal right at Chancellorsville and was surprised and routed by General Stonewall Jackson. Howard, only in command for a few days, should have protected his flank, and this oversight may have cost Hooker the battle. At Gettysburg, Howard briefly assumed command of the federal forces after the death of General John Reynolds. His actions at Gettysburg have been questioned, even though he did identify key defensive positions as the I and XI Corps were pushed through the town. He is generally credited for rallying elements of the I Corps, whose actions were key in preventing the federals from being seriously defeated on the first day. In autumn 1863, Howard's XI Corps was transferred to Chattanooga, along with General Joseph Hooker's XII Corps. Howard commanded the IV Corps in the Atlanta campaign, and with the death of General James McPherson was selected by General William Sherman to be commander of the Army of Tennessee. He led the right wing of Sherman's army on the March to the Sea and was promoted to brigadier-general in the regular army to rank from the date of the capture of Savannah, Georgia. Howard concluded his Civil War career in the campaign of the Carolinas, ending with the surrender of General Joseph Johnston after the battle of Bentonville. At the end of hostilities Howard was appointed commissioner of the "Freedman's" Bureau, an agency to assist providing for the welfare of freed slaves. The agency became notorious for fraud and corruption during the reconstruction period, but Howard personally was never found to be corrupt. Howard was one of the most devout Christians in the Army, and one of the very few never touching alcohol. After reconstruction duties with the Freedman's Bureau he led efforts to found Howard University, an institution of higher education for blacks. In the late 1870s and into the 1880s he was engaged in several Indian campaigns, most notably the pursuit and defeat of Chief Joseph of the Nez

Perce in 1877. He also served as head of the Military Academy after his promotion to major-general in 1886. Following his retirement in 1894 he continued his humanitarian efforts. Howard's Civil War career was curious, as he survived numerous tactical errors seriously affecting his command and the Federal army while at the same time gaining promotions to high rank.

Howard, Oliver Otis. *Carte de visite* by Brady, Washington. In this photogaph General Howard is shown as a colonel and before he lost his right arm. Author's collection.

HUMPHREYS

Humphreys, Andrew *Carte de visite* by Anthony, New York. Author's collection.

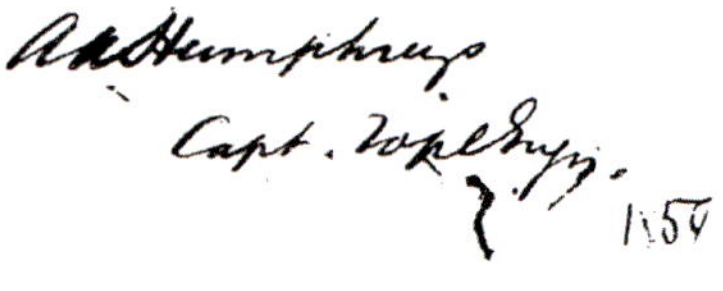

Humphreys, Andrew Jackson (1810-1883) was born in Pennsylvania, and even though his father and grandfather designed and built ships, he chose to attend the Military Academy, graduating thirteenth in the class of 1831. He was commissioned in the 2rd Artillery and was assigned drawing and topographical duties, but also served in action against the Seminole Indians. Humphreys was stationed for nearly a year in the Cherokee Nation with the disagreeable task of Indian removal.. He resigned from the army in 1836 and engaged in civil engineering, mainly planning and building lighthouses for the federal government. He was reappointed to the Army as a first lieutenant of Topographical Engineers in 1838, and until the Civil War served in numerous engineering projects, including important topographical and hydrographic studies of the Mississippi Delta. Promoted to captain in 1848, he was engaged in this period of his career in exploration and making railroad surveys to the Pacific Ocean. Just prior to the firing on Fort Sumter he was serving on an army board to examine and revise the course of instruction at the Military Academy. Promoted to major in August 1861, Humphreys joined General George McClellan's staff as chief topographical engineer and accompanied McClellan on the 1862 Peninsula Campaign, where existing maps of Virginia were found to be faulty and inadequate for military use. Appointed a brigadier-general of volunteers in March 1862, he left his staff position and in December 1862 assumed the command of a division in the V Corps that he ably led at Antietam and Fredericksburg. He was awarded a brevet to lieutenant-colonel in the engineers for gallantry in making a valiant assault on the Confederate position on Marye's Heights during the Battle of Fredericksburg. Humphreys remained with his division through the Battle of Chancellorsville, and then was given a division command in General Dan Sickle's III Corps. At the Battle of Gettysburg he resisted the ferocious assaults by General John B. Hood and General Lafayette McLaws to take advantage of the near disastrous decision by Sickles to extend forward the III Corps line. For action at Gettysburg he received appointment to major-general of volunteers. After Gettysburg, General George Meade asked Humphreys, a trusted friend, to become his chief of staff in order to rid himself of General Dan Butterfield, whom he mistrusted and disliked. Humphreys, though a successful field commander and desiring to remain one, reluctantly accepted the staff position. Both Meade and later Grant appreciated Humphreys' loyalty and superb management of the Army of the Potomac. He returned to field duty as commander of the II Corps in November 1864 when he replaced the exhausted and ill General Winfield Hancock. Humphreys was partially successful in reorganizing and revitalizing the premier fighting corps in the Army of the Potomac. He led the II Corps through all the actions leading to the surrender at Appomattox and received a brevet to major-general in the regular army for action at the Battle of Saylor Creek during the Appomattox Campaign. In 1866 he was made a brigadier-general in the regular army and Chief of Engineers, a post he held till his retirement in 1879. Humphreys was one of the few generals that demonstrated exemplary skills in both staff and field assignments. Sadly he has been mostly overlooked by scholars for his able role in the campaigns of the Army of the Potomac.

HUNTER

Hunter, David. *Carte de visite* by Brady, Washington. Author's collection.

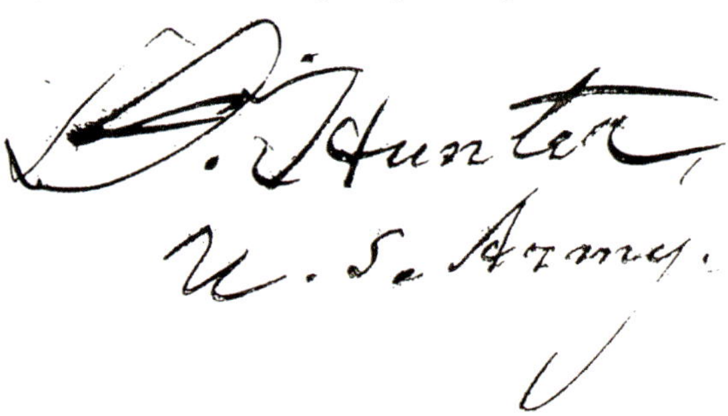

Hunter, David. *Carte de visite* by Brady, New York. Author's collection.

Hunter, David (1802-1886) was born in Washington D.C. He entered the Military Academy in 1818 and graduated twenty-fifth in the class of 1822. He was commissioned in the 5th Infantry and served in numerous frontier assignments till transferred in 1833 to the 1st Dragoons with promotion to captain. He resigned in 1836 and entered into land speculation in his wife's hometown of Chicago. Hunter returned to the Army in 1842 as a paymaster and served in that position for General Winfield Scott during the Mexican War. In 1860, while stationed at Fort Leavenworth, Kansas, Hunter adroitly began a correspondence about secession and military matters with newly elected President Abraham Lincoln. He became one of Lincoln's early military advisers and exploited his relationship with the president to gain appointment as a brigadier-general of volunteers. He then commanded General Irvin McDowell's lead division at the Battle of Bull Run, where he was seriously wounded. In August 1861 he was appointed major- general of volunteers, and in November Lincoln sent him to St. Louis, Missouri, to relieve General John Fremont in command of the Division of the West. He was subsequently relieved by General Henry Halleck in March 1862 and put in command of the Department of the South, with headquarters at Port Royal, South Carolina. In April 1862 his forces captured Fort Pulaski, and later that month Hunter found a large body of slaves on Cockburn Island in his department desirous of service or employment in the federal army. In May 1861 he issued an order that declared all slaves free in Georgia, Florida, and South Carolina. Hunter felt that martial law and slavery were incompatible, and that slave owners had no right to hold them as property. Lincoln immediately repudiated Hunter's order with a widely distributed proclamation declaring Hunter's order entirely void. At this time Lincoln was extremely concerned with holding the border states, and Hunter's proclamation would strengthen the influence of pro-slavery supporters in Kentucky and Missouri. However, before leaving the Department of the South Hunter organized the first regiment of black troops to enter the Federal army. Hunter's tenure as commander in the Department South came to an end after the defeat of federal forces at the Battle of Secessionville, a failed effort to capture Charleston. He was ordered back to Washington and presided over of a court of inquiry examining the causes and blame for the surrender of Harper's Ferry by Colonel Dixon Miles. He later served as president of the court-martial for General Fitz John Porter for disobedience of General John Pope's orders at the Battle of Second Bull Run. Hunter was later placed in command of the Department of West Virginia in May 1864, and was victorious at the Battle of Piedmont, cutting Southern supply and railroad lines in the Shenandoah Valley. At Lynchburg he was confronted by General Jubal Early and, disregarding Grant's orders, retreated west, virtually taking his command out of the war. Early was then able to march unimpeded up the Shenandoah and make a raid on Washington that required withdrawing Federal troops from the lines at Petersburg. Hunter resigned his command in August 1864 after a meeting with Generals Ulysses Grant and Philip Sheridan, at which Grant indicated that Sheridan was to command a campaign to rid the valley of Confederate forces, and that Hunter's services were not needed. Upon Lincoln's assassination, Hunter served as president of the committee that tried the conspirators. He was, in most respects, an inept general, but was able to cling to commands through his strong support of the abolition cause.

HURLBUT

Hurlbut, Stephen. *Carte de visite* by Day, Memphis, Tennessee. Author's collection.

Hurlbut, Stephen Augustus (1815-1882) was born in South Carolina. He studied and practiced law in Charleston before relocating to Belvidere, Illinois. He was active in the Illinois Republican Party and a strong supporter of President Lincoln. Hurlbut was sent on a secret mission to Charleston by Lincoln just before the firing on Fort Sumter to examine conditions in the Palmetto state. Upon the outbreak of the war he was rewarded for his political support with an appointment in May 1861 as a brigadier-general of volunteers. He served in several assignments in Missouri before being put in command of the 4th Division, spearheading General Ulysses Grant's move up the Tennessee River. Hurlbut's division reached Pittsburg Landing a week before the arrival of the rest of Grant's army and fought well at the Battle of Shiloh. Hurlburt was later appointed major-general of volunteers, and his division accompanied General Henry Halleck's snail paced advance on Corinth, Mississippi. After the Battle of Corinth Hurlburt's division defeated a retreating Confederate force at the Battle at Hatchie Bridge. He was credibly engaged in the Vicksburg Campaign, and in the reorganization of the Army of the Tennessee was made commander of the XVI Corps, with headquarters in Memphis. His time in Memphis was spent both in lining his pocketbook with cotton bribes and failing to prevent General Nathan Bedford Forest making numerous raids. After leaving New Orleans Hurlburt, on the way to his new command, stopped over in Memphis. Confederate General Bedford Forrest mounted a raid on Memphis to capture Hurlbut and General Washburn Cadwallader. He commanded forces attached to General William Sherman's Meridian Campaign, and in 1864 replaced General Nathaniel Banks in New Orleans. While commanding the Department of the Gulf Hurlbut continued lining his pockets from various financial schemes. Even though his corrupt practices had been known for some time in Washington, his blatant actions in New Orleans finally resulted in a special military commission that recommended his arrest and trial. Newly appointed Department of the Gulf commander General E.R.S. Canby ordered his arrest, but Washington overturned the order, and the matter was left to die in the waning days of the war. He was honorably mustered out of service in June 1865 and returned to Belvidere, where he continued to be a prominent Republican politician, despite charges of corruption and drunkenness. President Grant appointed him to a diplomatic post, as did President James Garfield. Between the two diplomatic posts in Peru and Chile he served in Congress in 1872 and 1874. It is hard to understand why the Lincoln Administration tolerated Hurlbut and his corrupt activities.

KEARNY

Kearny, Philip. *Carte de visite* by Gurney, New York. Author's collection.

Kearny, Philip (1815-1862) was born in New York to a prominent and wealthy family that denied him an opportunity for a military career. Kearny attended and graduated from Columbia University in 1833. Once he came into his inheritance he left law practice in 1837 and secured a commission as a lieutenant in the 1st Dragoons, commanded by his uncle, General Stephen Watts Kearny. A master equestrian, he applied for and was granted permission to attend the French Cavalry School at Saumur, after which he joined the First Chasseurs d'Afrique in the Algerian campaign against Arab chief Abdel-Kader. Six months later in 1840, he returned to the United States and was assigned as aide-de-camp to General Alexander Macomb, commander in-chief of the United States Army. Kearny remained in this position when Macomb retired and was replaced by General Winfield Scott. In 1845-46 he accompanied the South Pass Expedition and resigned from the army shortly before the beginning of the Mexican War. Upon the beginning of the war he recruited, and at personal expense armed and equipped a company of dragoons that acted as a personal body guard for General Scott. He was promoted to captain in 1846 and distinguished himself at the battles of Contreras and Churubusco, where he lost his left arm. At the end of hostilities he was stationed in New York until 1851, when he was engaged in the Rogue River Indian War in Oregon. In late 1851 he resigned again from the army and took a world tour. In 1859 he rejoined the Chasseurs d'Afrique, and in the war with Italy won the Legion of Honor for gallantry at the Battle of Solferiono. He returned to the United States shortly before the Civil War, and upon the beginning of hostilities offered his services to both the state of New York and to the federal government. When no federal command was immediately offered he became colonel of the 1st New Jersey. In 1861, President Lincoln appointed him a brigadier-general of volunteers in a brigade in General William Franklin's division. In the 1862 Virginia Peninsula Campaign at the Battle of Williamsburg Kearny began a series of remarkable combat actions, showing superb leadership. At Williamsburg he reinforced General Joseph Hooker's Division at a critical moment, turning defeat into victory. He performed similar feats throughout the Peninsula Campaign, and was given command of a division in General Samuel Heintzleman's III Corps. At the Battle of Chantilly he was killed when inadvertently riding his horse into Confederate lines while on a reconnaissance. What future role Kearny might have played in the federal army is open to question. He was a superb battlefield leader, but was often vocally critical of both colleagues and his superiors. Given the nature of the Civil War, a general leading from the front like Kearny had little chance to survive. General Winfield Scott was quoted as saying that Kearny was the bravest man he knew and the most perfect soldier.

Kearny, Philip. *Carte de visite* by unidentified photographer. This is copy of another *carte de visite*. Author's collection.

KEYES

Keyes, Erasmus. *Carte de visite* by Brady, Washington. Author's collection.

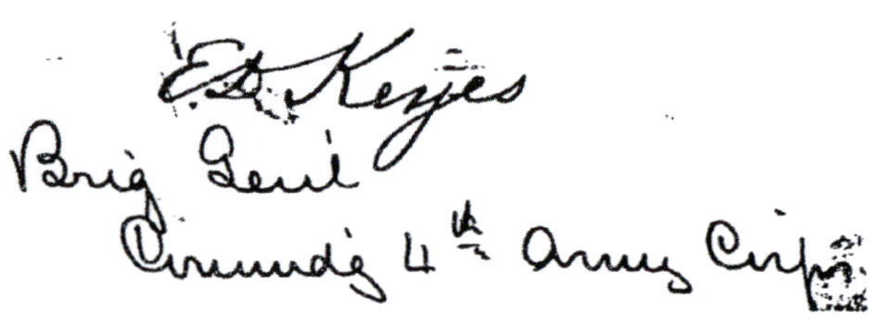

Keyes, Erasmus. *Carte de visite* by Brady, Washington. Author's collection.

Keyes, Erasmus Darwin (1810-1895) was born in Massachusetts. He was admitted to the Military Academy in 1828 and finished tenth in the class of 1832. Keyes was commissioned in the 3rd Artillery, and in the next three decades was to have an interesting and productive military career that ended prematurely during the first months of the Civil War. He acted as aide and military secretary to General Winfield Scott on three different occasions and fought Indians in Washington Territory and California, where he would relocate after the end of his military career. He served as a major of the 3rd Artillery in the Spokane Expedition and in the battles of Spokane Plains and Four Lakes. In 1860 he was commissioned as lieutenant-colonel of staff and was military secretary to General Scott at the beginning of the Civil War. Keyes, upon a request to Scott, was given command of a brigade in General Daniel Tyler's division and fought at the Battle of Bull Run. He was made colonel of the 11th U.S. Infantry in May 1861, and in August was appointed a brigadier-general of volunteers. In November 1861 he was given command of a division when General McClellan organized the Army of the Potomac for the 1862 Virginia Peninsula Campaign. President Lincoln and several of his cabinet officers urged McClellan to adopt the corps organization model, and when he hesitated they proceeded to name the corps commanders, with Keyes being assigned to command the IV Corps. In the Peninsula Campaign Keyes and his corps were not distinguished, but he was nonetheless breveted brigadier-general in the regular army for services at the Battle of Fair Oaks. Keyes and the IV Corps were not part of the Army of the Potomac sent to reinforce General John Pope's Army of Virginia prior to the Battle of Second Bull Run. Instead, Keyes was assigned to General John Dix's Department of Virginia, located at Fortress Monroe. At the beginning of the 1863 Gettysburg Campaign, Dix ordered Keyes to make a heavy demonstration near Tallysville, Virginia, in hopes of preventing additional Confederate troops from joining General Lee's forces in Maryland. His modest forces met the Confederates and then retired back toward Fortress Monroe. Keyes was censured by General Dix for retiring in the face of inferior forces, and he was removed from command of the IV Corps, which was soon disbanded. Keyes was not successful in obtaining a court of inquiry, and the politically powerful General Dix virtually ended Keyes' military career. He served on various boards and commissions for about a year and resigned on May 4, 1864. Keyes relocated to San Francisco, California, and became very successful in gold mining, grape growing, and banking. He was the author of several works describing events and people before and during the Civil War. It is unfortunate the Lincoln administration did not find a constructive use for Keyes' obvious talents in organization and administration.

KILPATRICK

Kilpatrick, Hugh Judson. *Carte de visite* by Fredricks, New York. Author's collection.

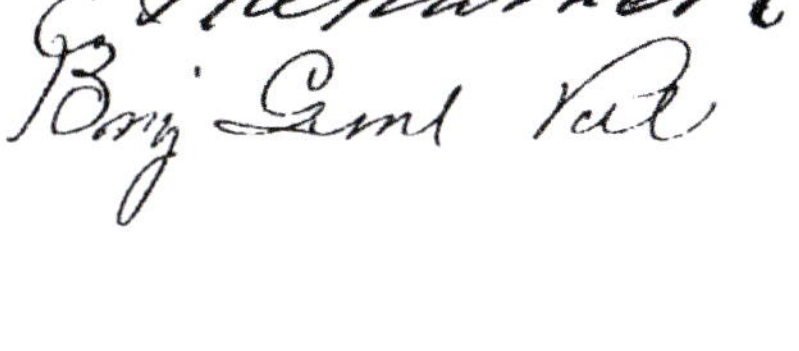

Kilpatrick, Hugh Judson. *Carte de vistie* by Brady, Washington. Author's collection.

Kilpatrick, Hugh Judson (1836-1881) was born in New Jersey. He was admitted to the Military Academy in 1856, graduating nineteenth in the class of 1861. He was commissioned in the 1st Artillery and quickly decided that his future in the Civil War was in volunteer service. Within a few days of commissioning he joined the 5th New York cavalry as a captain and was severely wounded in the skirmish at Big Bethel, becoming the first regular army officer having the distinction to be wounded in the war. He returned in February 1862 from medical leave and received an assignment as chief of cavalry for an expedition to Texas led by Brigadier-General Jim Lane, a U.S. Senator from Kansas. The expedition was soon abandoned, and Kilpatrick rejoined the 2d New York Cavalry as lieutenant-colonel. He participated in numerous raids and skirmishes in northern Virginia and became colonel of the regiment in December 1862. He then commanded a cavalry brigade in General George Stoneman's raid towards Richmond. At the cavalry battle of Beverley Ford, his performance resulted in appointment to brigadier-general of volunteers in command of a cavalry division in the Army of the Potomac. In the cavalry action at Aldie he was awarded a brevet to major in the Regular army. His division was later engaged in cavalry operations at Upperville, Hanover, Hunterstown, and at the Battle of Gettysburg. His judgment at Gettysburg was questioned when he sent newly promoted brigadier-general Elon Farnsworth's brigade in a suicide charge that resulted in the death of Farnsworth. Even after charges of reckless behavior Kilpatrick received a brevet to lieutenant-colonel for his actions at Gettysburg. He fought a series of cavalry actions against the Army of Northern Virginia in its retreat back to Virginia from Gettysburg. During the fall of 1863 his division engaged in actions in central Virginia, including a raid to destroy the Confederate gunboats *Satellite* and *Reliance*. He was engaged in the Battle of Brandy Station and Gainesville before taking a lengthy Christmas leave. Kilpatrick returned to his command, and in February 1864 mounted a raid on Richmond that ended in near disaster. Nearly reaching the gates of Richmond, he appeared to lose his nerve, and instead of freeing union prisoners held in Richmond he and his men almost became prisoners themselves. Colonel Ulric Dahlgren, commanding a separate section of the raid, was killed, and a set of papers were found on his body that, according to Confederate authorities, indicated Kilpatrick had ordered the burning of Richmond. In April 1864 General William Sherman requested, and Grant approved, a transfer of Kilpatrick to command the 3rd Cavalry Division in the Army of the Cumberland on its campaign into Georgia to capture Atlanta. He was badly wounded at the Battle of Resaca, but returned in time for the Battle of Atlanta and protected Sherman's lines of communication while constantly skirmishing with Confederate cavalry led by his West Point classmate General Joseph Wheeler. He was breveted a colonel in the regular army for actions at the Battle of Resaca. On Sherman's March to the Sea his division protected the flanks of the army and conducted several raids. In the invasion of the Carolinas Kilpatrick was nearly captured in his underwear by General Wade Hampton. Near the end of hostilities Kilpatrick was awarded brevets to brigadier and major general in the regular army. Kilpatrick, although sometimes a competent cavalry leader, consistently self-promoted, submitting fictitious accounts of his battle actions. He garnered political favor and was reckless in both the use of men and horses, justifying his nickname of "Kill Cavalry".

LEGGETT

Leggett, Mortimer. *Carte de visite* by Anthony, New York. Author's collection.

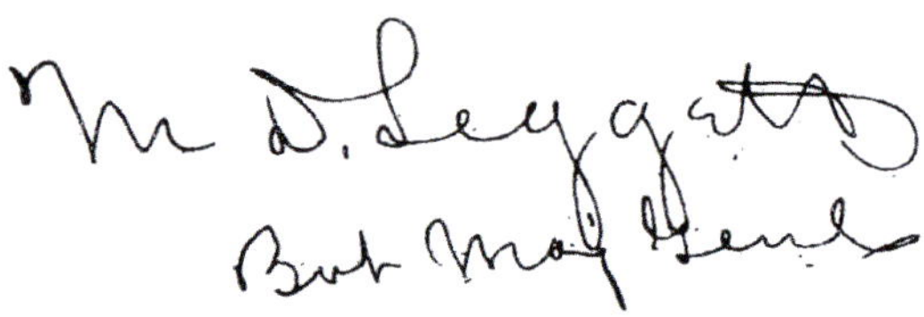

Leggett, Mortimer Dormer (1821-1896) was born in New York, but was raised in Ohio. He studied at Western Reserve College, later becoming both a superintendent of schools and lawyer in Akron, Warren, and Zanesville, Ohio. Besides careers in education and law, Leggett graduated from Willoughby medical school. For six years he was a professor of law at the Ohio Law College and a law partner of Jacob Cox, one of the first of the many Ohio Civil War generals. Leggett was also a personal friend of General George McClellan and spent the first months of the war as a volunteer aide-de-camp to McClellan in western Virginia. He became Colonel of the 78th Ohio in January 1862 and was engaged in the Battles of Fort Donelson and Shiloh, where his regiment was lightly engaged. Even though his brigade was not well battle tested, his superiors saw that Leggett had potential as a combat leader, and he was appointed brigadier-general of volunteers in November 1862. During the Vicksburg Campaign he distinguished himself in leading two brigades in General John Logan's division of the XVII Corps. His brigades in the Vicksburg campaign were engaged in the Battle of Champion's Hill, where he was wounded for the second time, but led the federal effort to mine under the Confederate lines. In the Atlanta Campaign Leggett commanded a division in the XVII Corps in the Army of the Tennessee. Before Atlanta, on July 21, 1864, Leggett's command made a historic assault on an important Confederate position on Bald Hill. In a furious fight Leggett captured the hill and held it against a series of Confederate counterattacks. In the annals of the federal army the hill is always referred to as "Leggett's Hill". Leggett, for a short period of time in 1864, led the XVII Corps and played a leading role in Sherman's March to the Sea, then followed him in the invasion of the Carolinas. He was appointed major-general of volunteers in August 1865. He resigned a month later and returned to his law practice in Zanesville. Later he was appointed by President Grant to be commissioner of patents. In 1884 he organized the Brush Electric company, which later became part of today's General Electric Company. Leggett, in many respects, was a true renaissance man of his time. He died in 1896.

LOGAN

Logan, John. *Carte de visite* by Brady, Washington. Author's collection.

Logan, John Alexander (1826-1886) was born in Illinois to a rural physician. He received sufficient education at the University of Louisville to be admitted to the bar and practice law. He briefly served as a lieutenant in the Illinois volunteers during the Mexican War. In the 1840s and 1850s Logan became a strong voice in the Illinois Democratic Party, in its stronghold in the southern part of the state commonly referred to as "Little Egypt". He was first elected to the Illinois legislature in 1856, and then elected in 1858 on a Free Soil party ticket to the U.S. Congress. In 1860 he was reelected, and as a civilian at the Battle of Bull Run helped to evacuate the wounded back to Washington. Returning to Illinois in September 1861, he recruited and was appointed colonel of the 31st Illinois Volunteers. President Lincoln felt that holding "Little Egypt" in the union was critical, and that it could not be done without the assistance of southern Illinois democrats like Logan. His wide network of political allies and ability to deliver fiery stump speeches made Logan an important key in Lincoln's plans and strategy for Illinois. Logan's regiment was first stationed at Cairo, Illinois, along with Ulysses Grant's 21st Illinois. In their first encounter, Grant recalled that he asked Logan to speak to his regiment, whose enlistment period was soon expiring. Logan delivered a strong pro-union speech with passion and humor that coaxed most of the regiment to reenlist, perhaps saving Grant's tenuous position in the army. Later Logan was engaged with Grant at the inconclusive Battle of Belmont, and while still with Grant at the Battle of Fort Donelson was wounded. He distinguished himself at the Battle of Shiloh, and in March 1862 was appointed a brigadier-general of volunteers. He commanded a division at Corinth and held several department commands, making movements through Northern Mississippi before the Vicksburg Campaign. He was appointed a major-general of volunteers in March 1863, partially due to Lincoln's desire to have Democrats and border state officers in the higher ranks. At Vicksburg, Logan was awarded the Medal of Honor for his assault on the Confederate works following the mine explosion. During the Atlanta Campaign Logan fought brilliantly, and temporarily assumed command of the Army of the Tennessee after the battlefield death of General James McPherson. Logan was a charismatic leader much loved by his troops, who would shout "Black Jack, Black Jack" as he rode by. Much to his chagrin, General William Sherman did not ask that he be made permanent commander of the Army of the Tennessee. Instead, he appointed General O.O. Howard, a less inspiring and competent leader. Sherman appreciated the fighting ability of Logan, but distrusted him as a politician and military administrator. Logan then returned to Illinois to campaign for the Republican Party and recruit new regiments, leading his XV Corps in the Carolinas campaign. After the war Logan returned to Congress as a Radical Republican, serving both in the House and Senate. Due to his bitter experience with General William Sherman he developed a strong dislike for "professional soldiers" and was a constant critic of the Army, most especially West Point. While in Congress he faithfully served his party and President Grant, but was often involved in many questionable business enterprises. His political style was hard and ruthless, and he used the technique of waving the "Bloody Shirt" to his political advantage. Logan was a frequent speaker at veterans' groups and wrote several books about the Civil War. He was one of, if not the best, of the civilian field generals.

Logan, John. *Carte de visite* by unidentified photographer, probably Brady. Author's collection.

MANSFIELD

Mansfield, Joseph. *Carte de visite* by Brady, Washington. Author's collection.

Mansfield, Joseph Keno (1803-1862) was born in Connecticut and entered the Military Academy in 1818, just before his fourteenth birthday. He graduated second of forty-seven in the class 1822. Mansfield was commissioned into the Corps of Engineers and served in various engineering assignments until the War with Mexico. Assigned as chief of engineers for General Zachary Taylor, he was cited for gallantry and meritorious services at the construction and defense of Fort Brown, Texas. He also received brevets of lieutenant-colonel and colonel for services at Monterey and Buena Vista. In 1853 he was appointed Inspector General of the Army with the staff rank of colonel. Prior to the outbreak of the Civil War he made numerous inspections of army facilities and units located in Oregon, Washington, California, Texas, Arizona, and New Mexico. In May 1861 he was appointed brigadier-general in the regular army and in charge of constructing the ring of fortifications providing for the defenses of Washington. On March 8, 1862, Mansfield directed the shore batteries during the battle between the Federal ship *Congress* and the Confederate ship *Virginia*. When the *Congress* struck its flag Mansfield kept firing on the *Virginia,* and was asked why he was violating naval protocols. He replied, "the *Congress* may have surrendered but I have not". Upon the return of General John Wool to Fortress Monroe Mansfield assumed command of Fort Hamilton and Newport News. He was engaged in the capture of Norfolk and Suffolk in May 1862, and received appointment to major-general of volunteers and was given a command in Bank's XII Corps in the Army of the Potomac. At the Battle of Antietam he was mortally wounded while leading his raw troops with his sword held high and cheering his men to victory. His valiant efforts led to the survival of the right wing of the Army of the Potomac in this crucial battle. He died of wounds on September 18, 1862. Mansfield, if he had lived and despite his age, probably would have been an effective corps commander.

McClellan, George. *Carte de visite* by Brady, Washington. General McClellan is shown with Ellen McClellan. Author's collection.

McClellan, George. *Carte de visite* by Anthony, New York. General McClellan is pictured with staff officers Henry Clarke, Stewart Van Vliet, and William F. Barry. Author's collection.

McClernand

McClernand, John. *Carte de visite* by Brady, Washington. Author's collection.

McClernand, John Alexander (1812-1900) was born in Kentucky, but moved to Shawneetown, Illionis. As a youth he studied and began the practice of law in 1832. He briefly fought in the Blackhawk War and later engaged in trade, founding a newspaper called the "Democrat". McClernand served in the Illinois legislature from 1836 to 1842, and then was elected as a Jacksonian Democrat to congress. He was an opponent of abolitionists and held a moderate position on the question of giving states the right to secede from the union. McClernand was again sent to Congress in 1859 as a strong supporter of Stephen Douglas, but resigned in 1861 to raise a brigade comprised of loyal southern Illinois troops. McClernand's efforts were rewarded by Lincoln with an appointment to brigadier-general of volunteers, as the President Lincoln considered him a key to keeping southern Illinois loyal to the union. McClernand and his brigade served in the Department of the Missouri and District of Cairo, and under the command of General Ulysses Grant fought at the Battle of Belmont. At the Battle of Fort Donelson he held the important right of the Federal line, but without orders engaged in a premature assault that was criticized by Grant. In March 1862 he was appointed major-general of volunteers, and at the Battle of Shiloh ably commanded a division in the Army of the Tennessee. He was a participant in General Henry Halleck's slow march to Corinth, and later commanded a district in Tennessee before returning to Illinois to recruit troops and garner support for the war effort. In late 1862 McClernand, while on leave from the army, made a trip to Washington to lobby Lincoln for an independent command raised in Illinois to move down the Mississippi River and capture Vicksburg, Mississippi. Lincoln and Secretary of War Edwin Stanton approved McClernand's plan, perhaps more for political than military reasons. The first part of the plan was the removal of General William T. Sherman and the turnover of his command to McClernand. True to his word, McClernand raised the troops and forwarded them to Memphis, but before he could take command, Halleck and Grant sent Sherman forward to the unsuccessful Battle of Chickasaw Bayou. Sherman's failure to take Chickasaw Bayou forced him to turn command over to McClernand. In an effort to bolster his military reputation McClernand turned back upriver and captured Arkansas Post. Under the overall command of Grant in the following Vicksburg campaign, McClernand fought well at the battles of Port Gibson, Champion's Hill, and Big Black. During the siege of Vicksburg Grant removed him from command in July 1863, when he violated an order regarding the distribution of unauthorized information. McClernand had issued a congratulatory order that lauded his troops, and according to Grant denigrated others. Some authorities claim that part of his removal was Grant's feeling that he did not adequately support troops engaged in the battle of Champion's Hill. McClernand did not help his case by making public charges about Grant's alleged drinking. In January 1864 Lincoln did give McClernand command of the XIII Corps, but due to ill health he resigned from volunteer service in November 1864 and returned to his law practice. He later served as a circuit judge and remained active in the Democratic Party. McClernand, while showing some military aptitude and at times adequately performing in the field, was a constant thorn in the side of his superior officers. Halleck, Grant, Sherman, and McPherson roundly despised him and did all in their power to rid themselves of a most contentious general.

McCook

McCook, Alexander. *Carte de visite* by unidentified photographer. Author's collection.

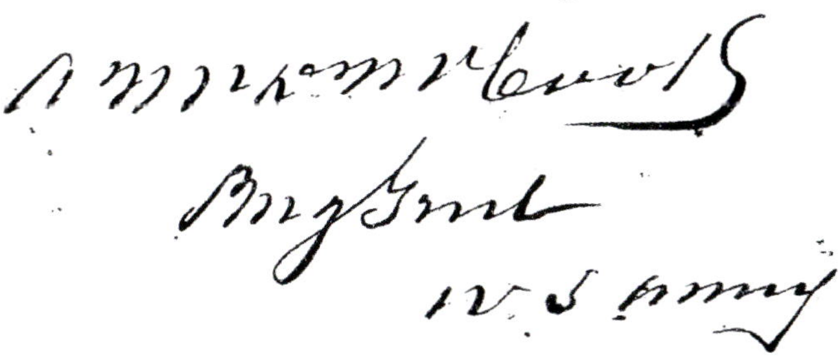

McCook, Alexander McDowell (1831-1903) was born in Ohio. He was the highest ranking officer in an extraordinary family, the "Fighting McCooks", that sent fourteen men to fight in the Civil War. McCook entered the Military Academy in 1847 and graduated thirtieth in the class of 1852. He was commissioned in the 3rd Infantry and spent his early army years fighting Indians in the Southwest. Most of these actions were against Apaches in New Mexico and Arizona. In 1858, McCook was promoted to first lieutenant and assigned to West Point as an assistant instructor of infantry tactics. Just weeks after the firing on Fort Sumter he was appointed Colonel of the 1st Ohio Volunteers as part of General Daniel Tyler's Division that fought at the Battle of Bull Run. McCook, for his actions at Bull Run, was breveted a major in the regular army. In September 1861 he was appointed brigadier-general of volunteers and assigned to command a brigade in the Army of the Ohio. He took part in General Don Carlos Buell's advance on Nashville and subsequent march to Pittsburg Landing to reinforce General Grant's troops at the Battle of Shiloh. Along with the Army of the Ohio, he participated in General Henry Halleck's lethargic march to besiege Corinth, Mississippi. For his services at the Battle of Shiloh he received a brevet to colonel and appointment to major-general of volunteers dated to July 17, 1862. After Corinth, he participated in operations in northern Alabama before marching into Kentucky with the Army of the Ohio to stop General Braxton's movement toward Lexington and Louisville. McCook, now in command of the I Corps in the Army of the Ohio, ably led his troops in the Battle of Perryville, receiving a brevet to brigadier-general in the regular army. McCook then commanded the XX Corps in the Army of the Cumberland at the Battles of Stone's River and Liberty Gap, and fought prior to General William Rosecran's Tullahoma Campaign. At the Battle of Chickamauga McCook commanded the XX Corps, which was badly routed by Confederate forces. Rosecrans blamed McCook and General Thomas Crittenden for the disastrous defeat of the Army of the Cumberland. McCook asked for and was granted a court of inquiry that officially exonerated him, but his Civil War career was beyond repair, and he awaited orders until November 1864, when he was given command of Eastern Arkansas. His only other duty, other than awaiting orders, had been defending Fort Stevens in Washington DC during Early's raid on the capital. In 1865 he represented the army in working with a Congressional Committee investigating Indian affairs in the western states. McCook resigned from the volunteers in October 1865, reverting back to the rank of captain in the 3rd Infantry. In March 1867 he was promoted to lieutenant-colonel of the 26th Infantry. He was an excellent administrative officer and served for a number of years on General Sherman's staff. He also commanded the Cavalry School at Fort Leavenworth, where he served as colonel of the 6th Infantry. Promoted to brigadier-general in 1890 and major-general in 1894, McCook retired in 1895. His last service was on a commission appointed by President McKinley to investigate the War Department during the war with Spain.

McDowell

McDowell, Irvin. *Carte de visite* by Brady, Washington. Author's collection.

McDowell, Irvin. *Carte de visite* by Brady, Washington. Author's collection.

McDowell, Irvin (1818-1885) was born in Ohio and educated in France. He was admitted to the Military Academy in 1834, graduating twenty-third in the class of 1838. McDowell was commissioned in the 2d Artillery, serving in garrisons on the northern border until assigned in 1841 as an instructor of infantry tactics at West Point. He remained in this post until the beginning of the War with Mexico, when he joined General John Wool as aide-de-camp and later as assistant adjutant general. He was with Wool's forces at the Battle of Buena Vista and was breveted captain for gallantry. He remained in Mexico with the "Army of Occupation" until ordered back for duty in the Department of Adjutant General, both in Washington and New York. He served briefly in the Department of Texas in 1860 before taking a leave of absence. McDowell was made brigadier-general of volunteers in May 1861, and President Lincoln, at the urging of General Scott and Secretary of Treasury Salmon Chase, placed him in command of the Army of the Potomac, quartered in the defenses of Washington. This unusual appointment of an army commander without a shred of experience leading troops in the field was partially due to Lincoln's inexperience in military policy in the early days of the war. Responding to political pressure from Lincoln, Congress, and the public for a military confrontation with the Confederates, McDowell reluctantly led the Army of the Potomac on July 21, 1862, to defeat at the Battle of Bull Run. The Army fell back into the defenses of Washington for reorganization, which McDowell had partially accomplished when he was removed from command in March 1862. Lincoln, without the knowledge of the new Army of the Potomac commander, George McClellan, appointed McDowell a major-general of volunteers and placed him in command of a corps in the Army of the Potomac. McDowell's III corps, much to the consternation of McClellan, was detached from the Army of the Potomac to protect Washington during McClellan's movement on Richmond in Spring 1862. In the Second Bull Run Campaign McDowell received command of the III Corps of the Army of Virginia commanded by General John Pope, and his conduct at the Battle of Second Bull Run was strongly criticized. Further damage to his reputation was caused when he appeared as a witness against General Fitz John Porter in his court-martial for disobeying orders in the same battle for which McDowell was also facing a court of inquiry for disobeying orders. Always well connected both in the army and Congress, McDowell was able to get himself exonerated, but was exiled within the army until 1864, when he was assigned to command the Department of the Pacific. In part due to the army seniority system McDowell was promoted to major general in 1872 and continued to command departments until his retirement in 1882.

McPherson

McPherson, James. *Carte de visite* by unidentified photographer. Author's collection.

McPherson, James Birdseye (1826-1864) Born in Ohio, McPherson attended Norwalk Academy before being appointed to the Military Academy in 1839, graduating first in the class of 1853. He was commissioned in the Corps of Engineers, and was retained at West Point as an instructor in engineering until being assigned to construct harbor defenses at Alcatraz Island, near San Francisco. In 1858 he was promoted to first-lieutenant, and then in August 1861, upon the request of General Henry Halleck commanding the Department of the West in St. Louis, was promoted to captain. McPherson then served on Halleck's staff as aide-de-camp with the staff rank of lieutenant-colonel. He acted as chief engineer, under General Grant, for the Army of the Tennessee at the battles of Fort Henry and Fort Donelson, and then rejoined Halleck's staff to supervise fortifications in the siege of Corinth. In May 1862 he was appointed general superintendent of military railroads in West Tennessee and received appointment to brigadier-general of volunteers. McPherson then served on the staff of General Grant at the Battle of Iuka before being assigned to command a brigade stationed at Jackson, Tennessee. When ordered to Corinth McPherson had to fight his way through several skirmishes with Confederates and arrived late for the Battle of Corinth, but did join in the pursuit of Confederate forces retreating toward Ripley, Mississippi. Upon the recommendations of General Grant and General Sherman he was appointed to major-general of volunteers in October 1862. In the battles leading to the siege of Vicksburg McPherson commanded the center of the Army of the Tennessee and demonstrated brilliant leadership of the XVII Corps. General Grant strongly urged his promotion to brigadier-general in the regular army, which Lincoln assented to in August 1863. Soon after, under the command of General William T. Sherman, he successfully led an expedition to victory at Canton, Mississippi, and then made a successful raid on Meridian, Mississippi. In the spring of 1864 he conducted operations in Louisiana and Mississippi, then later in 1864 was placed in charge of reorganizing and massing the Army of the Tennessee with other federal forces at Huntsville, Alabama, in preparation for the invasion of Georgia. During the Georgia Campaign he commanded the XV, XVI, and XVII Corps, and distinguished himself at the Battles of Resaca, Dallas, Altoona, Kolb's Farm, and Kennesaw Mountain. McPherson showed initiative and attacked and captured Dallas before being ordered to do so by Sherman. However, he showed excessive caution at Snake Creek, where he possibly could have dispersed General Johnston's forces and shortened the campaign to take Atlanta. In riding from left to right in front of his lines before the Battle of Atlanta he encountered a group of Confederate skirmishers and was shot and killed. In terms of command level, McPherson was the highest ranking Federal general killed in the Civil War. He was an extremely well liked officer and a firm friend and supporter of Generals Grant and Sherman. For the remainder of the war his name was a rallying cry for the Army of the Tennessee.

McPherson, James. *Carte de visite* by Baer and Young, Vicksburg, Mississippi. Author's collection.

Meade

Meade, George. *Carte de visite* by Brady, Washington. Author's collection.

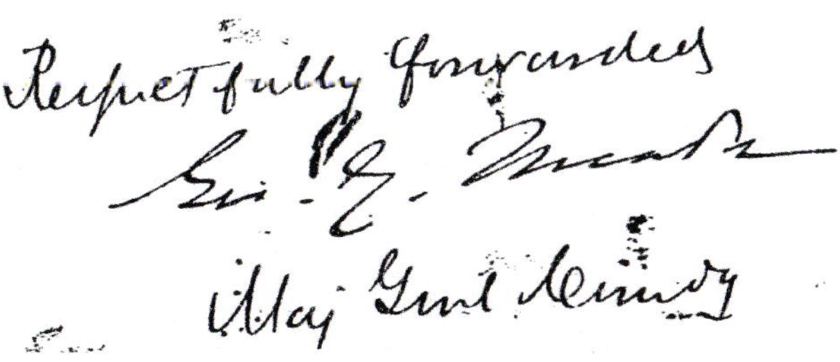

Meade, George. *Carte de visite* by Brady, Washington. Author's collection.

MERRITT

Merritt, Wesley. *Carte de visite* by Bray, Washington. Author's collection.

Merritt, Wesley. *Carte de visite* by Brady, Washington. Author's collection.

Merritt, Wesley (1834-1910) was born in New York. He was raised in St. Clair County, Illinois, and entered the Military Academy in 1855, graduating twenty-second in the class of 1860. Merritt was commissioned in the 2nd Dragoons and served in Utah until August 1861. In February 1862 he left his assignment in the defenses of Washington to serve as an aide to General Philip St. George Cooke, commander of the Army of the Potomac cavalry. When General Cooke left the army after the Peninsula Campaign Merritt served in the same capacity under General George Stoneman. In Stoneman's Raid during the Chancellorsville Campaign Merritt commanded the Cavalry Reserve Brigade, even though his rank was a captain in the 2nd Dragoons. He performed admirably at the Battle of Brandy Station, which was one of the largest cavalry battles waged and signaled to the Confederate cavalry the Federal cavalry was a much improved opponent. When General Stoneman was replaced by General Alfred Pleasonton, Merritt, Elon Farnsworth, and George Custer were quickly appointed from being young captains to brigadier-generals of volunteers. This occurred shortly before the Battle of Gettysburg, where Merritt commanded the Reserve brigade in General John Buford's cavalry division. He continued to lead the Reserve Brigade, comprised mostly of regulars, in the Bristoe and Mine Run campaigns. By the Battles of Yellow Tavern and Haw's Shop in May 1864, Merritt commanded a cavalry division. He returned to command the Reserve Brigade at Cold Harbor and in the early days of the siege of Petersburg. In August 1864 he was given command of the 1st Division in General Sheridan's Shenandoah Valley Campaign and won a brevet to major-general for action at Winchester, Fisher's Hill, and Cedar Creek. At the Battle of Tom's Creek he inflicted on General Thomas Rosser probably the worst defeat of the Confederate cavalry in the war. Merritt was made a division commander in the Cavalry Corps from January 26, 1865, till May 22, 1865. He was appointed as a major-general of volunteers in April 1865, but the appointment was never confirmed by the Senate. After service in the Department of Texas, Merritt mustered out of the volunteer service in February 1866. He became lieutenant-colonel of the newly formed 9th Cavalry and later the 5th Cavalry, serving on frontier duty engaged against hostile Indians. In the crucial year of 1876 he led the 5th Cavalry at the Battle of Slim Buttes during the Yellowstone and Big Horn Expedition. General Merritt remained in the army until after the Spanish American War. He retired in 1900. His quiet and unassuming manner is often compared to that of his colleague and oftentimes jealous rival, George Armstrong Custer.

MILES

Miles, Nelson. *Carte de visite* by Fredricks, New York. Author's collection.

Miles, Nelson Appleton (1834-1925) was born in Westminister, Massachusetts, and after a brief education at a local academy left there to clerk in a Boston mercantile store. While working as a clerk he received some military education from a retired French colonel. At this early age Miles decided upon a military career. At the outbreak of the Civil War he used his own financial resources and raised a company of infantry to serve in Colonel Henry Wilson's 22rd Massachusetts Volunteer Infantry. Miles was commissioned first-lieutenant and accompanied the regiment to the defenses of Washington. His first field experience was as an aide-de-camp on General O.O. Howard's staff, and in the 1862 Virginia Peninsula Campaign at the Battle of Seven Pines he was wounded, and received commendation from General Howard for his battlefield leadership. This action led to his receiving the lieutenant-colonelcy of the 61st New York, the first step in a brilliant combat career. Colonel Francis Barlow, another promising young officer in the 61st, was seriously wounded at Antietam, and Miles took command of the regiment. He was quickly elevated to brigade command in the II Corps, and was seriously wounded both at Fredericksburg and Chancellorsville while bravely leading from the front, both times receiving the commendation of General Winfield Hancock. At the Battle of Chancellorsville Miles was shot in the neck and abdomen, and finally in 1894 received the Medal of Honor for his bravery. When his wounds healed he returned to duty with the Army of the Potomac shortly after the Battle of Gettysburg as a brigade commander in General Francis Barlow's 1st Division of the II Corps led by General Winfield Hancock. He led his brigade in the poorly planned and fought battles of Bristoe and Mine Run, and later in the battles of the Wilderness and Spotsylvania, for which he was highly commended. Upon the request of Generals Grant and Meade, Miles received appointment to brigadier- general of volunteers for his fighting at the "Bloody Angle" during the Battle of Spotsylvania on May 8, 1864. During the Petersburg Campaign he received command of a division and was wounded for a fourth time. After the Battle of Ream's Station he was breveted a major-general of volunteers and given a division in the II Corps, which was in the forefront of the Appomattox Campaign. After the surrender he took command of Fortress Monroe, serving as Confederate President Jefferson Davis' jailor. He received widespread criticism for his seemingly harsh treatment of Davis, but was actually following the direct orders of Secretary of War Edwin Stanton. He was promoted to major-general of volunteers in August 1865, and in 1866, when the number of regiments in the regular army was increased, Miles received command of the black 40th Infantry regiment and was sent west. In 1868, Miles married the niece of Army General-in-Chief William Sherman and soon was promoted to Colonel of the 5th Infantry. Miles participated in many Indian campaigns, including his pursuit in 1876-77 of Sitting Bull and later the capture of the Apache chief Geronimo. He also supervised army forces that fought or massacred Big Foot's Sioux band at the Battle of Wounded Knee, ending the Indian Wars. During the Indian Wars he was promoted to brigadier general, and in 1895 became general-in-chief of the Army. He wrote extensively and served as the head of many patriotic organizations. Miles was fiercely ambitious in an unrelenting manner, highly political, and self-serving, while at the same time a highly effective Civil War and Indian War commander.

MILROY

Milroy, Robert. *Carte de visite* by Brady, Washington. Author's collection.

Milroy, Robert Huston (1816-1890) was born in Indiana. He entered Norwich Academy at the age of 24, and three years later received a degree in the arts and military science. He served as a captain with little distinction in the 1st Indiana Volunteers during the war with Mexico. Milroy then studied law at Indiana University, becoming a lawyer and judge prior to the Civil War. At the beginning of the war Milroy received a commission as Colonel of the 9th Indiana Volunteers, a three month regiment that later reenlisted in time to participate in federal operations in Western Virginia. In January 1862 he was placed in command of the Cheat Mountain District in the Mountain Department, and was appointed in February 1862 to be a brigadier-general of volunteer to date from September 1861. During his administration of the Mountain Department, his strict measures enforced against guerrillas and partisans resulted in Confederate President Davis securing the passage of a bill putting a $100,000 bounty on his head. In 1862 Milroy was attacked at McDowell, Virginia, by General Stonewall Jackson on his successful Shenandoah Campaign. His forces were saved from total collapse by timely aid from General James Shields. Milroy was given an "independent" brigade that fought at the Battle of Second Bull Run attached to General Franz Sigel's I Corps. Probably for political reasons, in November 1862 he was appointed to major-general of volunteers. While commanding 6,000 to 8,000 troops at Winchester, Virginia, in June 1863, he was attacked by the forces of General Richard Ewell on the Army of the Northern Virginia's march up the Shenandoah Valley to invade Pennsylvania. Milroy suffered a disastrous defeat, with his forces all but annihilated. Milroy and his staff escaped with some cavalry to the garrison at Harper's Ferry. After a court of inquiry he was not held to be culpable for one of the federal army's most one-sided defeats, even though he had clearly violated the orders of General Robert Schenck not to make an attack. After the Winchester debacle Milroy saw minor action in Tennessee under General George Thomas, including a successful minor skirmish against General Nathan Bedford Forrest following the Battle of Nashville in December 1864. In the post-war years he received an appointment as superintendent of Indian Affairs in the Washington Territory, dying there in 1890. Milroy was a good example of a political general; impatient with authority and full of abolitionist zeal seen by many as near fanaticism. He constantly quarreled with superiors and disobeyed orders, but never could be accused of lack of bravery and devotion to the federal cause. President Lincoln probably tolerated his military incompetence to placate the feelings of union supporters in Indiana. Lincoln was also probably aware that Indiana had very few high ranking general officers in the federal army.

MITCHEL

Mitchel, Ormsby. *Carte de visite* by Anthony, New York. Author's collection.

Mitchel, Ormsby MacKnight (1809-1862) was born in Kentucky, but was raised in Ohio. Mitchel was appointed to the Military Academy in 1825, graduating fifteenth in the class of 1820, which included Robert E. Lee. He was commissioned in the 2d Artillery and remained at West Point as assistant professor of mathematics till August 1831, when he was transferred to the garrison at Fort Marion, Florida. He resigned from the army in September 1832 and then embarked on a remarkable civilian career that included railroad engineering, academics, journal editor, adjutant general of the state of Ohio, and member of the Military Academy Board of Visitors. His most notable achievements were in the area of astronomical studies, where he gained a worldwide reputation. From 1834 to 1844 he was professor of Mathematics, Philosophy and Astronomy at Cincinnati College and founded the Mitchel Observatory, which was the first major observatory in the country. He was also extensively involved in establishing the United States Naval Observatory. He also was director of the Dudley Observatory in Albany, New York, and was a popular national lecturer on astronomy. At the outbreak of war Mitchel was quickly commissioned a brigadier-general of volunteers, and in September 1861 was placed in command of the Department of the Ohio. In December 1861, while commanding the 3rd Division of the Army of the Ohio, he was involved in winter operations in Tennessee and northern Alabama, including the occupations of Bowling Green, Kentucky, and Nashville, Tennessee. His only combat action was at Bridgeport, Alabama, on the way to occupy Huntsville, Alabama. Mitchel then seized the Memphis and Charleston Railroad, which effectively secured control of Northern Alabama for the federal army. The Army of the Ohio, coming under the command of General Don Carlos Buell, brought an end to Mitchel's career, as he and Buell quarreled over discipline in Mitchel's division and his recommendation to Buell to advance further south. Buell's primary complaint against Mitchel stemmed from his subordinate General John Turchin's 18th Ohio Volunteers pillaging and robbing the citizens of Athens, Alabama. Buell was also greatly displeased that Mitchel communicated directly with the Secretary of War. He tendered his resignation, which was first refused, but a request for transfer was accepted and he assumed command of the Department of the South in September 1862. He died of yellow fever at Hilton Head, South Carolina, in October, 1862.

Mitchel, Ormsby. *Carte de visite* by Brady, Washington. Author's collection.

Morell

Morell, George. *Carte de visite* by Brady, Washington. Author's collection.

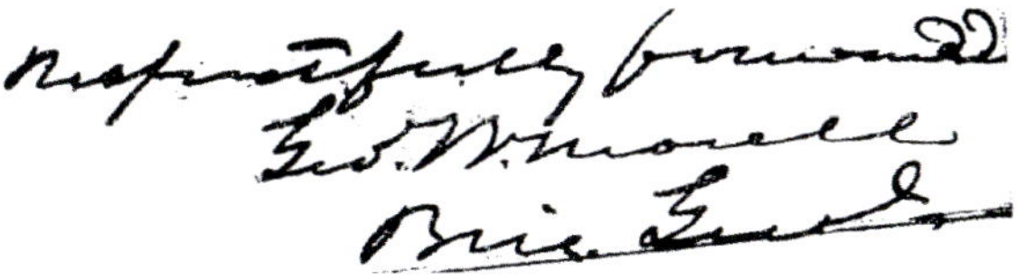

Morell, George Webb (1815-1883) was born in New York. Morell was admitted to the Military Academy in 1831, graduating first in the class of 1835. He was commissioned in the Corps of Engineers and saw normal engineer assignments until resigning from the army in 1837. Until the Civil War, Morell engaged in railroad construction and later as a lawyer and colonel in the New York Militia. In the first days of the war Morell served on the staff of General Charles Sanford of the New York Militia in organizing regiments to be sent to the defenses of Washington. Morell's first federal service was at Harper's Ferry, guarding the approaches to Washington. In August 1861 he was appointed a brigadier-general of volunteers, and in March 1862 served in the Peninsula Campaign as a brigade commander in General Fitz John Porter's Division. When Porter moved to command of the V Corps, Morell accompanied him and received command of a division. He was complimented for his skill and bravery in directing his division in the Battle of Seven Pines, and was with Porter at the Second Battle of Bull Run. At the Battle of Antietam he again demonstrated that he was an able commander. On July 4, 1862, Morell was appointed by President Lincoln, upon the recommendation of General George McClellan and General Fitz John Porter, to be a major-general of volunteers, but the appointment was never sent to the Senate for confirmation. The reason for lack of confirmation was the removal of McClellan from the Army of the Potomac and Porter's trial for dereliction of duty at the Second Battle of Bull Run. Morell was delegated to rear echelon assignments, the last being the draft rendezvous in Indianapolis. His testimony in the Porter court-martial did not please the carefully selected court martial or members of the Committee on the Conduct of the War. This testimony and his loyalty to Porter destroyed his career. He mustered out of volunteer service in December 1864.

MORGAN

Morgan, Edwin. *Carte de visite* by Churchill and Denison, Albany, New York. Author's collection.

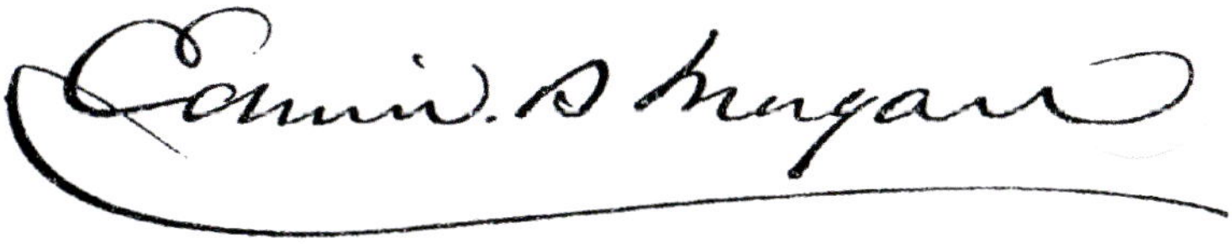

Morgan, Edwin Denison (1811-1883) was born in Massachusetts, but at age 26 moved to New York City to engage in the wholesale grocery business. By the age of 30 he had achieved success, and added underwriting and banking to his network of profitable enterprises. After amassing a fortune Morgan became interested in politics, and was elected to the New York City board of aldermen in 1849, to the state senate as an Anti-slavery Whig in 1850, and to governor of New York in 1858 as a Republican. He later became the first chair of the National Republican Committee and was reelected New York governor in 1860. President Lincoln, well aware of the need for New York to provide finances and manpower to the union cause, appointed Morgan to be a major-general of volunteers commanding the New York Military District. This provided him the power and influence to control civil and military affairs in New York in favor of the federal war effort. Morgan and Lincoln were both aware of strong anti-war sentiment amongst New York Democrats, partially due to the dependence of New York financial interests on the cotton trade. During his term of office he enrolled, equipped, and sent over 200,000 men to fight for the union cause. He declined to run for a third term, and instead was selected in March 1863 to fill a United States Senate seat. This caused him to resign his commission as a major- general of volunteers. He failed to win reelection in 1869 and declined nomination offers by President Andrew Johnson to make him Secretary of the Treasury. At first he supported Johnson's reconstruction policies, but later supported his impeachment. In his later years he engaged in philanthropy, making large gifts to education, religious, and medical groups.

MOTT

Mott, Gershom. *Carte de visite* by Sexton, Bordentown, New Jersey. Author's collection.

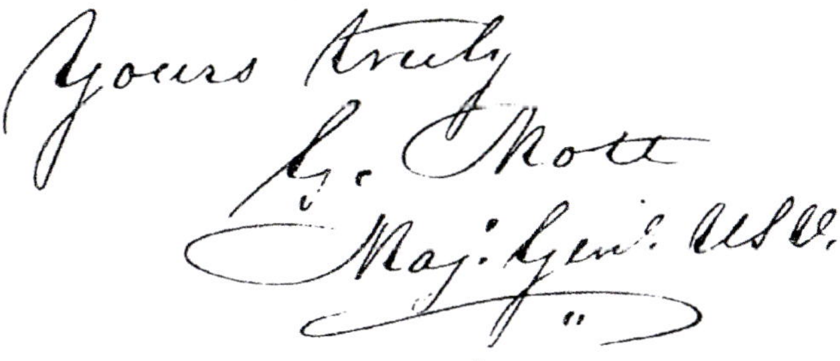

Mott, Gershom (1822-1884) Born in New Jersey, Mott engaged in business in New York City until being appointed a second lieutenant in the 10th U.S. Infantry during the war with Mexico. His regiment never left the country, and he was mustered out in 1848. Mott then engaged in business in Bordentown, New Jersey, until the commencement of the Civil War, at which time he was appointed lieutenant-colonel of the 5th New Jersey after it was mustered into federal service. Both Mott and the 5th New Jersey remained with the Army of the Potomac for the duration of the war. In May 1862 Mott became Colonel of the 6th New Jersey and led it through the battles in the Virginia Peninsula Campaign. He was wounded at the Second Battle of Bull Run, and in September 1862 was appointed a brigadier-general of volunteers and given command of the 3rd Brigade in the 2nd Division of the III Corps. Mott was wounded at the Battle of Chancellorsville while commanding his brigade under General Hiram Berry, who was killed in the battle. Due to his wounds he missed the Battle of Gettysburg, but in August 1863 received division command in General Winfield Hancock's II Corps in time for the Battle of the Wilderness. His division faltered badly on the second day of the battle, and General Meade and others believed him to be an inept leader. He had been ordered to support General Emory Upton's focused assault on Confederate lines that was initially successful, but Mott did not move his division quickly enough to support Upton, whose division took severe casualties while making their way back to federal lines. Mott's division was reorganized as a brigade, and he fought at North Anna and Cold Harbor as a brigade commander until returning to division command during the siege at Petersburg. However, he recovered a bit of his reputation at the botched Battle of the Crater and was awarded a brevet to major-general. He was again wounded on April 6, 1865, at Amelia Courthouse, and was not present at the Appomattox surrender. He received promotion to major-general of volunteers in September 1865 to rank from May 26, 1865. After the end of hostilities Mott served as commander of a provisional division, and on the military commission to determine the guilt of Captain Henry Wirtz, the commander of the infamous Andersonville prison. In 1868 he declined to accept a commission as a colonel in the regular army. He was mustered out of federal service in February 1866 and returned to commercial interests and holding positions in local and state offices.

Mower

Mower, Joseph. *Carte de visite* by Oak Gallery, Memphis. Tennessee. On the back of the carte is the signature of General Mower. Author's collection.

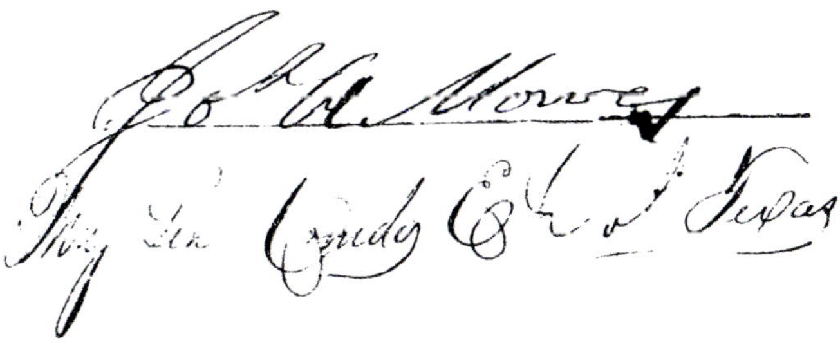

Mower, Joseph Anthony (1827-1870) was born in Vermont. Mower attended Norwich Academy, and worked as a carpenter before entering the Mexican War as a private in an engineering battalion in the regular army. In 1855, he was directly appointed a second-lieutenant in the 1st U.S. Infantry, and by September 1861 was a captain in the 9th U.S. Infantry, which was active in the early Missouri operations. He obtained the command of the 11th Missouri Volunteers in May 1862 and gallantly led the regiment in the battles of Farmington, Iuka, and Corinth, earning three brevets. At the Battle of Corinth he was wounded and left on the field, but escaped back into federal lines. During the Vicksburg Campaign, after being appointed to brigadier-general of volunteers in March 1863, backdated to November 1862, he served as a brigade commander in the 3rd Division of the XV Corps. Mower won another brevet for his actions in the capture of Jackson, Mississippi, and commendations for his fighting at the Battle of Milliken's Bend. After Vicksburg he was sent with General A.J. Smith's XVI Corps to support General Nathaniel Banks' ill-fated Red River Campaign. Mower led the attacking column in taking Fort DeRussy in March 1864, and defeated Confederate forces at Yellow Bayou while commanding the rear guard of Bank's army. He and his division ably fought later with General A.J. Smith and the XVI Corps at the Battle of Tupelo, which seriously damaged the forces of Confederate General Nathan Bedford Forrest. In August 1864 he was appointed major-general of volunteers and participated briefly in defeating the last effort by Confederate General Sterling Price to invade Missouri. He returned south to serve with General William T. Sherman in the Atlanta and March to the Sea, skillfully commanding the XVII Corps in South Carolina and the XX Corp at the Battle of Bentonville and in the process winning a brevet to major-general in the regular army. Mower was awarded the colonelcy of the 39th Infantry, a black regiment stationed on reconstruction duty, in the army reorganization of 1866. In 1869 he was transferred to the 25th Infantry and died of pneumonia in January 1870 while in command of the Department of Louisiana. Mower was a particular favorite of General Sherman and was constantly lauded by superiors. He was one of the most breveted officers in the federal army.

NEGLEY

Negley, James. *Carte de visite* by Morse, Nashville, Tennessee. Author's collection.

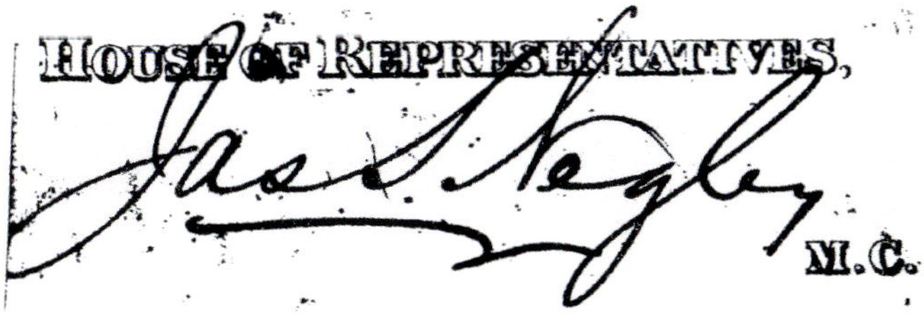

Negley, James Scott (1826-1901) was born in Pennsylvania and educated at Pittsburgh University. Negley served for about a year and a half as a private in the 1st Pennsylvania Volunteers during the Mexican War. In the years prior to the Civil War he was active in the Pennsylvania militia and became a prosperous and well known horticulturalist. Upon the firing on Fort Sumter he was appointed as a brigadier-general of Pennsylvania Volunteers, and with General Robert Patterson participated in the Battle of Falling Waters, where Patterson was unable to stop General Joseph Johnston from supporting General G.P.T. Beauregard at the Battle of Bull Run. After the ninety day enlistment period of his volunteer troops expired he was appointed a brigadier general of volunteers and sent to serve in the Army of the Ohio, commanded by General Don Carlos Buell. He then served under General Ormsby Mitchel in Northern Alabama and Tennessee. In an action at Sweedon Grove, while serving under Mitchel, his brigade surprised and defeated the Confederate cavalry led by General Wirt Adams. In October 1862 he was successful at the Battle of La Vergne, defeating the cavalry of General Nathan Forrest and General Richard Anderson. Negley was assigned to remain and defend Nashville during Buell's advance and pursuit of General Braxton Bragg's invasion of Kentucky that ended at the Battle of Perryville. Negley received division command in the Army of the Cumberland, and in the Battle of Stone's River was complimented by General George Thomas and appointed to major-general of volunteers. Negley's Division in the XVI Corps at the Battle of Chickamauga was given the assignment of holding Owen's Gap, but in the second day of the battle it was completely routed and joined the exodus of two-thirds of Rosecrans' army to the fortifications at Chattanooga. General Thomas Wood and General John Brannan, fellow division commanders in Thomas' XVI Corps, accused Negley of cowardice, desertion, and negligence, but a court of inquiry did not substantiate the charges. Negley was never again assigned a field command and spent the remainder of 1864 recruiting in the Pittsburgh area. He bitterly resigned in January 1865, claiming to be a victim of the West Point "clique" against civilian officers. In post war years he served several terms in Congress as a Republican and engaged in business interests in the New York area.

NELSON

Nelson, William. *Carte de visite* by Brady, Washington. Author's collection.

Nelson, William (1824-1862) was born in Kentucky. Nelson attended Norwich Academy before becoming a midshipman in the U.S. Navy in 1840. He commanded a naval battery in the siege of Vera Cruz and rose to the rank of lieutenant in 1855. In 1858 he commanded the *Niagara*, in which he returned back to Africa blacks that had been aboard the captured slaver *Echo*. He was stationed in Washington at the beginning of the war, but was soon promoted to lieutenant commander and placed in command of gunboats on the Ohio River. Nelson agreed with President Lincoln there was considerable union support in Kentucky and accepted an army assignment to recruit. He built Camp Dick Robinson as a recruiting and supply depot, and was appointed to brigadier-general of volunteers in September 1861. In November 1861, at the head of a mixed force of Ohio and Kentucky regiments, he stopped the movement of Confederate Colonel John Williams into Kentucky from Virginia. Commanding a division in General Don Carlos' Army of the Ohio, he was highly commended for his actions at the Battle of Shiloh, where he helped reorganize federal troops in the evening of the first day's battle. He gallantly participated in federal attacks on the second day that resulted in the withdrawal of Beauregard to Corinth, Mississippi. Nelson participated in General Henry Halleck's march to Corinth, but was ordered back north to oppose General Braxton Bragg's invasion of Kentucky. Now a major-general of volunteers, he was soundly defeated and slightly wounded at the Battle of Richmond. Afterwards, in early August 1862, he was placed in charge of the defenses of Louisville. Nelson asked for assistance in recruiting and defending the city and received the services of General Jefferson C. Davis. He directed Davis to form defense battalions, but within several days the two were in loud vocal disagreements, and Nelson ordered Davis out of the city. Davis, an officer in the regular army, was deeply angered and did not return to Louisville till late September 1862, after Nelson had been superseded by General Don Carlos Buell. Davis encountered Nelson in the Galt Hotel and the two engaged in heated conversation, with Davis demanding an apology. Nelson refused and Davis threw a crumpled visiting card in Nelson's face, with Nelson responding by slapping Davis in the face and leaving the hotel lobby. Davis was enraged and went upstairs, borrowed a pistol, and found Nelson and shot him at point blank range. The shooting was witnessed by numerous officers and civilians. General Buell imprisoned Davis, but department commander General Horatio Wright believed Davis' actions to be justified, and he was soon released. He was never brought to trial or court-martial, as army authorities declared there were no officers available to form a court. Bragg's invasion of Kentucky obscured the case, and probably there were few general officers with any feelings of friendship for "Bull" Nelson, a man with a history of being a violent bully.

NEWTON

Newton, George. *Carte de visite* by Brady, Washington. Author's collection.

Newton, John (1823-1895) was born in Virginia and entered the Military Academy in 1838, graduating second in the class of 1842. He was commissioned in the Corps of Engineers, and prior to the Civil War served solely in the engineers, building forts, harbors, and lighthouses. For several years he was stationed at West Point as an instructor in engineering. His only field experience was in General Albert Sidney Johnston's 1858 Utah Expedition. His first assignment in the Civil War was as chief engineer for the Department of Pennsylvania and the Department of Shenandoah before being promoted a major and named chief engineer of the defenses of Washington, commanding a brigade of volunteers. Newton was appointed brigadier-general of volunteers in August 1861, and led a brigade in General William Franklin's Division in the VI Corps of the Army of the Potomac. In the 1862 Virginia Peninsula Campaign he fought in the battles of West Point, Gaines' Mill, and Glendale. His brigade was part of the federal force that covered the retreat of the Army of Virginia into the Washington defenses after the Federal defeat at the Second Battle of Bull Run. Newton was later moved to command of the 3rd Division in the VI Corps at the battles of South Mountain and Antietam, where he was breveted a lieutenant-colonel for gallantry. He continued to command a division at the Battle of Fredericksburg, and was one of seven generals that complained directly to President Lincoln about General Ambrose Burnsides' incompetent leadership. Burnside was furious with the group, and gave Lincoln the option of dismissing them from the army or accept his resignation. Newton later testified against Burnside before the Congressional Committee on the Conduct of the War. Lincoln, in the end, removed Burnside and kept most of the complaining generals, but their careers were tarnished for the rest of the war. In Newton's case, he continued in command of his division at Chancellorsville, but received his punishment later when his appointment as major-general of volunteers, issued in April 1863, was revoked in March 1864. With the death of General John Reynolds on the first day of battle at Gettysburg, Newton was selected by General George Meade to command the I Corps, even though he was a division commander in the VI Corps. His leadership of the I Corps at Gettysburg earned him a brevet to colonel in the regular army. Upon the dissolution of the I Corps after the Mine Run Campaign in the winter of 1864 Newton transferred to the western theater, where he commanded a division in the IV Corps led by General O.O. Howard. His division fought in the important battles of the Atlanta Campaign, with Newton receiving a brevet to brigadier-general in the regular army. He did not accompany Sherman on the March to the Sea, but in October 1864 was placed in command of the Department of Key West and remained in Florida until January 1866, when he mustered out of volunteer service. He returned to the Corps of Engineers as a lieutenant-colonel, and in 1884 Newton was made Chief of Engineers with the rank of brigadier-general.

Oglesby

Oglesby, Richard. *Carte de visite* by unidentified photographer. Author's collection.

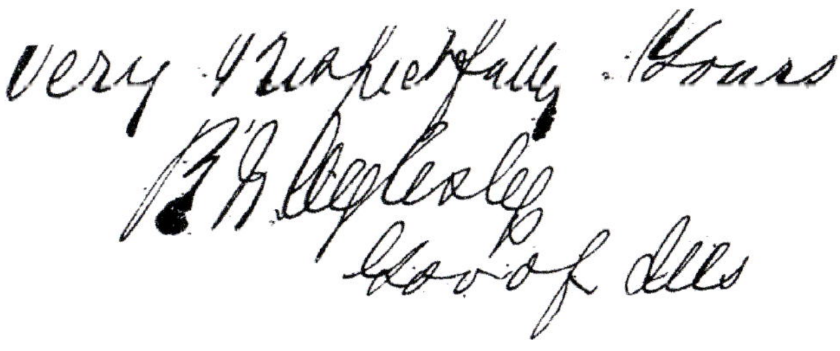

Oglesby, Richard James (1824-1899) was born in Kentucky, but read for and practiced law in Decatur, Illinois, before serving as a lieutenant with the 4th Illinois Volunteers in the Mexican War, fighting in the battles of Cerro Gordo and Vera Cruz. Upon returning from the Mexican War Oglesby enrolled in the University of Louisville law school, graduating in 1849 before departing to the gold fields in California. In 1856-57 he toured Europe, Egypt, and the Holy Land, and upon returning joined the newly formed Republican Party. He then ran and failed in 1858 to become a U.S. congressman. During the Republican Chicago convention in 1860 he coined the term "Lincoln the Rail Splitter". In 1860 he was elected to the Illinois state senate, but resigned in 1861 to accept command of the 8th Illinois volunteers. Oglesby's brigade was active in Missouri and formed part of General John McClernand's Division in the Army of the Tennessee, present at the battles of Fort Henry and Fort Donelson. He was appointed to brigadier- general of volunteers for bravery and leadership after the Battle of Fort Henry, where his brigade was the first to enter the Confederate fortifications. He participated in General Henry Halleck's advance and siege of Corinth, and at the later Battle of Corinth in October 1862, where he was severely wounded and did not return to the army until April 1863. Oglesby was promoted to major-general of volunteers to date from November 29, 1862, and took command of the left wing of the XVI Corps, stationed in Northern Mississippi and Western Tennessee. On May 18, 1864, he resigned from volunteer service to run for the governorship of Illinois. Oglesby was a strong and consistent supporter of Lincoln, but later as a Republican radical opposed the reconstruction policies of President Andrew Johnson. He was easily elected Illinois governor, succeeding Richard Yates, and held office until 1869. Oglesby was one of the last to have a conversation with Lincoln before the assassination, and was at his deathbed and supervised the transportation of the body for internment in Springfield. In 1872 he was again elected governor, but resigned in 1873 to become a United States Senator. In 1884 he was elected for his third and last term as Illinois governor. Oglesby was also one of the founders of the Grand Army of the Republic organization and died in 1899.

ORD

Ord, E.O. *Carte de visite* by Fredricks, New York. Author's collection.

Ord, E.O. *Carte de visite* by Brady, Washington. This photograph shows Ord and family in the Confederate White House in Richmond. Author's collection.

Ord, Edward Otho Cresap (1818-1883) was born in Maryland, but was raised in Washington. He entered the Military Academy in 1835 at the age of sixteen. Ord finished seventeenth in the class of 1839 and was commissioned in the 3rd Artillery. He, like most other junior officers, fought in the Florida Indian wars against the Seminoles lodged deep in the Everglades. Ord was given garrison and survey duties until he was transferred to California in 1846, and remained in the Monterey garrison during the war with Mexico. Promoted to captain in 1850, he was engaged in numerous actions against Indians in Oregon and Washington, including the 1856 Rogue River War, Yakima War in 1855, and the 1858 Spokane Expedition. While at Fort Monroe, Virginia, and assigned to Artillery School, he was detailed to Harper's Ferry to serve with Colonel Robert E. Lee, putting down the John Brown insurrection. Ord, who was married to the daughter of a slave owner, was present at John Brown's hanging. In 1861 Ord was again ordered to Fort Vancouver, Washington Territory, and later was reassigned to Benecia Barracks and San Francisco, California. He returned to Washington in late 1861 to receive command of a brigade in the Army of the Potomac with the rank of brigadier-general of volunteers. He was in command of troops at the Battle of Dranesville, Virginia, in December 1861, and on May 1862 received the command of a division after being appointed a major-general of volunteers. In May 1862 he was transferred from the Department of the Rappahannock to command troops stationed at Corinth, Mississippi. In August 1862, under General Ulysses Grant, he participated in the battles of Iuka and Hatchie, where he was severely wounded. While on medical leave he served on a commission to investigate General Don Carlos Buell's campaigns in Kentucky and Tennessee. Grant, after relieving General John McClernand shortly before the surrender of Vicksburg, asked Ord to return to duty. In May 1863 he was commanding McClernand's old XIII Corps and was engaged in the latter parts of the siege of Vicksburg and the capture of Jackson, Mississippi. Late in 1863 and early in 1864 he held various commands in the Gulf and Shenandoah Valley. For the remainder of the war he commanded the VIII Corps and the XVIII Corps in operations before Richmond. In the assault and capture of Fort Harrison he was again severely wounded and did not return to duty until December 4, 1864. Then, in January 1865, he replaced Army of the James commander General Benjamin Butler. Upon Butler's relief he commanded the Army of the James, as well as the Departments of Virginia and North Carolina. He was engaged in the various operations of the Petersburg siege and played a central part in the pursuit of the Confederate army until its capitulation at Appomattox. Ord was appointed a brigadier-general in the regular army in July 1866, and served in various departmental commands till his retirement as a major-general in 1881. Ord was a steady and reliable commander holding the confidence of General Grant, who requested him to command at several important junctures of the war. In 1883 he died of yellow fever while on a voyage to Vera Cruz, Mexico. Ord was a very competent corps commander, perhaps not always showing a great deal of initiative, but he functioned well under the direction of General Grant.

OSTERHAUS

Osterhaus, Peter. *Carte de visite* by Brady, Washington. Author's collection.

Osterhaus, Peter Joseph (1823-1917) was born in Koblenz, Germany. He received a military education in Berlin and was one of many German born officers that fled to the United States after the 1848 revolutions in Europe. First settling in Belleville, Illinois, in 1849, Osterhaus engaged in business and eventually moved to St. Louis, Missouri. At the onset of the Civil War he helped organize and was appointed major of a battalion comprising part of the 2d Missouri Infantry, which took an active role in actions at Dug springs and at the important Battle of Wilson's Creek. In December 1861 he received a commission as Colonel of the 12th Missouri, and later a brigade under General John Fremont. In the federal victory at the Battle of Pea Ridge he led a division of General Samuel Curtis' Army of the Southwest. In June 1862 he was commissioned brigadier-general of volunteers, then led his brigade in the federal victory at Arkansas Post. In January 1863 Osterhaus was given command of the 1st Division of the XV Corps in the Army of the Tennessee and fought in the battles preceding the actual siege of Vicksburg. At the Battle of Big Black he was wounded, but returned to the army in time to participate in the capture of Jackson, Mississippi. He then accompanied General William T. Sherman in the relief of General George Thomas and the Army of the Cumberland at Chattanooga. Serving under General Joseph Hooker at the Battle of Missionary Ridge, Osterhaus' division was among the first over the top of the ridge and was successful in driving General Braxton Bragg from the southern end of his line of fortifications. He was placed under command of General William T. Sherman for the Atlanta campaign and fought well, and was in temporary command of the XV Corps. In July 1864, despite objections from General Sherman alleging that he had been absent on leave seeking rank, Osterhaus was appointed to be a major-general of volunteers. Osterhaus, despite his disagreements with Sherman, remained on the March to the Sea and fought in the early actions of the Carolina campaign. In January 1865 he was made chief of staff to General E.R.S. Canby in the Military Division of West Mississippi. After the capture of Mobile and surrender of the Confederates in the Trans-Mississippi in late May 1865, Osterhaus held departmental commands in the west until he mustered out of federal service in January 1866. He received a diplomatic post to France in 1866 and served there eleven years, until receiving his last diplomatic post in Mannheim, Germany. In 1905 he was made, by Act of Congress, a brigadier-general in the regular army, and several days later placed on the retired list. He died in Germany in 1917. Osterhaus was perhaps the best of the foreign born federal generals.

Osterhaus, Peter. *Carte de visite* by Brady, Washington. Author's collection.

PALMER

Palmer, John. *Carte de visite* by Schwing and Rudd, Army of the Cumberland. Author's collection.

Palmer, John. *Carte de visite* by Bonsall, Cincinnati, Ohio. Author's collection.

Palmer, John McCauley (1817-1900) was born in Kentucky, but was raised in Alton, Illinois, near St. Louis. After attending Shurtleff College he studied law, and in 1839, after moving to Carlinville, Illinois, was admitted to the bar. He entered politics in 1840, supporting Martin Van Buren, and later was elected as a Free Soil Democrat, serving as a county judge and state senator. Palmer, always an opponent of slavery, joined the Republican Party, and in 1859 failed in a bid for a congressional seat. He was a delegate to the 1860 Republican Convention in Chicago and to the failed 1861 Washington Peace Conference that attempted to reconcile differences between the North and South. When war came Palmer immediately mustered in as Colonel of the 14th Illinois Infantry and accompanied General John Fremont on his capture of Springfield, Missouri. Palmer, probably due to political influence, was promoted to brigadier-general in December 1861. He commanded the 2d Division of General John Pope's Army of the Mississippi in capturing Island No. 10 and New Madrid. He reverted back to brigade command during General Henry Halleck's slow movement to Corinth, and afterwards commanded the 1st Division of the Army of the Mississippi in holding Nashville. In December 1862 he was transferred to division command in the XIV Corps of the Army of the Cumberland and fought with it on the left wing at the Battle of Stone's River. He was again transferred in January 1863 to the XXI Corps and appointed to major-general of volunteers in March 1863 to date from November 1862. He fought bravely at Chickamauga and then led the XIV Corps in the Chattanooga campaign. During the Georgia campaign Palmer became embroiled in an argument with General William Sherman after being subordinated to General John Schofield, whose promotion to major-general was confirmed later than Palmer's. He asked to be relieved and was placed in command of the Department of Kentucky, remaining in that post until he was mustered out of volunteer service in January 1866. In post-war years he practiced law in Springfield, Illinois, was elected governor, and later returned to the Democratic party in the 1880s and was elected to the United States Senate in 1891. In 1896, Palmer ran for president on the Gold Democrat Ticket in opposition to William Jennings Bryan's Free Silver ticket. His running mate was former Confederate General Simon Bucker, a one-time opponent at the Battle of Chickamauga.

PARKE

Parke, John. *Carte de visite* by Brady, Washington. Author's collection.

Parke, John. *Carte de visite* by Brady, Washington. Author's collection.

Parke, John Grubb (1827-1900) was born in Pennsylvania, and attended the University of Pennsylvania before being admitted to the Military Academy in 1845, graduating second in the class of 1849. He was commissioned in the Topographical Engineers, spending his career prior to the Civil War conducting surveys in New Mexico and Southern California for a route for the future Southern Pacific Railway. At the start of the Civil War Parke was stationed in Washington territory and did not arrive in Washington until September 1861. Parke's Civil War service began as a brigadier-general of volunteers, accompanying the expedition of General Ambrose Burnside to North Carolina in December 1861. He was engaged in the combat at Roanoke Island, Battle of New Bern, and commanded the bombardment and reduction of Fort Macon. For his actions at the Battle of New Bern he was breveted a lieutenant-colonel in the regular army and appointed a major-general of volunteers. He then served as chief of staff to General Burnside, commanding the IX Corps in the Maryland Campaign. Parke saw combat at the Battle of South Mountain and the Battle of Antietam, where he temporarily assumed division command when General Isaac Rodman was killed. He resumed his chief of staff position with Burnside during the pursuit of Lee's army. Parke remained as chief of staff when General Burnside became commander of the Army of the Potomac, and when Burnside was relieved he moved with him to the Department of the Ohio. He later took command of the IX Corps from Burnside and led it successfully at Vicksburg and in the capture of Jackson, Mississippi. After Vicksburg the IX Corps was returned to the Department of the Ohio, and Parke was engaged in East Tennessee at the Battle of Blue Springs and in the defense of Knoxville. In March 1864 General Burnside resumed command of the IX Corps, marching it from Tennessee to join the Army of the Potomac before the 1864 Overland Campaign in Virginia. Parke again served as chief of staff through the battles of the Wilderness and Spotsylvania. During the Petersburg siege Burnside approved a plan to mine under Confederate lines. The subsequent explosion was successful, but Burnside's division commanders failed to exploit it, instead turning the action into a Federal bloodbath and Confederate victory. Parke assumed command of the IX Corps after General Grant ordered Burnside's removal for the disaster at the Battle of the Crater. Parke ably led the IX Corps in the battles of Hatcher's Run and Fort Stedman. He also commanded the Army of the Potomac for a brief period while General George Meade was on leave. During this time he repulsed the last offensive attack by Confederate forces. For this action he was breveted a brigadier-general in the regular army. His corps was active in the Appomattox campaign, and he was present at the surrender. Parke was not only a superb engineer and administrator, but a talented combat commander. However, he seemed to be content to serve as Burnsides' chief staff officer for a good part of the war. After the war he resumed his duties in the Corps of Engineers till being appointed in 1887 as commandant of the United States Military Academy. He retired in 1889 as a colonel and assistant chief of Engineers.

PECK

Peck, John. *Carte de visite* by Brady, Washington. Author's collection.

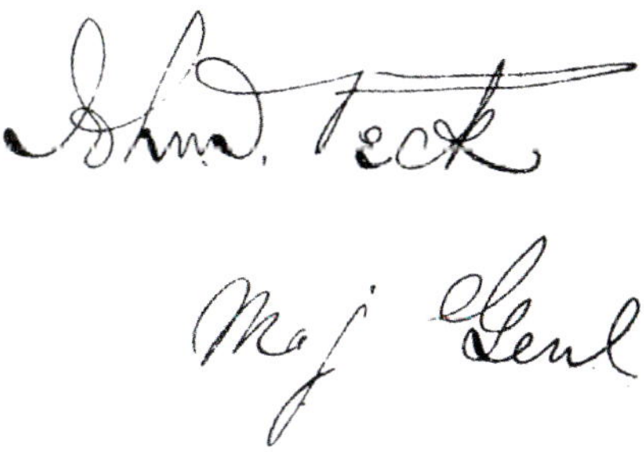

Peck, John James (1821-1878) was born in New York. He was admitted to the Military Academy in 1839, graduating eighth in the class of 1843 that included Ulysses Grant. He was commissioned into the 2d Artillery and performed garrison duty until the beginning of the war with Mexico. He participated in the occupation of Texas and numerous battles before the capture of Mexico City in 1847. Peck received brevets to captain and major for gallantry and service at the battles of Contreras, Churubusco, and Molino Del Rey. Beginning in 1849 he saw extensive service in New Mexico, scouting and skirmishing with Navaho Indians. In 1851 and 1852 he was on recruiting service and took an extended leave in 1852, resigning from the army on March 31, 1853. Until the Civil War Peck engaged in various pursuits, including railroads and banking, and served as the president of the Syracuse, New York, school board. He entered politics, serving as a delegate to the Democratic national conventions in 1856 and 1860, and was twice nominated to Congress. Peck was appointed a brigadier-general of volunteers by President Lincoln in August 1861, and served in the defenses of Washington until joining General George McClellan's 1862 Peninsula Campaign, commanding the 2d Division of General Erasmus Keye's IV Corps. He fought credibly in the Seven Days Campaigns and was promoted to major-general of volunteers in July 1862. Placed in command of all troops in Southeastern Virginia in September 1862, in April 1863 Peck beat back assaults by General James Longstreet's superior forces attempting to capture Suffolk. In later actions at Norfleet House and Fort Huger Peck demonstrated his ability as a solid field commander. He was seriously wounded in the Suffolk operations, and was incapacitated for a number of months before taking command of the District of North Carolina. In July 1864 he commanded the Department of the East, responsible for regulating affairs with Canadian provinces along the northern border. Mustered out of Federal service in August 1865, he returned to Syracuse and was one of the founders of the New York State Life Insurance Company in 1867. He served as president of the company until his death in 1878.

PLEASONTON

Pleasonton, Alfred. *Carte de visite* by Brady, Washington. Author's collection.

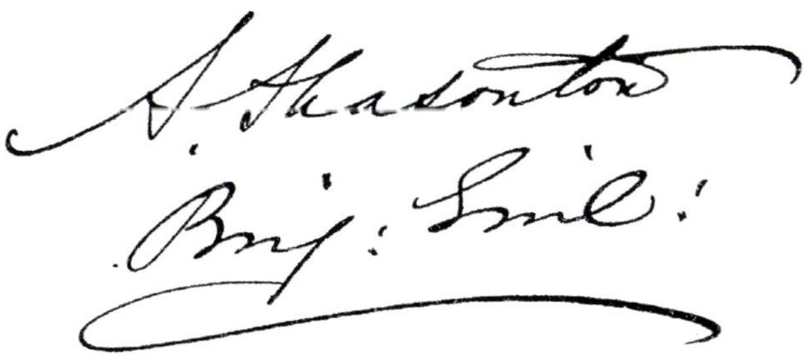

Pleasonton, Alfred (1824-1897) was born in the District of Columbia. Pleasonton gained admission to the Military Academy in 1840, graduating seventh in the class of 1844. He received his commission in the 1st Dragoons and served on frontier duty till the beginning of the war with Mexico. He was lightly engaged in a few battles, but did receive a brevet to first lieutenant for gallantry at the battles of Palo Alto and Resaca. He returned in 1848 to frontier scouting duty in New Mexico, and was involved in 1852 in a heavy skirmish with Navaho Indians at Canyon del Muerto. Transferred to the 2nd Dragoons in 1855, he was involved in fighting Indians in Florida till joining the 1856 Sioux Expedition. Pleasonton next accompanied his regiment and General William Harney in quelling the Kansas disturbances, and afterwards, in June 1860, was ordered to the Department of Oregon as assistant adjutant general. At the commencement of the Civil War Pleasonton led the 2nd Dragoons from Utah on their epic march to Washington, arriving there in October. He served in the defenses of Washington till February 1862, when he was promoted to major in the 2nd Dragoons. He caught the attention of General George McClellan in the Peninsula Campaign, resulting in an appointment to brigadier-general of volunteers commanding the 2nd Brigade in the Cavalry Division of the Army of the Potomac. He was engaged in various cavalry actions, including Poolville, South Mountain, Antietam, and Warrenton. He was also with the cavalry as it covered the Army of the Potomac's retreat from Fredericksburg. At this juncture of the war, the cavalry of the Army of the Potomac was substantially inferior to that of Confederate General Jeb Stuart's horsemen. Pleasonton was made responsible for keeping abreast of Stuart, and soon became notorious for making unreliable reports regarding Stuart's movements. He was also unable to stop the second raid by Stuart around the Army of the Potomac. At Chancellorsville, the commander of the Cavalry Corps, General George Stoneman, chose not to utilize Pleasonton on a major raid and left him with the main army in command of a brigade. However Stoneman's Raid, due to rainy weather, high water, and other reasons failed in its intent. Pleasonton, however, during the Chancellorsville battle, received laurels for sending a regiment in an almost suicidal charge to save Federal artillery pieces at Hazel Grove. General Jospeh Hooker, furious at General Stoneman, replaced him with Pleasonton as Chief of the Cavalry Corps of the Army of the Potomac. In May and June 1863 he engaged Confederate cavalry at Brandy Station, Beverly Ford, Aldie, Middleburg, and Upperville. At Brandy Station Pleasonton commanded nearly 11,000 horsemen in the largest cavalry battle of the war and nearly penetrated Stuart's screen of the Army of Northern Virginia at Culpepper. Although not a victory for Pleasonton, the Battle of Brandy Station clearly demonstrated that Federal cavalry were no longer inferior to Stuart's horsemen. At Gettysburg Pleasonton, now a major-general of volunteers, chose to remain with the Army of the Potomac headquarters, leaving fighting in the field up to subordinate commanders, such as General Judson Kilpatrick and General John Buford. The junior captains that Pleasonton had recently appointed to brigadier generals (Wesley Merritt, George Custer, and Elon Farnsworth) all played key roles in the cavalry actions at Gettysburg. A serious failing at Gettysburg on the part of Pleasonton was that after the first day he failed to replace General John Buford's brigade, which left an open approach to the far right of the Federal line. As usual, during the Gettysburg campaign Pleasonton had been unable to provide valuable and credible intelligence to the army. In February 1864 he disapproved Kilpatrick's proposed raid on Richmond that was later endorsed by the Lincoln administration. The raid was unsuccessful, and Colonel Ulric Dahlgreen, son of

Admiral Dahlgreen, was killed while carrying documents allegedly indicating the purpose of the raid to be the burning of Richmond. In March 1864, new general-in- chief General Ulysses Grant replaced Pleasonton with General Philip Sheridan. His new assignment was as commander of the cavalry forces of General William Rosecrans, commanding the Department of Missouri. Pleasonton's operations against the invasion of Missouri by General Sterling Price were successful at the Battle at Jefferson City. In cooperation with General Samuel Curtis, he pursued Price's forces and fought battles at Little Blue and Big Blue Rivers in eastern Kansas. These actions nearly destroyed Price's army, but Pleasonton and Curtis hesitated launching a final pursuit. He was mustered out of the volunteers in January 1866 and returned to his permanent rank of major. In the regular army reorganization of 1866 Pleasonton was offered the lieutenant-colonelcy of the 20th Infantry, which he refused. This left him in the 2nd Cavalry subordinate to Colonel Thomas J. Wood and Lieutenant Colonel Innis Palmer. Pleasonton felt he outranked Wood and Palmer and resigned in January 1868. He retired as a major and held some minor federal posts and was involved in some railroad enterprises.

Pleasonton, Alfred. *Carte de visite* by Brady, Washington, Author's collection.

Pope

Pope, John. *Carte de visite* by Brady, Washington. Author's collection.

Pope, John (1822-1892) was born in Kentucky and raised in southern Illinois. In 1838 Pope was admitted at age sixteen to the Military Academy. He graduated seventeenth in the class of 1842 and was commissioned in the Topographical Engineers. Pope served in Florida between 1842 and 1844, and during the war with Mexico received brevets to first-lieutenant and captain for gallantry and meritorious service at the battles of Monterey and Buena Vista. After the war, between 1851 and 1853, he performed duty as chief topographical engineer in the Department of New Mexico, surveying potential Pacific railroad routes through New Mexico. Promoted to first-lieutenant in 1853, he began an important engineering task in finding water for the arid "Llano Estacado" (the current Texas panhandle) by using artesian wells. At the beginning of the Civil War he was a captain serving in lighthouse construction duty. Through Illinois political connections he was one of a group of officers selected to accompany newly elected President Lincoln to Washington. Probably due to his father's political prominence in southern Illinois, Pope was appointed a brigadier-general of volunteers in June 1861 and given command of the District of Missouri, then part of the Western Department commanded by General John C. Fremont. Amidst the tumultuous military climate in Missouri he was transferred to the southwestern and central districts of Missouri. In December 1861 at Blackwater, Missouri, he led forces that bested Confederate General Sterling Price, almost forcing him out of the state. In February 1862 Pope received command of the Army of the Mississippi, and in cooperation with a naval flotilla commanded by Admiral Andrew Foote captured Island No. 10 and New Madrid, Missouri, opening up the northern part of the Mississippi River to federal traffic. Pope and his Army of the Mississippi were transported in late April 1862 to join General Henry Halleck on his turtle-like advance on Corinth, Mississippi. Pope was appointed to major-general of volunteers in May 1862, and most certainly had caught the eye of President Lincoln, who was desperately searching for successful "fighting" generals. Lincoln appointed him commander of the Army of Virginia on June 27, 1862, with the responsibility of protecting Washington and creating demonstrations to protect General George McClellan's Virginia Peninsula Campaign. Pope's Army of Virginia was comprised of nearly all federal forces in the eastern theater. The loud and bombastic Pope, in the first days of his command, issued circulars infuriating most men and officers in the army, destroying any chance of a harmonious command. One of the circulars stated that his headquarters was to be in the saddle, drawing quips that Pope did not know his headquarters from his hindquarters. Another of the communications unfavorably compared the fighting ability of the eastern armies to those in the west. Pope also became embroiled in arguments with some of his generals over his harsh treatment of secessionists. General McCellan's withdrawal to Harrison's Landing in late July 1862 created an opportunity for General Lee to quickly move his army toward Washington and destroy the numerically smaller Army of Virginia. For fifteen days in August 1862 the Army of Virginia fought the successive battles of Cedar Mountain, Bristoe, Groveton, Second Bull Run, and Chantilly. Pope was decisively defeated by the Army of Northern Virginia, but in a deliberate and orderly manner drew back into the Washington defenses. Generals Lee, Longstreet, and Stonewall Jackson had masterfully deceived Pope in locating their forces, and in a classic movement of splitting and reuniting forces had routed Federal forces. Pope blamed his defeat not on his poor use of tactical skills on the Manassas plains, but on McClellan and some of his generals he thought to be disloyal. General McClellan had resisted and been slow in obeying the direct orders of General-in-Chief Henry Halleck and President Lincoln to quickly dispatch Army of the Potomac divisions to support Pope. In retaliation against McClellan Pope demanded the court-martial of General Fitz John Porter, a McClellan loyalist, for disobeying his orders for an assault that was clearly impossible. In the bitter aftermath of Second Bull Run Pope asked in October 1862 to be relieved, and was transferred to the Department of the Northwest and spent the rest of the war dealing with Indian problems, including the Sioux uprising in Minnesota. In 1865 he mustered out of volunteer service, and as a brigadier-general was assigned various departmental commands. Until his retirement in 1886, he was one of the relatively few army generals with a realistic perception of the problems facing Native Americans and how they might be resolved. He was also an effective departmental administrator and wrote an insightful autobiography.

Pope, John. *Carte de visite* by Webster, Louisville. Author's collection.

PORTER

Porter, Fitz-John. *Carte de visite* by Brady, New York. Author's collection.

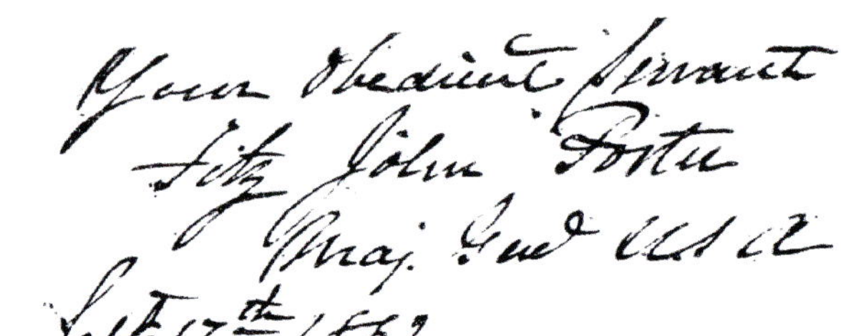

Porter, Fitz-John (1822-1901) was born in New Hampshire. The son of Commander John Porter of the United States Navy, he entered the Military Academy in 1841 after attending Exeter Academy. Porter graduated eighth in the class of 1845 and was commissioned into the 4th Artillery. His performance in the Mexican War was commendable, gaining him brevets to captain and major. He fought in most of the major battles and was wounded at the Belen Gate during the assault on Mexico City. Between 1849 and 1855 he served as an instructor and adjutant at the Military Academy. Until the commencement of the Civil War Porter served in the Adjutant General's office as assistant Adjutant General in the Department of the West, and in 1857 as the Assistant Adjutant General on the Utah Expedition. His first Civil War service was as chief of staff of the Department of Pennsylvania and with the forces of General Robert Patterson and General Nathaniel Banks in Shenandoah Valley movements. In May 1861 he was promoted to colonel of the 15th U.S. Infantry, and in August 1861 was appointed a brigadier-general of volunteers dated back to May 17, 1861. He took part in General Robert Patterson's action at Falling Waters, Virginia, and in October 1861 was placed in command of a division in the Army of the Potomac. His division remained in the Washington defenses until the beginning of the 1862 Virginia Peninsula campaign. General George McClellan, commanding the Army of the Potomac, placed Porter in charge of the siege at Yorktown and in command of a division in the III Corps. He ably directed its operations at New Bridge, Hanover Court House, Mechanicsville, Gaines' Mill, and Malvern Hill. For his commendable performance, McClellan requested his appointment to major-general of volunteers. He was also breveted a brigadier-general in the regular army for actions on the Chickahominy. In late July 1862, Porter's V Corps was ordered from Harrison's Landing to the support of General John Pope and the Army of Virginia during the Second Bull Run campaign. Porter was vocal about his displeasure in being ordered to support General Pope and was later accused by Pope of disobeying orders to promptly join the Army of Virginia. Pope also accused him of disobeying orders to make an assault that was clearly impossible. Porter left the defenses of Washington in September 1862 and returned to the Army of the Potomac to fight with General George McClellan at the Battle of Antietam. Porter alone led the V Corps in the Battle of Shepardstown before being relieved of command to appear before a military commission in Washington. A court-martial was ordered, with members of the court being hand-picked by Secretary of War Edwin Stanton, who intensely disliked General McClellan. Most members of the court-martial selected by Stanton later received brevets or promotions. Porter then paid the price for his loyalty to McClellan, and in August 1863 was cashiered and dismissed from the army and forbidden to hold any post with the federal government. The outcome of the court-marital created great controversy inside and outside the army. Porter made repeated efforts to have the case reopened, and in 1878 an inquiry led by General John Schofield found that Porter had acted correctly in not making the assault, and probably saved the Army of Virginia from an even worse disaster. The controversy was finally resolved by congressional action signed by President Grover Cleveland in 1886 that reappointed Porter a colonel with a commission date of May 14, 1861. Most authorities attribute Porter's court-marital not to his actions on the field, but for his close relationship and devotion to General George McClellan, who consistently showered him with praise and preference. After his dismissal from the army he engaged in various business interests, including commissioner of police, commissioner of public works, and fire commissioner of New York City.

POTTER

Potter, Robert. *Carte de visite* by Brady, Washington. Author's collection.

Potter, Robert Brown (1829-1887) was born in New York. The son of Episcopal Bishop Alonzo Potter, he attended Union College and entered the legal profession in New York City. At the outbreak of the Civil War Potter was a recent widower with a small child, but joined the New York Militia's New York Rifles as a private. In October 1861 he received the lieutenant-colonelcy of the 51st New York Volunteers, which was ordered to accompany General Ambrose Burnside's expedition to North Carolina. He fought at Roanoke Island and New Bern, where he was wounded. He returned with Burnsides' IX Corps to ably fight at Cedar Mountain and became a colonel in August 1862. At Antietam he was credited with breaking the bottleneck at Burnsides' Bridge, a key to federal success in that sector of the field. He continued with the IX Corps at Fredericksburg, and was in garrison at Cincinnati in March 1863 when he received appointment to brigadier-general of volunteers. Leaving garrison duty, he served with the IX Corps, now led by General John Parke at Vicksburg, and in the capture of Jackson, Mississippi. For a short time he held nominal command of the corps. After actions in East Tennessee and in the defense of Knoxville Potter was ordered, along with the IX Corps, to join General Ulysses Grant's 1864 Overland campaign. Potter, now a division commander, fought in the battles of the Wilderness, Spotsylvania, and Petersburg, with his division suffering nearly twenty-five hundred casualties. One of the regiments of Potter's division were Pennsylvania coal miners, and during the siege of Petersburg tunneled under enemy lines and detonated a huge amount of black powder that initiated the Battle of the Crater. In this federal disaster Potter was the only division commander personally accompanying his troops. He was also the only general that fought with his troops, and was subsequently not reprimanded. He received appointment to major-general of volunteers and was soon seriously wounded in the last assault at Petersburg. Potter was seriously disabled, and served in several business ventures before retiring and living in England till his death in 1873.

PRENTISS

Prentiss, Benjamin. *Carte de visite* by Anthony, New York. Author's collection.

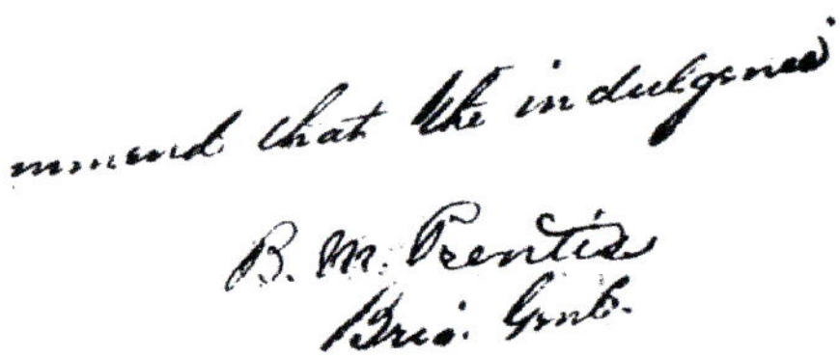

Prentiss, Benjamin Mayberry (1819-1901) While born in Virginia, Prentiss, as a child, moved to Missouri and then to Quincy, Illinois. He served in the Quincy area militia against Joseph Smith's Mormons in 1844-45, and in the war with Mexico served as a captain in the 1st Illinois Volunteers, receiving a mention for gallantry at the battle of Buena Vista. Returning to Quincy, he was a commission merchant and unsuccessful congressional candidate. Upon the start of the Civil War, he organized and was appointed in April 1861 to be Colonel of the 10th Illinois Volunteers enlisted for three months. While stationed with his regiment at Cairo, Illinois, he and General Ulysses engaged in a feud as to which held higher rank and right to command. The outcome was that he was appointed a brigadier-general of volunteers, and transferred to Missouri to fight guerillas attempting to disrupt railroads and telegraph lines. He successfully fought Confederate forces at Pilot Knob and routed another force at Mt. Zion. In April 1862 Prentiss received command of the 6th Division in General Ulysses Grant's Army of the Tennessee, joining it at Pittsburg Landing three days before the Battle of Shiloh. His camp at Shiloh occupied the most isolated ground, and on the eve and morning of the battle, at the urging of one of his regimental commanders, he ordered a probe outside the federal perimeter. Prentiss discovered the advancing Confederate attack, and was the first federal unit hit by Confederate General Albert Sidney Johnson's army. He was able to pull his troops into a defensive position along a sunken road, later to be called the "Hornet's Nest", and fought valiantly for six hours until compelled to surrender the remnants of his remaining troops. Prentiss' stubborn stand at the Hornets' Nest slowed the Confederate advance, allowing time for General Ulysses Grant and General William T. Sherman to organize defensive lines. Prentiss was not released from captivity until October 29, 1862, and was appointed major-general of volunteers. He then was ordered to serve on the court-martial of General Fitz-John Porter, facing charges lodged against him by General John Pope for his lack of support at the Battle of Second Bull Run. This gained him no popularity with many general officers, including Grant and Sherman. He was then sent to command the District of Eastern Arkansas with headquarters at Helena. He was attacked there by Confederate General Theophilus H. Holmes on July 4, 1863, and successfully repulsed his attackers. Feeling that he had been shelved and would receive no more suitable commands, he resigned from the army in October 1863, citing health and personal reasons. Unlike many civilian generals, Prentiss did not seem to have any strong political sponsors. He returned to Quincy and practiced law, and later moved to Kirksville, Missouri, where he was also engaged in practicing law. In 1881 he moved to Bethany, Missouri, serving as postmaster till his death in 1901.

RENO

Reno, Jesse. *Carte de visite* by McClees, Philadelphia. Author's collection.

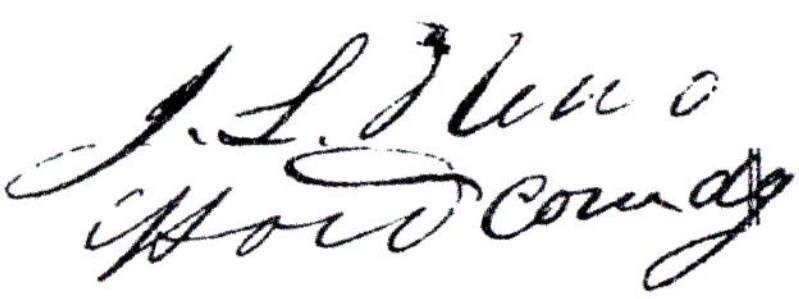

Reno, Jesse Lee (1823-1862) was born in Virginia and admitted to the Military Academy in 1842, graduating eighth in the class of 1846. He was commissioned as a second-lieutenant in the Department of Ordnance. During the war with Mexico he served with a howitzer battery at the Siege of Vera Cruz, receiving a brevet to first-lieutenant for gallantry and meritorious service. He also received brevet to captain for bravery and service at the battles of Cero Gordo and Chapultepec. Upon his return he was assigned as an instructor at the Military Academy. In 1850 he served on a board preparing a "System of Instruction for Heavy Artillery". In 1854 Reno was ordnance officer for Colonel Albert Sidney Johnson's Utah Expedition. He was commanding the Mount Vernon Alabama Arsenal when it was seized by a rebel group on January 4, 1861. Reno was then ordered to command the federal arsenal at Fort Leavenworth, Kansas, where he remained until promoted to brigadier-general of volunteers and brigade command in General Ambrose Burnside's North Carolina Expedition. He was engaged in the capture of Roanoke Island, New Bern, and at Camden. Reno, from April through August 1862, commanded a division and served as commander of the Department of North Carolina. Appointed major-general of volunteers in July 1862, he was engaged with his division in the movement to join Pope's Army of Virginia on the Rappahannock line. He took command of the IX Corps while its regular commander, General Ambrose Burnside, was in charge of General Pope's left wing. He fought credibly at the Second Battle of Bull Run, and days later at the Battle of Chantilly. In the following Maryland Campaign Reno's division, in pursuing General Stonewall Jackson, went through Frederick, where Reno is said to have offered to purchase a national flag from union supporter Barbara Fritchie that she had waved in front of General Stonewall Jackson. Instead, she presented Reno with a homemade bunting flag that he kept until his death a few days later in Fox Gap, at the Battle of South Mountain. While in the midst of an assault up South Mountain Reno was killed while riding up and down his lines encouraging his men. Reno was a popular officer, and showed great promise as a field commander. With Reno's death General Ambrose Burnside lost one of his most aggressive generals and a best friend. The history of the IX Corps might have been different if Reno had survived. He was one of the very few union generals with a background in ordnance.

REYNOLDS, JOHN

Reynolds, John. *Carte de visite* by McClees, Philadelphia. Author's collection.

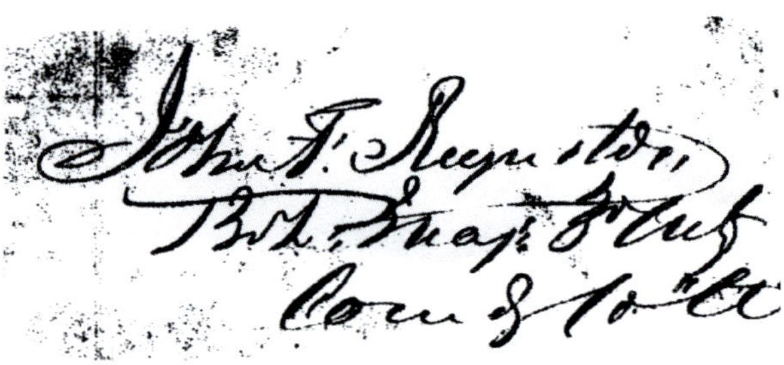

Reynolds, John Fulton (1820-1863) was born in Pennsylvania. The son of a newspaper editor, he entered the Military Academy in 1837, graduating twenty-sixth in the class of 1841. He was commissioned into the 3rd Artillery and posted to various artillery garrisons until the war with Mexico. In 1846 Reynolds was promoted to first-lieutenant and credibly served in the Mexican War, earning brevets to captain and major for gallantry at the battles of Monterey and Buena Vista. Upon the conclusion of the war he began a series of assignments in artillery garrisons in the east and on the frontier. In 1852 and 1853 he served as aide-de-camp to General David Twiggs, stationed in San Antonio. Other postings included Utah in 1854; Benicia Barracks, California, in 1855; Fort Orford, Oregon, in 1856; Fort Leavenworth, Kansas, in 1858; Colonel Albert Johnston's Utah Expedition in 1859; and Fort Vancouver, Washington Territory, in 1860. In early 1861 he returned east and was selected as commandant of cadets at the Military Academy. At the beginning of the Civil War he was made lieutenant-colonel of the reactivated 14th U.S. Infantry and brigadier-general of volunteers to date from May 14, 1861. Reynolds served in the defenses of Washington with the Pennsylvania Reserve Corps, and was military governor in Fredericksburg, Maryland, till joining General George McClellan's 1862 Virginia Peninsula campaign as a brigade commander. On June 27, 1862, shortly after the retreat of McClellan's right wing following the action at Gaines Mill, Reynolds and division commander General George McCall were captured and spent several weeks in Richmond's Libby Prison before being exchanged. For his actions at the battles of Mechanicsville, Glendale, and Gaines Mill he received a brevet to brigadier-general in the regular army. Commanding a division in the Pennsylvania Reserves, he was engaged at the Second Battle of Bull Run and then commanded the Pennsylvania State Militia in the Maryland Campaign. On November 29, 1862, he was appointed major-general of volunteers and assigned command of the 1st Corps in the Army of the Potomac. He led the I Corps at the Battle of Fredericksburg in December 13, 1862, his I Corps division commanded by his subordinate, General George Meade, was the only federal unit to make a lodgment in the Confederate lines on Mayre's Hill. Reynolds' battered I Corps was held in reserve and saw minimal action at the Battle of Chancellorsville. After Chancellorsville, President Lincoln is said by most authorities to have offered command of the Army of the Potomac to Reynolds. Being always distrustful of politics and politicians, Reynolds refused Lincoln's offer. A second reason for his refusal was that Lincoln would not grant him total discretion in operating the Army of the Potomac. Instead Reynolds' subordinate, General George Meade, took command of the Army of the Potomac three days before the Battle of Gettysburg. On the first day of the battle, cavalry under General John Buford encountered the vanguard of the Army of Northern Virginia outside Gettysburg and attempted to delay their advance. Upon receiving communication from Buford, General Meade ordered Reynolds to quickly move his small 8,000 man I Corps to Gettysburg and join up with the XI Corps and the III Corps. Reynolds, immediately upon arrival at about mid-morning, relieved General Howard, commander of the XI Corps, and began to deploy troops to defensive positions when he was shot in the back of the neck by a musket ball and instantly killed. Reynolds was buried in his hometown of Lancaster, Pennsylvania, about forty miles from Gettysburg. The fiancé of this bachelor general entered into a Maryland convent, remaining there for the rest of her life. Reynolds was a respected corps commander and most likely would have been one of General Ulysses Grant's best corps commanders if he had lived.

Reynolds, Joseph

Reynolds, Joseph. *Carte de visite* by unidentified photographer. Author's collection.

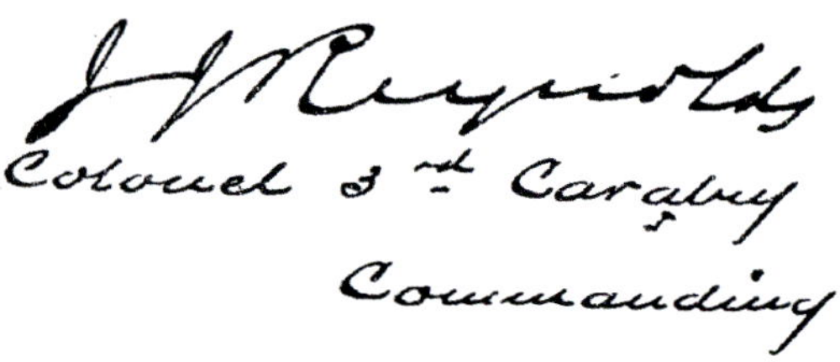

Reynolds, Joseph, J. (1822-1899) was born in Kentucky. He was admitted to the Military Academy in 1839, graduating tenth in the class of 1843. Commissioned in the 4th Artillery, he served in garrison duty until ordered to West Point in 1846 as an assistant professor of Geography, History and Ethics. He remained at West Point until sent to Fort Washita, Indian Territory, in 1856. After a leave of absence he resigned from the army in 1857 after accepting an appointment as Professor of Mechanics and Engineering at Washington College, St. Louis, Missouri. At the beginning of the Civil War he was a merchant in Lafayette, Indiana. In April 1861, as Colonel of the 10th Indiana Volunteers, he commanded the recruiting depot at Camp Morton, Indiana. Reynolds was deployed in July 1861 as a brigadier-general of Indiana Volunteers to the Cheat Mountain District in West Virginia. In early 1862 he again resigned from the army when his brother died, but returned to duty in September 1862. In November 1862 he was appointed a major-general of volunteers and joined the Army of the Cumberland for the Tullahoma Campaign, fighting credibly at the Battle of Chickamauga and receiving a brevet to brigadier-general in the regular army. Afterwards he was designated as chief of staff to General George Thomas, the new commander of the Army of the Cumberland. He remained with General Thomas until January 1864, when he became commander of the defenses of New Orleans and of the XIX Corps. He assisted in organizing the forces led by General E.R.S. Canby in the capture of Mobile, and in October 1864 was in command of the Mississippi River from New Orleans to Memphis. He later commanded the Department of Arkansas and the Military Division of West Mississippi before being mustered out of the volunteer forces in September 1866. He was reappointed to the Army as lieutenant-colonel of the 26th Infantry and served for many years in different posts in Texas. As a colonel he also commanded the 25th Infantry and the 3rd Cavalry. In the 1876 Powder River Expedition against the Sioux and Cheyenne under General George Crook, Reynolds made a winter attack on a Sioux village and prematurely ordered a retreat, leaving behind his dead and wounded. Crook was infuriated with Reynolds and several other officers, and brought all before a court-martial. Reynolds then resigned from the army and resided in Washington, D.C. until his death in 1899.

RICHARDSON

Richardson, Isarel. *Carte de visite* by Brady, Washington. Author's collection.

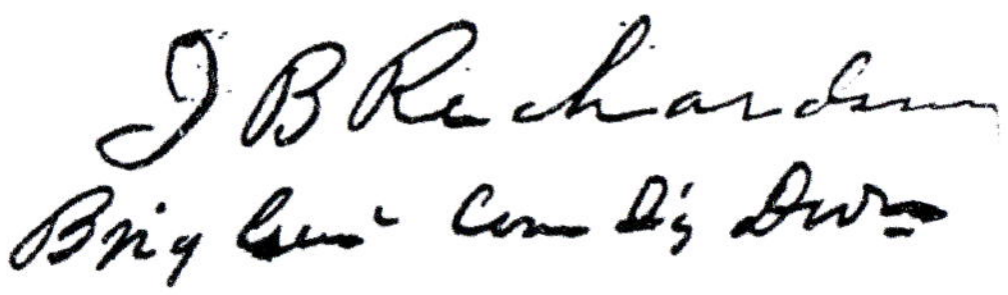

Richardson, Israel Bush (1815-1862) was born in Vermont to the family of Revolutionary War hero General Israel Putnam. He was admitted to the Military Academy in 1836, and five years later graduated thirty-eighth in the noted class of 1841, in which twenty-three of its fifty-two members achieved the rank of general. This was in spite of the fact that sixteen members had died before the beginning of the Civil War. Richardson was commissioned in the 3rd Infantry, and in 1841 was sent to fight in the interminable Florida Indian Wars. He served on frontier duty till the war with Mexico, where he fought in most of the major actions, receiving brevets to captain and major for gallantry in four separate battles and gaining the nickname "Fighting Dick". Richardson was stationed in 1850-1851 in Texas, and then spent three years posted in several New Mexico posts before resigning in 1855 from the army. He then engaged in a successful farming enterprise in Pontiac, Michigan, until the beginning of the Civil War. In the early days of the war Richardson organized the 2nd Michigan Infantry and was mustered into federal service as its colonel in May 1861. He commanded his regiment and a brigade at the Battle of Bull Run but did not take part in the heaviest fighting. Richardson, however, was able to hold his raw troops together in the retreat back to the Washington defenses after the federal defeat. He received appointment to brigadier-general of volunteers dated to May 1861, and ably commanded a division in the II Corps led by General Edwin Sumner during the Virginia Peninsula Campaign, with which he fought credibly at the Seven Days Battles, Yorktown, Williamsburg, Fair Oaks, and Malvern Hill. Richardson, during the Peninsula Campaign, was able to invoke strong discipline in undisciplined regiments, and led his division into battle with steeled courage. For his efforts on the Peninsula he was appointed to major-general of volunteers. Briefly assigned to the I Corps, he returned to the II Corps to fight in the Second Battle of Bull Run, South Mountain, and at Antietam in the Maryland Campaign. During the first day at Antietam his division, aided by the division of General William French, repulsed the assault of Confederate General D.H. Hill on the "Bloody Lane". While directing his artillery he was wounded by a spherical case shot on September 17, 1862, and died of his wounds at General McClellan's headquarters in Pry House on 3 November.

Rosecrans

Rosecrans, William. *Carte de visite* by Brady, Washington. Author's collection.

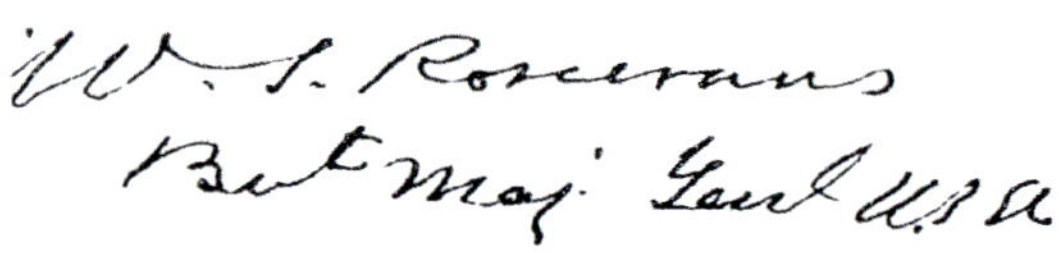

Rosecrans, William Starke (1819-1898) was born in Ohio. He began to work at fourteen, but through individual study was able to gain admittance to the Military Academy in 1838. He graduated fifth in his class, and was commissioned in the Corps of Engineers and stationed in brief engineering assignments until becoming an instructor at the Military Academy from 1843 to 1847, thus missing involvement in the war with Mexico. After leaving the Military Academy he continued being engaged in routine engineering assignments until his resignation as a first- lieutenant from the army in 1854. After resigning from the army he practiced civil engineering in Cincinnati, Ohio, and manufactured kerosene lamps. He was also president of a coal company in Coal River, Virginia. A few days after the outbreak of war Rosecrans joined the personal staff of his friend, General George McClellan, with a state militia rank of Colonel of engineers and responsible for training and equipping "Home Guards". On June 10, 1861, he received an appointment as colonel of the 23rd Ohio Volunteers and commanded Camp Chase, Ohio, for a few weeks before being deployed with McClellan's forces to West Virginia. As a brigade commander he took part in the action at Rich Mountain, and upon McClellan leaving West Virginia, Rosecrans was given command of the Department of Ohio and later the Department of West Virginia. In May 1861 he was appointed to brigadier-general of volunteers. In September 1861, Confederate Generals John Floyd and Henry Wise threatened the federal possession of the Kanawha Valley, which forced Rosecrans to assemble his forces and make a forced march to meet Floyd at Carnifix Ferry. He routed the Confederate force and received thanks from the legislature of Ohio. He next was assigned the command of the left wing of General Pope's Army of the Mississippi in General Halleck's slow march to Cornith, Mississippi. When Pope was transferred to the Army of the James Rosecrans assumed command of the Army of the Mississippi, comprised of the divisions of General Eleazar Paine and General David Stanley. He fought Confederate Generals Sterling Price and Earl Van Doren at two partially successful actions at Iuka and Corinth. Rosecrans had been appointed to major-general of volunteers in March 1862, and in late October 1862 was given command of General Don Carlos Buell's Army of the Cumberland. The day after Christmas Rosecrans marched his army of 47,000, divided into three wings commanded by General Alexander McCook, General George Thomas, and General Thomas Crittenden, out of Nashville and towards Murfreesboro, Tennessee. Rosecrans met General Braxton Braggs several miles from the town along the Stone River. A bloody battle ensued, with Rosecrans' forces suffering severe casualties. The Battle of Stone River was a virtual stalemate that forced Bragg to withdraw his forces to Shelbyville and Tullahoma, Alabama. Rosecrans chose not to pursue Bragg, but instead to occupy Murfreesboro.

Before and after the Battle of Stone's River, Rosecrans was constantly requesting and then demanding from President Lincoln and Secretary of War Edwin Stanton troop reinforcements, artillery, and horses. This led to the creation of much ill will in Washington and lack of trust in Rosecrans' ability to lead the Army of the Cumberland. Upon the constant urging of President Lincoln, in June 1862 Rosecrans embarked on a masterpiece of military maneuver, first driving Confederate forces from their bases at Shelbyville and Tullahoma and causing them to cross to the south side of the Tennessee River. Rosecrans, also through the use of a demonstration at Decatur, Alabama, drew Bragg out of Chattanooga. He then crossed the Tennessee to Chattanooga and threatened Bragg's line of communication with Atlanta. Having no other choice Bragg withdrew south of Chattanooga, allowing

Rosecrans to get between the Confederates and Atlanta. Bragg, with his superior numbers, then turned and attacked Rosecrans' separated forces split into three elements located on roads leading into Chattanooga. The resulting Battle of Chickamauga, although a serious defeat for the federals, could have been worse if General George Thomas, commanding the center of Rosecrans' line, had not stood like a "Rock", allowing the escape of the army to Chattanooga. The battle on the first day was a virtual draw, but on the second day Rosecrans made a catastrophic error when he mistakenly believed there to be a gap in the federal lines and ordered General Thomas Wood's division from its position, allowing General James Longstreet's troops to break through and force about two-thirds of the army, including Rosecrans and his staff, to flee the field on a dead run to the Chattanooga fortifications. President Lincoln then replaced the discredited Rosecrans with General George Thomas.

Rosecrans, William. *Carte de visite* by Brady, Washington. General Rosecrans is usually seen in a Napoleonic pose. Author's collection.

He was then sent to command the ever troublesome Department of the Missouri, where with limited forces he was able to just barely contain General Stirling Price's last invasion of Missouri. He was relieved of this command in December 1864 and sat out the rest of the war awaiting orders. He was mustered out of volunteer service in January 1866 and resigned from the army in March 1867 in disgust at his treatment. Rosecrans received the post of Minister to Mexico in 1868 from President Andrew Johnson, but was removed when Grant became president. He returned to his ranch in California and later became a congressman and Chair of the Military Affairs Committee of the House of Representatives, opposing Grant's attempt to collect back pay. Rosecrans showed brilliance in tactical maneuvers, but often lacked skill and ability in battlefield command. He was also a constant complainer and many times showed a lack of inertia to engage his army.

Rosecrans, William. *Carte de visite* by Anthony, New York. Author's collection.

ROUSSEAU

Rousseau, Lovell. *Carte de visite* by Brady, Washington. Author's collection.

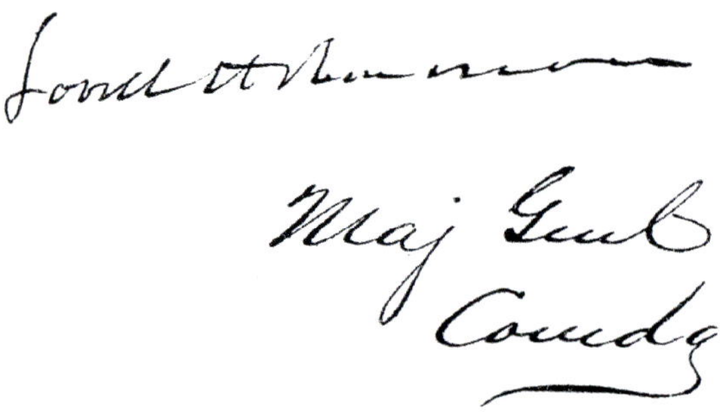

Rousseau, Lovell. *Carte de visite* by Wenderoth and Taylor, Philadelphia. Author's collection.

Rousseau, Lovell Harrison (1818-1869) was born in Kentucky, and he received a common education before studying for the law. In 1841, having moved to Bloomfield, Indiana, he was admitted to practice law. Rousseau shortly became politically active and was elected to the Indiana house and senate, but left in 1847 to serve during the Mexican War as a captain in the 2nd Indiana Volunteers, receiving commendation for his actions at the Battle of Buena Vista. In 1849 he returned to Kentucky and established a law practice in Louisville, developing a reputation as a criminal lawyer. Elected unopposed to the Kentucky senate in 1860, he did all in his power to keep Kentucky in the union. With the outbreak of war Rousseau was mustered in as Colonel of the 5th Kentucky Infantry, and in October 1861 was selected by Lincoln for appointment as a brigadier-general of volunteers. He led the 2nd Brigade of the 2nd Division of the Army of the Ohio the second day of the Battle of Shiloh and was complimented for his action in retaking the headquarters of General John McClernand. He then valiantly led a division in General Alexander McCook's Corps in the Army of the Ohio at the Battle of Perryville. While in command of the 3rd Division of the Army of the Cumberland he fought with distinction at the Battle of Stone's River. He continued to serve under General George Thomas, but was not engaged at the Battle of Chickamauga. For the remainder of the war he commanded districts in Tennessee. However, he did mount and execute an important cavalry raid in July 1864 that destroyed rail lines between Montgomery and Opelika, Alabama. He commanded Fort Rosecrans during the siege of Nashville by Confederate General John B. Hood, and later was military commander of Nashville and Tennessee. He resigned from the army November 30, 1865, and took his seat in Congress to which Kentucky had elected him. At first a radical Republican, he moderated his views regarding reconstruction policy after listening to the extreme views concerning reconstruction and the Freedman's Bureau voiced by many radical congressmen. He was involved in a caning incident in the capitol corridors with Republican J. B. Grinnell of Iowa that resulted in his censure. Rousseau resigned from Congress, but during the intersession was enthusiastically reelected by his Kentucky constituents and returned to the same congress, holding the same committee positions. As a supporter of President Andrew Johnson, he was made a brigadier-general in the regular army in March 1867 and was sent to Alaska to accept the formal turnover of the territory from Russia. In 1869 he was given command of the Department of Louisiana and died in New Orleans on January 7, 1869.

SCHENCK

Schenck, Robert. *Carte de visite* by Brady, Washington. Author's collection.

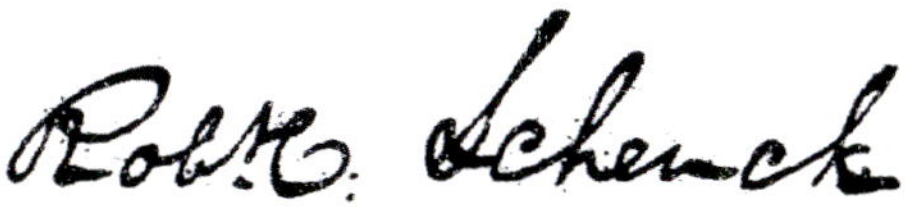

Schenck, Robert Cumming (1809-1890) was born in Ohio. Schenck graduated from Miami University in 1829, remaining there for three years to tutor French and Latin. He then studied for and practiced law in Dayton, Ohio, until elected in 1842 to the United States Congress. He served four terms, resigning in 1851 to accept a two year appointment as Minister to Brazil. After leaving his diplomatic post Schenck engaged in law practice and the management of the Fort Wayne Railroad. He also became a staunch Republican, and provided personal time and resources for the election of Abraham Lincoln. At the onset of war Schenck patriotically volunteered his services to Ohio Governor William Dennison and was appointed a brigadier-general in the Ohio militia. In several weeks he was sent to command state troops in western Virginia. Lincoln appointed Schenck a brigadier-general of volunteers on June 4, 1861, in time to be engaged at the Battle of Bull Run on June 17, 1861, with General Daniel Tyler's division of the Army of Northeastern Virginia. He was then transferred to the command of General William Rosencrans to drive Confederate forces out of western Virginia. In Spring 1862 Schenck succeeded General Frederick Lander and commanded inferior forces to those of General Stonewall Jackson at the Battle of McDowell. Schenck was bested by Jackson and was pushed out of the Shenandoah Valley toward the Allegheny Mountains. Later his brigade was attached to the right wing of hapless General John C. Fremont's army in its June 1861 defeat by General Stonewall Jackson at the Battle of Cross Keyes. His command was then merged with the Army of Virginia, and he briefly led the I Corps until General Fitz Sigel returned to duty. Schenck led a division at the Second Battle of Bull Run and received a wound that removed him from field duty for the rest of the war. Appointed to major-general of volunteers, he was assigned command of the Middle Department and the VIII Corps with headquarters in Baltimore. His command played a small logistical and supportive role in the Gettysburg campaign. He resigned from the army in December 1863 to return to Congress and was reelected in 1864, 1866, and 1868, then defeated in 1870. While in Congress he served as chairman of the Military Affairs Committee. In 1870 he accepted a diplomatic post as Minister to the Court of St. James, but before departing for England concluded his work with the Alabama Claims Commission. While in England he was charged with complicity in the Emma Mine fraud that forced him to resign in 1876. After an investigation he was exonerated but never returned to public life. He practiced law in Washington and became an author and world expert on draw poker.

SCHOFIELD

Schofield, John. *Carte de visite* by Morse, Nashville, Tennessee. Author's collection.

Schofield, John McAllister (1831-1906) was born in New York. He moved to Freeport, Illinois, and entered the Military Academy in 1849, graduating seventh in the class of 1853 along with Philip Sheridan, John B. Hood, and James McPherson. He was commissioned in the 1st Artillery, and first served at Fort Moultrie, South Carolina, and then in Florida. Schofield returned to the Military Academy in 1855 as a first lieutenant and Assistant Professor of Natural and Experimental Philosophy till 1860, at which time he was granted a years' leave of absence to teach physics at Washington University in St. Louis. At the onset of the war he left Washington University, and in April and May 1861 became mustering officer for the state of Missouri. With the permission of the War Department he accepted appointment as major in the 1st Missouri Volunteers and served as chief of staff to General Nathaniel Lyons in his operations at Dug Springs and the Battle of Wilson's Creek on August 10, 1861, in which Lyons was killed. In fall 1861 he was ordered to convert the 1st Missouri Volunteer Infantry into an artillery unit, and in November 1861 led Battery A in the battle of Fredericktown, Missouri. President Lincoln appointed Schofield a brigadier-general of volunteers in November 1861, and the state of Missouri concurrently appointed him brigadier-general in the Missouri Militia. From October 1862 to April 1863 Schofield commanded the St. Louis District and the Army of the Frontier, with operations in southwest Missouri and northwest Arkansas. Some of his actions in suppressing partisans and southern supporters resulted in controversy and political notoriety, but he was appointed major-general of volunteers in April 1863 and given division command in the XIV Corps of the Army of the Cumberland. Schofield served only for a month before returning to Missouri to command the Department of Missouri. He was constantly engaged in guerrilla and partisan warfare that brought political wrath down on his head from both Federal and Confederate supporters. He was responsible for forwarding troops to Grant at Vicksburg and secured the federal line along the Arkansas River. In January 1864 he was relieved and sent to command the Department of Ohio and Army of the

Ohio, fighting in every battle of the Atlanta Campaign. As Sherman began his March to the Sea, Schofield was ordered back in November 1864 to support General George Thomas at Nashville. General John B. Hood, in an attempt to destroy Sherman's line of supply and invade Tennessee, also marched north and tried to get in between Schofield and Thomas. By adept maneuvering and hard night marching Schofield was able to evade Hood, finally entrenching his forces at Franklin, Tennessee. At the Battle of Franklin Hood repeatedly attacked Schofield, and the battle evolved into one of the bloodiest battles of the Civil War in relation to the number of hours fought. Hood's army was seriously damaged at Franklin, both in men and commanders, as one of his best field generals, Patrick Cleburne, was killed while charging federal lines. Schofield, in the evening of the battle, was able to again evade Hood and withdraw his forces to Thomas' fortifications at Nashville. On December 15, 1864, Schofield's forces were part of the Battle of Nashville, in which Hood's army was nearly destroyed. He pursued Hood until January 24, 1865, when he was ordered to cooperate with General William Sherman's North Carolina Campaign. After the surrender of General Joseph Johnston he briefly remained as commander of the Department of North Carolina until he was ordered on a special mission to France to negotiate for the removal of French troops from Mexico. From 1866 to 1868 he commanded the Department of the Potomac and the 1st Military District of Virginia as a brigadier-general in the regular army. In June 1868 President Andrew Johnson appointed him Secretary of War, and he remained in that post till made a major-general in the regular army and placed in command of the Department of the Missouri, remaining there until May 1870, when he transferred to the Division of the Pacific. In 1881 he assumed command of the United States Military Academy. After leaving West Point he commanded the Division of the Pacific, and in 1883 returned to the Division of Missouri. At the death of General Philip Sheridan in 1888, Schofield was appointed by President Grover Cleveland to command the United States Army. He retired from service in 1895 with the rank of lieutenant-general.

SCHURZ

Schurz, Carl. *Carte de visite* by Brady, Washington. Author's collection.

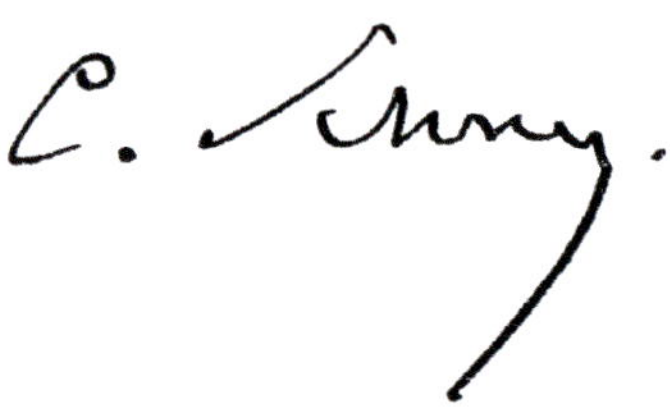

Schurz, Carl (1829-1906) was born in Liblar, Prussia, and educated at the University of Bonn. He served briefly as a junior officer in the 1848 uprising against Prussian authorities and was expelled from the country. After spending time in Scotland, England, and Paris, usually as a newspaper correspondent and teacher, he arrived in Philadelphia, spent three years there, and then finally in 1855 settled in Watertown, Wisconsin. Quickly becoming active in politics, he became a staunch Republican and a key force in convincing the large German population in Wisconsin to oppose the extension of slavery. Soon mastering the English language, Schurz was an effective orator in both English and German. His first political speech in English was made during the senatorial canvas in Illinois between Stephen Douglas and Abraham Lincoln. The speech was used as a political document and widely circulated by Republican advocates. Schurz soon opened a law office in Milwaukee, and was an important contributor to the Republican platform at the 1860 Chicago Convention. He campaigned widely for Lincoln, speaking in both German and English, and upon Lincoln's election was offered the post of Minister to Spain. The firing on Fort Sumter found Schurz still in Washington, and he convinced Lincoln and Secretary of War Cameron to award him a colonel's commission for the purpose of going to New York and raising a regiment of German speaking cavalry that later became the 1st New York (Lincoln) Cavalry. Schurz soon left for his post in Spain, but desperately desired a battlefield command, and in January 1862 resigned and returned to the United States. President Lincoln, to please German supporters of the federal cause, reluctantly rewarded him in April 1862 with a commission as brigadier-general of volunteers. Predictably, he was given division command in fellow German General Franz Sigel's IX Corps and was lauded by superiors for his performance at the Second Battle of Bull Run. This may have been the reason he was appointed a major-general of volunteers dated March 14, 1863. Schurz remained with the IX Corps when Sigel was relieved by General O.O. Howard and commanded a division at Chancellorsville, where the XI Corps was badly routed. At Gettysburg the XI Corps was again routed on the first day of the battle. The role Schurz and Howard played in the two routs has been debated for over a century, but it certainly can be said that Schurz was not a highly adept field commander, and that Howard was prone to making tactical errors. At Gettysburg he commanded the XI Corps for a short while when Howard assumed control of the field before the arrival of General John Reynolds. After Gettysburg Schurz and the XI Corps were sent west in late 1863, where he led his division at Chattanooga, but had a falling out with General Joseph Hooker over his battlefield performance and was relegated to rear echelon assignments. He left the Army in 1864 to campaign extensively for the Union ticket and Abraham Lincoln. After the election Schurz accepted an assignment to assist General Winfield Hancock in raising a Veteran's Volunteer Corps, with the assumption that he would be given command of a division. For various reasons the effort failed and Schurz spent the last few weeks of the war in North Carolina as chief of staff to General Henry Slocum. After the war President Andrew Johnson dispatched him on an inspection tour of Freedman's programs in southern states. He was elected United States Senator from Missouri in 1869, vigorously opposing Grant's policies, and in 1872 supported Horace Greeley for president. He returned in 1876 to support the Republican Rutherford B. Hayes and was given the cabinet post of Secretary of the Interior. Upon leaving the Hayes administration he edited a newspaper in New York City and continued to travel and advocate causes, such as civil service reform.

SCOTT

Scott, Winfield. *Carte de visite* by Gurney, New York. General Scott, often called "Old Fuss and Feathers" is seldom seen in a plain uniform. Author's collection.

Scott, Winfield. *Carte de visite* by Brady, Washington. Author's collection.

Scott, Winfield (1786-1866) was born in Virginia. He studied two years at the College of William and Mary before studying law. Upon admission to the bar in 1806 Scott moved to Charleston, South Carolina, but shortly accepted a commission in 1807 as a captain of light artillery. In the years leading up to the War of 1812 Congress had increased the size of the army, and at the start of the war Scott was made a lieutenant-colonel of artillery, participating in several battles before being captured and released. He was wounded at the Battle of Lundy's Lane, for which he was breveted a major-general and received a gold medal. Scott was made a brigadier-general in the regular army in March 1814. In 1832 he led federal and state troops in the Black Hawk War, and in the same year went to Charleston, South Carolina, to rebuff its nullification challenge. Scott's diplomacy may have prevented the Civil War. In 1835 he led Federal forces in the Creek War that resulted in the later removal of the Cherokees to the Indian Territory, and in 1841, with the death of General Alexander Macomb, Scott became general-in-chief of the army with the full rank of major-general. At the beginning of the Mexican War, Scott remained in Washington until ordered to the field and captured Vera Cruz, then successfully fighting a number of battles on the route to the capture of Mexico City. With the capture of Mexico City the war was virtually over, and Scott received the thanks of Congress, much to the disgust of President Polk, who had resisted sending Scott, a Whig, to lead the army to victory in a war initiated by the Democratic party. Polk, distrusting the Democratic party's enthusiasm for the war, appointed generals that were not Democrats. In 1848 Scott was a candidate for the Whig presidential nomination. In 1852 he ran as the Whig nominee and was defeated by Franklin Pierce, another Mexican War general. He remained as General-in-Chief of the Army with the brevet rank of lieutenant-general until the Civil War. As the war approached Scott quickly made known to the country his loyalty to the union, as he was a native Virginian. Lincoln, immediately upon his election, sought advice from General Scott, both in terms of strategy and personnel selections. Scott by this time was afflicted with numerous ailments, and at age seventy-five was only able to carry out a portion of his duties. The war strategy recommended by Scott, called the "Anaconda Plan", visualized the blockade of southern ports and maintaining control of the Mississippi River, thereby strangling the southern economy and cutting the communications between Confederate states. He also envisaged a four year war that would require hundreds of thousands of troops. Scott recommended General Irvin McDowell and General Robert Patterson to lead federal forces at the Battle of Bull Run, which turned into a rout and forced Lincoln to look elsewhere for a commander of the Army of the Potomac. General George McClellan, victor in several small battles in West Virginia and highly thought of by Scott, was appointed commander of the Army of the Potomac, and within a short period of time came into conflict with Scott. The old general, well knowing that he could not compete with or control McClellan, gracefully retired to a residence at West Point, New York. However Lincoln still sought Scott's advice, and once during the war traveled to West Point to visit Scott. He died in May 1866.

SEDGWICK

Sedgwick, John. *Carte de visite* by Brady, Washington. Author's collection.

Sedgwick, John (1813 to 1864) was born in Connecticut, and taught school several years before being admitted to the Military Academy in 1833, graduating twenty-fourth in the class of 1837. His classmates were Joseph Hooker, Jubal Early, Braxton Bragg, and John Pemberton, all of whom would be prominent generals in the Civil War. Sedgwick was commissioned in the 2nd Artillery, and was immediately sent to fight Indians in Florida. In 1838 he took part in the removal of the Cherokees to the Indian Territory, then served in artillery posts until the outbreak of the war with Mexico in 1846. He received brevets to captain and major for services at the battles of Conreras, Churubusco, and Chapultepec. Promoted to captain of artillery in 1849, he served in artillery garrisons until 1855, when the army expanded the number of its cavalry regiments. Sedgwick, although a career artillerist, obtained a majors' commission in the new 1st Cavalry commanded by Colonel Robert E. Lee. In the next six years Sedgwick saw duty in the "Bleeding" Kansas troubles and the 1857 Cheyenne Expedition, where he took part in the skirmishes at Grand Saline and Solomon's Fork. He accompanied his regiment in the Utah Expedition and returned to duty at Fort Leavenworth and Fort Riley, from which he led the Kiowa and Comanche Expedition of 1860. The beginning of the Civil War found Sedgwick stationed at Fort Wise, Colorado. When Colonel Robert E. Lee and Lieutenant-Colonel William J. Hardee defected to the confederacy Sedgwick advanced to Colonel of the 1st Cavalry. He was appointed brigadier-general of volunteers in August 1861 and served in the Washington defenses. In March 1862 he received a division command in General Edwin Sumner's II Corps of the Army of the Potomac, and in the Virginia Peninsula Campaign was engaged in most of the battles until he was seriously wounded at Glendale. His actions at the Battle of Fair Oaks were commended, and in July 1862 he received appointment to major-general of volunteers. He returned from convalescence and joined the retreat from the Second Battle of Bull Run, then later fought at the Battle of Antietam, where he was twice wounded, refusing to be taken from the field. For Antietam, he was cited by General McClellan for gallantry. Once again returning to action from wounds, Sedgwick led the VI Corps during the Battle of Chancellorville. Acting under a questionable order from General Joseph Hooker, Sedgwick was successful against Confederate General Jubal Early's forces at Salem Creek and was able to get the VI Corps back to the left bank of the Rappahannock River to join the rest of the defeated Army of the Potomac. He commanded the VI Corps in the Gettysburg campaign, arriving on the field for the second day's battle after an extraordinarily fast forced march. The VI Corps was not extensively involved in the battle, as it formed most of the Army of the Potomac's reserve. In November 1863, at the Battle of Rappahannock Bridge, Sedgwick commanded both the V Corps and the VI Corps in capturing a good portion of a Confederate division. This received compliments from General George Meade in a special order. In General Ulysses Grant's 1864 Richmond Campaign the VI Corps fought well under its highly popular commander, always referred to as "Uncle John". At the Battle of Spotsylvania Sedgwick was shot in the head by a sharpshooter and died instantly. His last words were that "they couldn't hit the side of an elephant at this range". General Sedgwick was a talented corps leader that inspired the devotion of his staff, officers, and enlisted men.

SHERIDAN

Sheridan, Philip. *Carte de visite* by Brady, Washington. Author's collection.

Sheridan, Philip Henry (1831-1888) was born either in Pennsylvania, New York, or Ireland. Sheridan grew up in Ohio and clerked in a country store before gaining admittance in 1848 to the Military Academy. He spent an extra year at the academy after a quarrel led to a fight, resulting in his being expelled for a year. He returned and graduated thirty-fourth in the class of 1853, and was commissioned in the 4th Infantry. Prior to the Civil War Sheridan served on the frontier in Texas, California, Oregon, and Washington. While at Fort Yamhill, Oregon, he is reputed to have married an Indian wife and had at least one son, for which he provided support and an education. With the outbreak of war Sheridan had just been made a first-lieutenant due to the resignation and defection of many 4th Infantry officers. He was transferred to the 13th Infantry as captain and ordered to St. Louis to audit claims submitted by General John Fremont prior to departing the Army of the Southwest. After reconciling the books he served ably on the staff of General Henry Halleck as chief quartermaster of the Army of the Southwest. While still serving on staff duty, Sheridan accompanied Halleck on the slow march from Pittsburgh Landing to Corinth, Mississippi. In May 1862, Sheridan was appointed colonel of the 2rd Michigan Cavalry and soon made a raid on Booneville, Mississippi, pursuing rebels from Corinth to Baldwin, Mississippi. Sheridan was appointed a brigadier-general of volunteers in July 1862 and received command of the 11th Division in the Army of the Ohio in October 1862 as it marched into Kentucky to stop Bragg's invasion. He fought credibly at the Battle of Perryville and was on the march to relieve Nashville. In November 1862, now in command of a division in the Army of the Cumberland, Sheridan was engaged in the crucial Battle of Stone River. He then accompanied General Rosecrans on the Tullahoma Campaign and crossed the Cumberland Mountains and the Tennessee River to reach Chickamauga, where his division was badly mauled. However, Sheridan was able to assemble a portion of his 11th division in time to join with General George Thomas in making a near last stand on Muleshoe Ridge. Sheridan remained with General Thomas and the Army of the Cumberland and fought magnificently in the assault on Missionary Ridge, with his division being in the lead pursuing Bragg's retreating forces. He remained on Tennessee occupation duty until April 1864, when he was named by General Ulysses Grant as Chief of the Cavalry Corps of the Army of the Potomac. Sheridan changed much of the function of the Army of the Potomac cavalry operations from being a support for infantry operations and conducting scattered raids to a mass armed force engaged in independent operations. Sheridan fought at the battles of the Wilderness, Spotsylvania, Cold Harbor, and Yellow Tavern, where on May 11, 1864, Confederate General Jeb Stuart was wounded and later died in Richmond. Sheridan's cavalry corps was constantly involved in tearing up railroad lines behind Confederate lines and engaging in large scale cavalry actions against the depleted rebel cavalry. In June 1864 Sheridan made an important raid on Charlottesville, Virginia, and in June 1864 fought the indecisive Battle of Trevilian Station. In a period of ninety days Sheridan established himself as a national media hero and elevated the cavalry into a primary federal battle force. In August 1864 Sheridan received command of the Army of the Shenandoah and a promotion to brigadier-general in the regular army. In brilliant use of combined infantry and cavalry forces, Sheridan was able to expel General Jubal Early's forces from the Shenandoah Valley after the battles of Opequan, Fishers' Hill, Cedar Creek, and Middletown. At Cedar Creek, General Early surprised Sheridan's army and might have been able to destroy it, but hesitated in his attack, giving Sheridan time enough to return from a Washington visit to rally his troops. His famous ride on his big black horse Rienzi is a classic story in Unites States military history. Upon instructions from General Grant, he implemented a scorched earth policy in the Shenandoah Valley to insure that it could never again be used as the Confederate "Bread Basket". Sheridan's scorched earth efforts, along with those of General William T. Sherman's in his March to the Sea, established the concept of "total war". In November 1864 Sheridan was appointed a major-general in the regular army, and in November mounted an extensive three week raid from Winchester to Petersburg, followed by actions at Waynesboro and North Anna Bridge. In Grant's Richmond Campaign Sheridan commanded cavalry forces at the Battles of Dinwiddie Court House, Five Forks, and Saylor's Creek, and was instrumental in bringing the final action at Appomattox Station on April 8, 1865. General Grant, only days after the surrender at Appomattox, ordered Sheridan to take command of the Military Division of the Gulf, as he and Secretary of War Stanton were concerned about conditions in Mexico, where liberals were in a life and death struggle with Emperor Maximillan and his French garrison. He skillfully used federal military presence to convince the French to withdraw from Mexico. Sheridan was also placed in command of the Fifth Military District, encompassing Texas and Louisiana, and responsible for the reconstruction policies of the federal government. His harsh treatment of civilians led President Andrew Johnson to remove him in less than a year. Sheridan then assumed command of the Department of the Missouri in September 1867 and engaged in conducting a winter Campaign against the Sioux. In March, with the election of General Grant to the presidency, General William Sherman became general in chief of the army, and Sheridan was promoted to Lieutenant-General, commanding the Division of the Missouri with headquarters at Chicago. In the 1870s he directed much of the military effort to subdue Native Americans and facilitated the building of the transcontinental railroad. The slaughter of the buffalo, continuous armed expeditions, and movement of settlers to the Great Plains finally forced tribes on to reservations. With Sherman's retirement in 1884 he became commanding general of the army until his premature death in 1888.

Sheridan, Philip. *Carte de visite* by Hoag and Quick, Cinncinatti, Ohio. Author's collection.

Sheridan, Philip. *Carte de visite* by Brady, New York. Author's collection.

SHERMAN

Sherman, William Tecumseh. *Carte de visite* by Matthew Brady, Washington. Author's collection.

Sherman, William Tecumseh (1820-1891) was born in Ohio. Orphaned at nine, he was adopted by Thomas Ewing, an Ohio lawyer and political figure who once served as Secretary of the Interior. Through the efforts of his foster father Sherman was appointed to the Military Academy in 1836, graduating sixth in the class of 1840. His first duty stations were in the south fighting Seminoles and garrison stations in Alabama and South Carolina, where he greatly enjoyed southern social life. Sherman, always a keen observer, was to use his knowledge of the terrain and culture in southern states to great advantage during the Civil War. In 1846, while on recruiting duty in Pittsburgh, he was ordered to California to serve as assistant adjutant general for General Stephen Kearny and later Colonel Richard Mason. This caused him to miss serving in Mexico. He returned to the "states" in 1850 and was promoted to captain, and also commissary general at St. Louis. In 1853, disenchanted with the Army and in need for income to support a growing family, he resigned from the army and became a partner in the banking house of Lucas, Turner and Company, based in San Francisco, California. He returned east in 1857 to work with the firm in New York, and when it collapsed he opened a law and realty office in Leavenworth, Kansas, with foster brothers Hugh and Thomas Ewing, Jr. This arrangement did not work well, and in July 1859 Sherman accepted the superintendent's position at the Louisiana Military Academy in Baton Rouge. Sherman enjoyed his brief time at the academy, but felt compelled to resign in January 1861 when the Louisiana state militia seized the federal arsenal in Baton Rouge. In 1861 he moved his family from Ohio to St. Louis when he obtained the presidency of a street railway company. Sherman's brother, John, just elected United States Senator, invited him to Washington, where they met with newly elected President Abraham Lincoln, and in conversation attempted to convey to him the strong feelings against the federal government held by southern leaders in St. Louis and those Sherman knew in Louisiana. He told Lincoln the country was sleeping on a volcano, and using ninety day volunteers was like "attempting to put out a burning house with a squirt gun". Lincoln's response, which angered Sherman, was, "Oh I guess we will just keep house". Sherman returned to St. Louis, but after seeing street riots in the city accepted a commission as Colonel of the 13th U.S. Infantry and commanded a brigade in General Daniel Tyler's Division at the Battle of Bull Run. Sherman stayed in the defenses of Washington organizing troops until appointed a brigadier-general of volunteers, then replacing the ailing General Robert Anderson as commander of the Department of Kentucky. Sherman, never discrete, was quoted in several newspapers as saying that he would need sixty thousand troops to drive the rebels out of Kentucky and 200,000 to force his way down the Mississippi Valley. Secretary of War Cameron felt that Sherman, always high strung, had gone insane. He was replaced by General Don Carlos Buell and sent to St. Louis to serve with his friend General Henry Halleck. He briefly prepared troops at Benton Barracks, and during Grant's move on Fort Donelson and Fort Henry, Sherman was in charge at Paducah, Kentucky, and forwarded supplies and reinforcements to Grant's Army of the Tennessee. Also while at Paducah he organized the 5th Division of the Army of the Tennessee from raw recruits and moved them up the Tennessee River to Pittsburg Landing. Sherman was greatly distinguished at the Battle of Shiloh, holding a key position in the battle and assisting Grant to reorganize the disorganized Federal units on the first day and assaulting Confederate lines on the second day. Sherman was wounded in the hand on the first day and had four horses shot from under him by the second day. For his actions at Shiloh he was appointed a major-general of volunteers. Sherman then joined in Halleck's slow march to Corinth, and while on this expedition convinced his friend Grant, who had been humiliated by Halleck, not to resign from the army. After Corinth Sherman assumed command of the Department of Memphis, where he engaged in restoring business, civilian control, and suppressing guerilla warfare. In October 1862 General Grant embarked on his first movement to capture Vicksburg and open up the Mississippi River. The plan was for Grant to march overland toward Vicksburg and join Sherman, who would be moving south from Memphis. Grant's movement was aborted after a raid by General Earl van Dorn destroyed Grant's supply base at Holly Springs. Sherman was then defeated at the Battle of Chickasaw Bayou and was forced, over Grant's objections, to turn his command over to General John McClernand. Lincoln and Stanton, for cloudy reasons, had commissioned McClernand to raise troops in Illinois and assume command of an effort to take Vicksburg. Sherman, after his defeat at Chickasaw, convinced McClernand to return back up the river to attack Fort Hindman at Helena, Arkansas. McClernand, eager for a victory, defeated Hindman at the Battle of Arkansas Post and established control of the Arkansas River. In the second Vicksburg Campaign in 1863, lasting some 109 days, Sherman served as Grant's second in command and played a key role in the capture of Jackson, and later Meridian. In the fall of 1863 Grant ordered Sherman, now a brigadier-general in the regular army, to advance and open communications with Chattanooga, where General Thomas was under siege by General Braxton Bragg. Sherman's men were successful in establishing the "Cracker Line" to Nashville, but were less successful in attacking Tunnel Hill at the Battle of Missionary Ridge. However, Grant praised Sherman's effort, which likley drew Confederate troops from the center of Bragg's lines on Missionary Ridge. After the Battle of Chattanooga he was ordered to relieve General Ambrose Burnside, who was besieged at Knoxville. When Grant was appointed Lieutenant-General and General-in-Chief in 1864 Sherman, a newly appointed major-general in the regular army, was given command of the Division of the Mississippi. On May 6, 1864, his movement to capture Atlanta was comprised of the Army of the Cumberland, the Army of the Ohio, and the Army of the Tennessee. After a series of successful battles in Georgia, Sherman ordered a frontal assault at Kennesaw Mountain that turned into a bloodbath. Sherman, in later years and in his memoirs, expressed regret over the assault. As he approached the outskirts of Atlanta his favorite subordinate, General James McPherson, commanding his left wing, was killed. Sherman captured Atlanta, remaining there about a month before sending General George Thomas back to Nashville to protect his long communication and supply lines. Sherman also ordered Thomas to contain Confederate General John Hood. On November 14, 1864, Sherman embarked from Atlanta on his famous March to the Sea, receiving no supply or communications with other federal forces. He reached the Atlantic and captured the city of Savannah, presenting it to President Lincoln as a Christmas gift. Sherman then turned north, capturing Charleston and Columbia, South Carolina. Continuing north to Fayetteville, North Carolina, and a final battle at Bentonville, Sherman received the surrender of General Joseph Johnston. In giving terms of surrender to Johnston Sherman dictated those agreed upon in a final meeting with Grant and President Lincoln. Secretary of War Stanton refused the terms, forcing Grant to travel to Durham with an acceptable set. This humiliated Sherman, and he refused to shake hands with Stanton at the Grand Review in Washington a few weeks later. After the war Sherman commanded the Division of the Mississippi until General Grant became President and promoted Sherman to be General in Chief of the army. Sherman detested politics, politicians, and Washington. In 1874 he moved his headquarters from Washington to St. Louis and did not return to the capital until 1876. He did much to professionalize the army with the establishment of the Army Command School at Fort Leavenworth. Sherman made constant trips to the field to inspect Army posts around the country and to coordinate operations against hostile Indians. Upon his request he was retired in 1884 and died in 1891. Sherman's great strength was in his strategic views and planning. His weakness was often in battlefield tactics and personal tact.

Sherman, William Tecumseh. *Carte de visite* by Brady, Washington. Author's collection.

Sherman, William Tecumseh. *Carte de visite* by Brady, Washington. General Sherman with his generals in 1864 during the Atlanta Campaign. Author's collection.

Sherman, William Tecumseh. *Carte de visite* by unidentified photographer, probably a copy of a Brady of General Sherman on horseback before Atlanta. Author's collection.

Sherman, William Tecumseh. *Carte de visite* by Brady, Washington. General Sherman with his generals in 1864 during the Atlanta Campaign. Author's collection.

SHIELDS

Shields, James. *Carte de visite* by Fredricks, New York. Author's collection.

Shields, James (1810-1879) was born in Ireland. Shields immigrated to the United States in 1826 and settled in Kaskaskia, Illinois. He had received a classical education in Ireland, then studied and practiced law in America. Upon entering politics as a Democrat, he served as an Illinois state legislator with Abraham Lincoln. Shields also served as state auditor, land office commissioner, and justice of the state supreme court. Lincoln, in a humorous letter to the editor of a Springfield newspaper, offended Shields and they almost fought a duel. During the Mexican War Shields fought as a major-general of Illinois volunteers and was wounded at the Battle of Cerro Gordo. At the Battle of Chapultepec he was commended for gallantry by General Winfield Scott. After the Mexican war he was selected in 1848 as a United States Senator for Illinois, serving till 1855, when he moved to take up a land grant in Minnesota. In 1858 Shield was selected United State Senator from Minnesota but only served one year. He then moved to California and was involved in superintending a mine in Mexico when the Civil War broke out. He returned as soon as possible to New York and Washington to lobby Lincoln and Irish nationalist groups for their support in acquiring an army appointment. President Lincoln responded to the appeals of his old antagonist and appointed him a brigadier-general of volunteers in August 1861. His appointment was partially attributable to Lincoln's early war efforts to place foreign born officers in charge of foreign born troops. Since Shields was born in Ireland he was a natural choice to lead New York Irish troops. He took over the command of General Frederick Lander's brigade in the Department of West Virginia for a few days before being appointed commander of a division in the II Corps of the Army of the Potomac. He was assigned in May 1862 to cooperate with General John C. Fremont in removing General Stonewall Jackson from the Shenandoah Valley. General Fremont's movement was delayed at Cross Keyes, and Shields engaged Jackson at Port Republic and was badly defeated. Shields then joined a growing group of federal generals routed by General Stonewall Jackson in the Shenandoah Valley. He then awaited orders until his resignation in March 1863. He resided briefly in San Francisco before moving to Missouri to practice law and serve as a railroad commissioner. He returned to electoral politics, and was selected in 1879 to fill an unexpired term in the United States Senate from Missouri. Shields was a dynamic speaker and popular lecturer on many subjects, especially Irish Independence. He died in 1879 while on a speaking tour in Ottumwa, Iowa.

SICKLES

Sickles, Daniel. *Carte de visite* by Fredricks, New York. Author's collection.

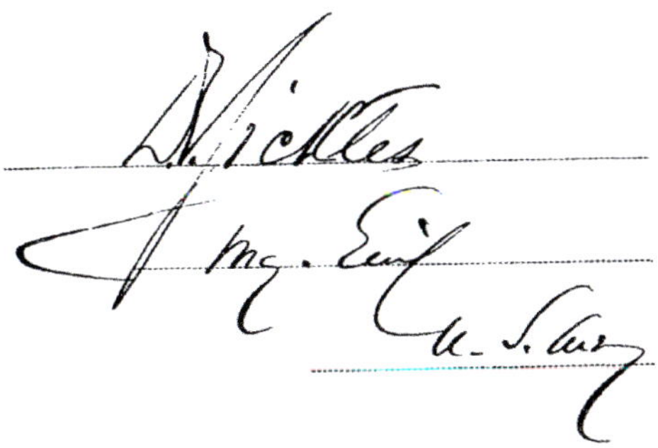

Sickles, Daniel Edgar (1819 to 1914) was born in New York City. Sickles attended New York University, and as a lawyer was part of the New York City Tammany Hall political machine. In 1847 he was New York corporation counsel, but left the position to become the secretary of the United States Legation in London, England. From 1857 to 1861 he served as a congressman, achieving national notoriety in 1859 when he shot the son of Francis Scott Key in Lafayette Square, just across from the White House. Sickles claimed Key and Sickles' wife were involved in an extramarital relationship, and in a sensational trial Sickles' defense attorney, Edwin Stanton, was successful in pleading temporary insanity for his client. Sickles soon regained his sanity and forgave his young wife, outraging the public but keeping the name "Dan Sickles" in the public eye. At the beginning of the Civil War in June 1861 Sickles was made colonel of the 70th New York Volunteers and later brigadier-general of volunteers, commanding the 2rd Brigade in General Joseph Hooker's division of the Army of the Potomac. Sickles constantly mixed politics and the army, a good example of this being that he single handed, without Democratic New York Governor Edwin Morgan's permission, raised the New York "Excelsior Brigade". When Governor Morgan balked at mustering the regiment Sickles had to make a direct appeal to President Lincoln to have it taken into federal service. Sickles, although often insubordinate to his commanders, was fearless in battle, but was often absent from his command, partaking of politics in New York and Washington. He fought in the 1862 Virginia Peninsula Campaign as a brigade commander and then led a division at the Battle of Fredericksburg. By this time he and Mrs. Lincoln had become good friends, and the president often heard Sickles' version of the Army of the Potomac affairs. He became a major-general of volunteers in November 1862 when General Joseph Hooker took command of the Army of the Potomac. Sickles and Hooker's chief of staff, General Daniel Butterfield, were accused by numerous general officers of turning Hooker's headquarters into a grog bar and brothel. Sickles' own division headquarters enjoyed a similar reputation. At the Battle of Chancellorsville, Sickles or officers in his command reported that Stonewall Jackson's famous left flank assault was actually a retreat, leading Hooker to order two-thirds of his troops forward to pursue the Confederates. This left Howard's XI Corps in an exposed position, and they were surprised and badly routed by Jackson's forces. After Hooker's removal Sickles remained with the III Corps, taking it to Gettysburg, where according to most authorities he made one of the major blunders in the war. General Meade, on the second day of the battle, ordered the III Corps to create a line on Cemetery Ridge extending to cover the federal left near the Round Tops. Sickles felt this line was too long and low, and against orders moved his corps forward to the Peach Orchard. This put both the left flank of the II Corps and the III Corps in the air. General James Longstreet executed a ferocious assault on Sickles' corps, which was barely beat back by the heroic efforts of several III Corps brigades and reinforcements from the II Corps. Early in the retreat Sickles sustained a serious leg wound that required almost immediate amputation. Sickles later defended his movement by claiming that if he had remained on Cemetery Ridge Longstreet's assault would have broken the federal line. In 1867, in the midst of Reconstruction, political friends of Sickles were able to get him breveted as a major-general in the regular army. Two decades later he received the Congressional Medal of Honor for his role at Gettysburg. General George Gordon Meade and Sickles locked horns for years in acrimonious debate over the Battle of Gettysburg before Congress and in publications until Meade's death. Sickles received no more field commands, and for the remainder of the war performed special missions for Secretary of War Edwin Stanton. In 1866 he was made colonel of the 43nd U.S. Infantry, and in 1869 was retired as major-general in the regular army.

President Ulysses Grant appointed Sickles, probably to placate Republic radicals, Minister to Spain, where he became an intimate friend of former Spanish Queen Isabella. In his later years he became a "professional" veteran. He chaired the New York State Monuments Commission, and was involved with the Grand Army of the Republic at every national encampment until his death in 1914.

Sickles, Daniel. *Carte de visite* by Brady, Washington. Author's collection.

Sigel

Sigel, Franz. *Carte de visite* by Brady, Washington. Author's collection.

Sigel, Franz Henry (1824-1902) was born in Germany and schooled at the Military Academy of Karlsruhe. During the unsuccessful 1848 revolution Sigel served in the Prussian army. He served as Minister of War and fled Prussia to Switzerland, England, New York, and then to St. Louis, Missouri, where in 1861 he was employed as a teacher and director of schools. Before the Civil War, while teaching in New York he held a major's commission in the 5th New York Militia. Lincoln, ever mindful of large foreign communities, saw Franz Sigel as a key to involving the large anti-slavery German born population in the federal cause. Militarily Sigel was one of Lincoln's worst choices of foreign born generals, but politically he was a popular recruiter and unifying force in holding the German born population to the union. One of the most popular slogans in the German community was "I fights mit Sigel". In May 1861 he was appointed colonel of the 3rd Missouri Volunteers, commanding a brigade in the Army of Southwest Missouri, and was appointed brigadier-general of volunteers in August 1861. He served with General Nathaniel Lyon in taking control of Camp Jackson in St. Louis, and at the Battle of Wilson's Creek assumed field command when Lyons was killed. His best Civil War performance was at the Battle of Pea Ridge in March 1862 where, under General Samuel Curtis, he commanded two divisions and personally led his artillery in decimating the troops of General Earl van Dorn. In June 1862 he was transferred to the eastern theater as a major-general of volunteers and placed in command of General John C. Fremont's IX Corps. He was engaged in the Second Battle of Bull Run, but was not engaged in the Battles of Antietam or Fredericksburg. While commanding the District of West Virginia in May 1864 he was defeated at New Market by the smaller forces of General John Breckinridge, which included young cadets from the Virginia Military Academy who bravely charged Sigel's lines. His movement down the Shenandoah Valley from Winchester was part of a coordinated move by Grant to put pressure on General Lee's Army of Northern Virginia by all the federal armies. Grant was dismayed when generals Sigel, David Hunter, and Benjamin Butler all failed to accomplish their assigned objectives. After the embarrassment at New Market Sigel was removed from command and resigned from the army on May 4, 1865. He then engaged in various pursuits, including holding public office as a pension agent. He died in 1902. In retrospect, Sigel was probably not as inept as many authorities have portrayed him. At the Battle of Pea Ridge he demonstrated ability as a field commander, but strangely at other times seemed indecisive and lacked aggressive force. His failures in leading large commands did create in the public mind that German troops were inept and would not fit, and a public joke was "I runs wit Sigel".

SLOCUM

Slocum, Henry. *Carte de visite* by Brady, Washington. Author's collection.

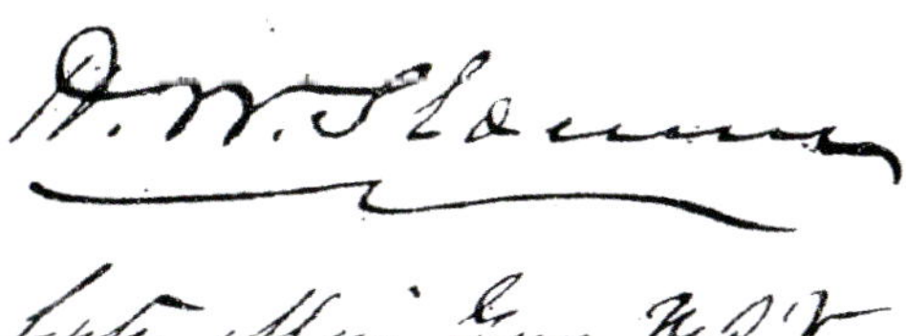

Slocum, Henry. *Carte de visite* by unidentified photographer. Author's collection.

Slocum, Henry Warner (1826-1894) was born in New York. Slocum attended a private academy and taught school before being admitted to the Military Academy in 1848, finishing seventh in the class of 1852. He was commissioned into the 1st Artillery and sent to the Seminole Wars in 1852 and 1853. While serving in garrison in Charleston, South Carolina, he studied law, and began the practice of law upon resigning from the army in October 1856. While residing and practicing law in Syracuse, New York, Slocum was active in the New York State Militia serving as a colonel. At the outbreak of the Civil War he was appointed colonel of the 27th New York Volunteers and led his regiment, a part of General David Hunter's division, in the Battle of Bull Run, where he suffered a leg wound. Upon returning from his injury he commanded a brigade in General William Franklin's division of the Army of the Potomac. When Franklin became commander of the VI Corps Slocum received command of a division. He was promoted to brigadier-general of volunteers in August 1861 and major-general of volunteers in July 1862 on becoming a division commander. In the 1862 Virginia Peninsula Campaign his division reinforced General Fitz John Porter at the Battle of Gaines Mill and was engaged in the Seven Days battles. Slocum's division was selected to reinforce General John Pope's Army of Virginia at the battle of Second Bull Run and covered its retreat to the Washington defenses. At the Battle of Antietam he took over the XII Corps upon the battlefield death of General Joseph Mansfield. Slocum and the XII Corps did not participate in the Battle of Fredericksburg, being held in reserve. However, in the Chancellorsville Campaign the XII Corps lost over 2,500 men and Slocum, along with General Darius Couch, second in command of the Army of the Potomac, were highly critical of General Hooker. At the Battle of Gettysburg Slocum's XII Corps held the extreme right of the union line, beginning at Culp's Hill and extending to the Baltimore Pike. He was thought by General George Meade to have been slow in moving his division to the federal lines before repelling a strong assault by Confederate General Richard Elwell at daylight on July 3rd. After General Rosecrans' defeat at Chickamauga, the XI and the XII Corps, under General Joseph Hooker, were sent to reinforce federal forces at Chattanooga. Upon learning that he was to serve under Hooker Slocum tendered his resignation, but it was refused. He reluctantly agreed to a compromise that one division of the XII Corps would serve under him in protecting the important Nashville and Chattanooga Railroad, while the second would serve with Hooker. In April 1864 he was sent to command the District of Vicksburg when the XII and the XI Corps were consolidated into the XX Corps, still commanded by Hooker. When General James McPherson was killed before Atlanta, the command of the Army of the Tennessee was given by General Sherman to General O.O. Howard. Both Generals John Logan and Joseph Hooker felt they had been slighted and Hooker resigned, declaring that he would not serve under his junior. Slocum was then returned to command the XX Corps, which was in the advance in entering Atlanta. He commanded the left wing of General Sherman's army in the March to the Sea, as well as in the Carolina campaign. Slocum resigned in September 1865 and returned to Syracuse, unsuccessfully running for New York Secretary of State. He later moved to Brooklyn, practiced law, and served three times in Congress as a Democrat. While in Congress he constantly advocated the overturning of General Fitz John Porter's court-martial stemming from the unverified charges of General John Pope.

SMITH, ANDREW

Smith, Andrew Jackson. *Carte de visite* by Gutekunst, Philadelphia. Author's collection.

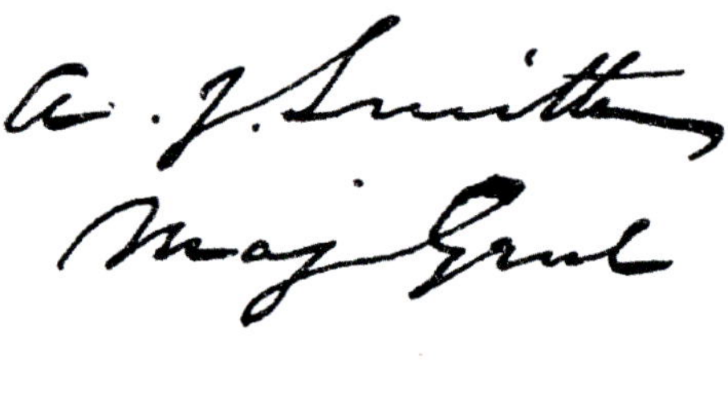

Smith, Andrew Jackson (1815-1897) was born in Pennsylvania. Smith entered the Military Academy in 1834, graduating thirty-sixth in the class of 1838. He was commissioned in the 1st Dragoons and served in various frontier posts, including the 1845 Expedition to the South Pass of the Rocky Mountains. Smith did not see action in Mexico, but instead served in garrison at San Diego and San Francisco. In the 1850s he was constantly engaged in Oregon and Washington subduing hostile Indians. He fought in the Rogue River Expedition in 1856 and skirmishes with the Snake Indians in 1860. Smith was stationed at Fort Walla Walla, Washington territory, at the beginning of the Civil War. In May 1861, while still at Walla Walla, he was promoted to major and traveled south to take command of the 2nd California Cavalry. Later he was requested by General Henry Halleck, commander of the Department of the Missouri, to be his chief of cavalry. Smith accepted in November 1861 and served in this role until the end of Halleck's siege of Corinth. In March 1862, when appointed to brigadier-general of volunteers, he briefly commanded a division based in Kentucky that was part of the Department of the Ohio. Afterwards, he was assigned divisional command in the XIII Corps of the Army of the Tennessee. Smith commanded a division in General William T. Sherman's December 1862 Yazoo Expedition, which ended in defeat at Chickasaw Bluffs. A month later Smith's division served in the XVIII Corps, now led by General John McClernand, in its successful capture of Arkansas Post. In the Vicksburg Campaign he commanded his division at the battles of Grand Gulf, Champion's Hill, Port Gibson, and Big Black River, as well as during the assaults on the Vicksburg fortifications. In August 1863 he was given divisional command in the XVI Corps, and in March 1864 was sent on a temporary assignment to accompany General Nathaniel Banks in the ill-fated Red River Expedition. He was credibly engaged in the capture of Fort DeRussy and the Battle of Pleasant Hill. Returning to the Army of the Tennessee, he defeated General Nathan Bedford Forrest at the Battle of Tupelo, for which he was appointed major-general of volunteers. Smith's division then was sent north to reinforce the Department of the Missouri, which again was threatened by an invasion of General Sterling Price. Once Price was contained Smith was ordered to move his division by rail to reinforce General George Thomas at Nashville. His division arrived in time for the Battle of Nashville and pursued Hood's army to Pulaski, Tennessee. Smith received command of the XVI Corps in February 1865, and was sent to New Orleans to cooperate with General E.R.S. Canby in the capture of Mobile. He received brevets to brigadier-general and major-general in the regular army for the battles of Tupelo and Nashville. He mustered out of the volunteer forces in January 1866 and was appointed colonel of the new 7th United States Cavalry. He served as commander of the Department of the Missouri from September 1867 to March 1868, resigning from the army in 1869. After retirement Smith served as the St. Louis, Missouri, postmaster and auditor for many years. Smith was an exceptional division commander in the union army and has been virtually ignored by Civil War scholars. Generals Sherman and Grant used Smith's division as a rapid deployment group shifted by either rail or boat, much as divisions are today by air. Smith often referred to his troops as the "lost tribes of Israel".

Smith, Andrew Jackson. *Carte de visite* by Gutekunst, Philadelphia. Author's collection.

SMITH, CHARLES

Smith, Charles Ferguson. *Carte de visite* by Anthony, New York. Author's collection.

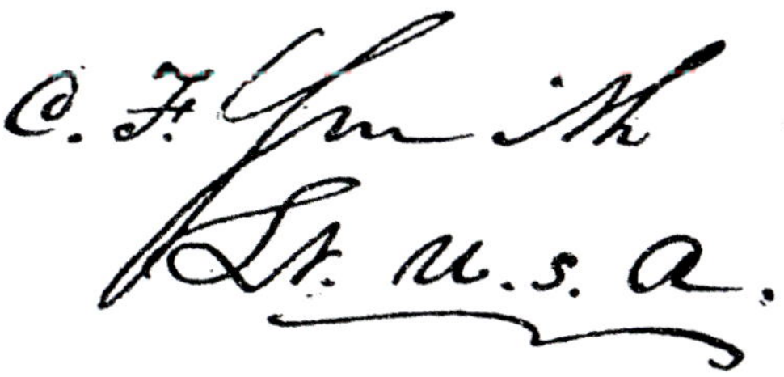

Smith, Charles Ferguson (1807-1862) was born in Pennsylvania. He entered the Military Academy in 1820, graduating nineteenth in the class of 1825. Smith was commissioned in the 2rd Artillery and served garrison duty until returning to West Point for nine years. During that time he rose from an assistant instructor of infantry to commandant of cadets, serving in that role from 1838 to 1842. In his nine years at West Point Smith had the opportunity to become well acquainted with many future Civil War generals, including Ulysses Grant in the class of 1843. Smith was one of the most distinguished officers in the war with Mexico, obtaining brevets up to colonel for gallant conduct at five different battles. After the capture of Mexico City he was appointed acting inspector-general, commanding the police guard in Mexico until 1848. In 1854 he was promoted to major in the 1st Artillery, then to Lieutenant-Colonel of the 10th Infantry in 1856, and commanded the Red River Expedition into the Idaho country. He then accompanied Colonel Albert Sidney Johnson's expedition to Utah in 1857, and then commanded a garrison in Utah till April 1861, when he was called back to command the Department of Washington. His stay in Washington was brief, as his views on the war were not well accepted by the Lincoln administration and Congress. At the urging of General John C. Fremont, in September 1861 he was appointed brigadier-general of volunteers and commanded the Department of Western Kentucky with headquarters at Paducah, Kentucky. He was assigned in a subordinate role to his former pupil, General Ulysses Grant, during the attacks on Fort Henry and Fort Donelson. At Fort Donelson Smith's division, with him leading from the front, made a brilliant charge that soon led General Simon Buckner, a former pupil of Smith's, to surrender the garrison's thousands of Confederate troops. He was appointed to major-general of volunteers in March 1862, and due to a misunderstanding between General Henry Halleck in St. Louis and General George McClellan in Washington, Smith and not Grant was placed in the command of the advance up the Tennessee River to locate Confederate General Albert Sidney Johnson's forces then concentrating at Corinth, Mississippi. The problem between the two generals was resolved when Smith stumbled getting out of a boat at Savannah, Tennessee, injuring his shin. He soon died on April 25, 1862, from infection and dysentery. General Smith, at fifty-five, was one of the older field commanders in 1862, but likely would have had a distinguished record if he had lived.

SMITH, GILES

Smith, Giles. *Carte de visite* by unidentified photographer. Author's collection.

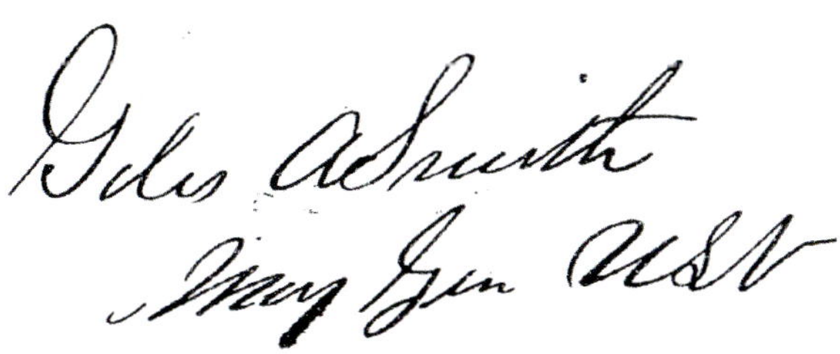

Smith, Giles Alexander (1829-1876) was born in New York, but at eighteen moved to Ohio, where he was engaged in business in Cincinnati before moving to Bloomington, Illinois, to operate a hotel until the beginning of the Civil War. His first service in the Civil War was as a company officer in the 8th Missouri Volunteers commanded by his brother, Morgan Smith. As major and lieutenant-colonel of the 8th Missouri Volunteers he was engaged against Missouri guerillas, defeating them at St. Charles and Mexico City. He also fought with the 8th Missouri at the capture of Fort Donelson and took part in some of the heaviest action at the Battle of Shiloh. He succeeded his brother as colonel of the 8th Missouri in June 1862, and later commanded a brigade in Sherman's failed Yazoo Expedition. He then accompanied General McClernand's expedition to capture Arkansas Post in January 1863. He was appointed to brigadier-general of volunteers in August 1863 and served as a brigade commander during the Vicksburg Campaign with the Federal XV Corps, where he was highly praised for his rescuing a gunboat at Steele's Bayou. At the Battle of Chattanooga, while commanding a brigade in the XV Corps, he was seriously wounded in Sherman's assault on the north end of Missionary Ridge. In the Atlanta campaign he led a division in the XVII Corps that was engaged at Resaca and Leggett's Hill. At the Battle of Atlanta Smith's division withstood a furious assault from the forces of General William J. Hardee which, if successful, would have seriously threatened General James McPherson's total command. Smith was breveted a major-general of volunteers in September 1864 and continued with his division on the March to the Sea and the Carolinas Campaign. From May to December 1865 he commanded a black division in the XXV Corps sent to Texas under the command of General Philip Sheridan to deter any hostile acts on the part of the Mexican Emperor Maximilian and his French allies. Smith was made a major-general of volunteers November 24, 1865, the last of the Civil War appointments to that rank. Generals Wager Swayne and Benjamin Grierson were appointed major-generals in 1866, but their appointments were backdated prior to Smith's.

SMITH, WILLIAM

Smith, William F. *Carte de visite* by Brady, Washington. Author's collection.

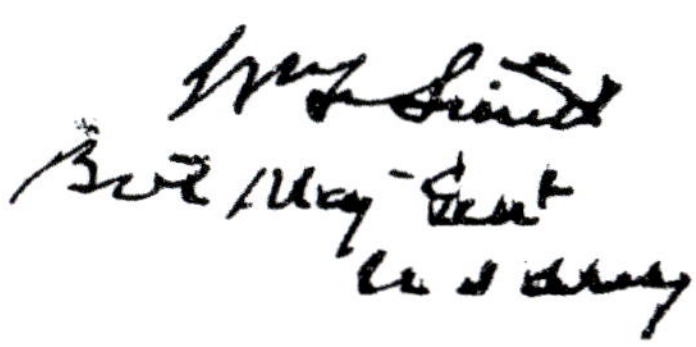

Smith, William Farrar (1824-1903) was born in Vermont and entered the Military Academy in 1841, graduating fourth in the class of 1845. He was commissioned in the Topographical Engineers and missed the Mexican War, being retained at the Military Academy as assistant professor of mathematics from 1846 to 1848. Prior to the outbreak of the Civil War he served in engineering assignments, most notably in mapping the boundary between the United States and Mexico. He again, in 1855 and 1856, was assigned to the Military Academy as senior assistant professor of mathematics. In April 1861, when war began, he was serving as a captain of engineers on the Lighthouse Board. His first war service was mustering troops in New York and then serving on the staff of General Benjamin Butler at Fort Monroe until June 30, 1861, becoming Colonel of the 3rd Vermont Volunteers. Smith was engaged at the Battle of Bull Run, serving on the staff of General Irvin McDowell. While in the defenses of Washington in August 1861 he was appointed a brigadier-general of volunteers, and in March 1862 was given a division command in the VI Corps, capably leading it through most of the battles of the 1862 Virginia Peninsula Campaign. Before the Maryland Campaign in July 1862, he was appointed major-general of volunteers and commanded a division at the Battle of South Mountain and the Battle of Antietam. He commanded the VI Corps at the Battle of Fredericksburg, and a few days later, with General William B. Franklin, drafted a letter to President Lincoln castigating Army of the Potomac commander General Ambrose Burnside. They additionally forwarded to the President their plan as to how the advance on Richmond should be conducted. This, along with other disloyal acts on the part of other Army of the Potomac generals, disturbed Lincoln and outraged some members of his cabinet. An immediate consequence for Smith in bypassing the chain of command was that his appointment to major-general was not confirmed by the United States Senate. This caused him to lose his corps and division command in the Army of the Potomac. He was shunted off to lesser commands in the Department of West Virginia and commanded a division of Pennsylvania militia in the Gettysburg campaign. In August 1863 he was sent west as chief engineer for the Department of the Cumberland. Later his good friend General Ulysses Grant arranged his transfer to the Military Division of the Mississippi, where he constructed the famous "Cracker Line", supplying General George Thomas' forces at Chattanooga with supplies and rations prior to their attack on Missionary Ridge. Smith's engineering skills played a significant role in the Chattanooga campaign, and he was highly praised by Generals Grant, Sherman, and Thomas. His long friendship with Grant resulted in being given another chance at field command. Upon Grant's request he was again appointed a major-general of volunteers by Lincoln, and was this time confirmed by the Senate. When Grant became general-in-chief of the army he made Smith commander of the XVIII Corps in General Benjamin Butler's Army of the James. There was some speculation that Grant had brought Smith east to replace General George Meade. At the Battle of Cold Harbor the XVIII Corps was attached to the Army of the Potomac, and afterwards Smith publicly criticized General Meade. In the Petersburg Campaign Smith committed a serious error on June 15, 1864, when in sight of Petersburg he hesitated and failed to attack, perhaps prolonging the war by many months. When General Winfield Hancock arrived on the field late in the day he and Smith got involved in an argument which, along with Smith's continued remarks about the competency of Butler, forced Grant to relieve him from command of the XVIII Corps. He resigned his commission in the volunteers in November 1864 and resigned from the Army in March 1867. His post-war years were spent as president of the International Telegraph Company, New York Police Commissioner, and in government employ designing river and harbor improvements. He was also a prolific writer on the history of the Civil War.

Smith, William F. *Carte de visite* by Fredricks, New York. Author's collection.

STAHEL

Stahel, Julius. *Carte de visite* by Brady, Washington. Author's collection.

Stahel, Julius (1825-1912) was born in Hungary and educated in Budapest. Stahel joined the Austrian army, but resigned to take part in the Hungarian Revolution. When Austria, with the help of Prussia, suppressed the revolutionaries, Stahel was forced to flee in 1849 to Berlin, London, and finally to the United States, where he was a journalist and teacher in New York City. At the beginning of the Civil War he was editor of a prominent German language newspaper in New York. In April 1861 Stahel and future Civil War general Louis Blenker were instrumental in organizing the 1st German Rifles (the 8th New York Volunteers), with Blenker as colonel and Stahel as lieutenant-colonel. The regiment was on hand for the Battle of Bull Run but was held in reserve at Centerville. In August 1861 he became Colonel of the 8th New York Volunteers, and in November 1861 was appointed brigadier-general and a brigade commander in General Blenker's division in the Army of the Potomac. Later he transferred to a brigade command in General John C. Fremont's operations against General Stonewall Jackson in the Shenandoah Valley and was engaged in Fremont's defeat at Cross Keys. At the Battle of Second Bull Run, Stahel assumed division command when General Robert Schenck, in Sigel's I Corps, was wounded. When the Army of Virginia was disbanded he was given command of the cavalry in the defenses of Washington, which included the Loudoun Valley during the Antietam and Fredericksburg campaigns. He was appointed major-general of volunteers in March 1863, likely more for political reasons than military competence. In the spring of 1864 he joined General David Hunter's unsuccessful operations in the Shenandoah Valley, in which he was forced to retreat to West Virginia. Stahel had a share in Hunter's fiasco, but distinguished himself at the Battle of Piedmont, winning the Medal of Honor, one of the few major-generals to do so. He was essentially without a command until he resigned in February 1865. In the post-war years he served in the consular service in Japan and China, later becoming associated with the Equitable Insurance Company in New York. Stahel was among the many foreign born generals, and probably should have held only cavalry commands, as he showed some aptitude in that branch.

STANLEY

Stanley, David. *Carte de visite* by Webster, Louisville. Author's collection.

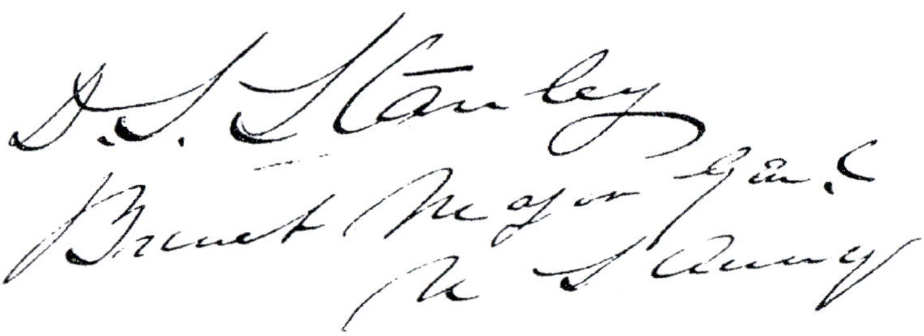

Stanley, David Sloane (1828-1902) was born in Ohio. Stanley apprenticed to study medicine, but entered the Military Academy in 1848, graduating ninth in the class of 1852. He was commissioned in the 2nd Dragoons, serving on frontier duty prior to the Civil War in Kansas, Texas, Indian Territory, and Arkansas. In April 1861 he was stationed as a captain in the 1st Cavalry at Fort Washita, in the Indian Territory, and successfully evacuated his command to Fort Leavenworth, Kansas. He remained in the western theater and took part in the Missouri Campaign, and in August 1861 guarded the wagon trains at the Battle of Wilson Creek. Stanley was appointed brigadier-general of volunteers in September 1861, and after recovering from a broken leg was placed in command of the 1st Division in the Army of the Mississippi in March 1862. He was engaged at the Battles of Island No. 10 and New Madrid, then joined General John Pope's Army of the Mississippi, attached to General Henry Halleck's slow movement toward Corinth. Stanley returned to cavalry duty in November 1862 as chief of cavalry in the Army of the Cumberland under General William Rosecrans. He was instrumental in enlarging the number of regiments and improving mounted effectiveness in the field. Stanley was appointed major-general of volunteers November 29, 1862, and was engaged at the Battle of Stone River. He was with his cavalry in the Tullahoma campaign, but was on sick leave and missed the Battle of Chickamauga. Upon returning to duty he was given command of the 1st Division and then the IV Corps in the Army of the Cumberland. In the Atlanta campaign he drew the wrath of General William Sherman for tardiness, and failing to check General William Hardee at Jonesboro. Stanley felt that Sherman had unjustly criticized him, as he had specifically followed his orders. After the Battle of Atlanta Stanley's IV Corps, along with General John Schofield's XII Corps, was sent back in November 1864 to join General George Thomas at Nashville. Thomas' assignment from Sherman was to block General John B. Hood's intentions to invade Kentucky and Ohio. Before reaching Thomas, Stanley and Schofield were forced to fight the battles of Spring Hill and Franklin, in which Stanley was seriously wounded leading a charge that prevented a potential federal disaster. For gallantry at the Battle of Franklin Stanley received the Medal of Honor. He continued on with General Schofield to the defenses at Nashville and was lightly engaged in the Battle of Nashville. He mustered out of volunteer service in February 1866 and was appointed in July 1866 as Colonel of the 22nd U.S. Infantry, stationed in Dakota Territory. He led the 1873 Yellowstone Expedition into western Montana which had the effect of hastening the settlement in that area. His second in command on the expedition, Lieutenant-Colonel George Custer of the 7th Cavalry, claimed that Stanley was an incompetent drunkard, and Stanley nearly placed Custer under arrest. In 1879 Stanley was transferred to Texas to eliminate Indian raids and promote better relations with Mexican military forces. His last field command was as Department Commander in New Mexico in 1882, where he was able to peacefully resolve potential conflict with the Navaho and Ute tribes. In March 1884 he was promoted brigadier-general in the regular army and retired in 1892. In retrospect, Stanley in the Civil War was a brave and efficient cavalry officer, but possessed only modest abilities in leading infantry.

STEEDMAN

Steedman, James. *Carte de visite* by Brady, New York. Author's collection.

Steedman, James Blair (1817-1883) was born in Pennsylvania. Steedman received little education and engaged in the trade of a printer. He moved to Ohio at the age of nineteen and served in the Texan army during the Mexican War, then migrated to the California goldfields before returning to Ohio and becoming owner of the *Toledo Times* newspaper. He was a strong supporter of Democrat Stephen Douglas, and in the Buchanan Administration received a political appointment as printer of public documents. He was an unsuccessful candidate for Congress, and in April 1861 was appointed Colonel of the 14th Ohio Volunteers, a ninety day regiment sent to West Virginia to take part in the Battle of Philippi. In September 1861 Steedman reorganized the regiment, and was sent to Kentucky in January 1862 to join General George Thomas in time to fight at the Battle of Mill Springs. Then he and General Thomas joined General Henry Halleck's advance on Corinth. He was appointed brigadier-general of volunteers in July 1862, commanding a brigade in the III Corps of the Army of the Ohio. At the Battle of Perryville his brigade arrived on the field at a critical moment, and likely turned the direction of the battle. He was still attached to General Charles Gilbert's III Corps at the Battle of Murfreesboro, but did not participate in the Battle of Stone's River. During General William Rosecrans' Tullahoma campaign Steedman commanded a division in General Gordon Granger's Reserve Corps. At the Battle of Chickamauga, Granger and Steedman valiantly reinforced the remaining forces of General George Thomas, preventing a total disaster for the federal army. During the battle Steedman rallied his men on Snodgrass Hill and was injured when his horse was shot from under him. On Horseshoe Ridge he carried a regimental standard and instructed one of his officers to make sure his name was spelled correctly in his obituary. He miraculously survived, even though he provided the enemy with a huge target at six feet four inches in height. While Steedman's personal bravery was lauded, his appointment to major-general of volunteers was delayed by his leanings toward the Democratic Party, and that his Toledo newspaper, until April 1864, opposed emancipation. During the Atlanta campaign he was assigned rear echelon duties and did not see front line field action. Steedman was part of the detachment of the Army of the Cumberland that was sent back to Nashville with General George Thomas to stop the advance of Confederate General John B. Hood. At the Battle of Nashville in December 1864 he ably commanded a provisional group of eight regiments. He was military governor of Georgia during reconstruction and left the army in July 1866, having been appointed by President Andrew Johnson to be collector at the port of New Orleans. He later returned to Ohio and was a newspaper editor.

STEELE

Steele, Frederick. *Carte de visite* by unidentified photographer. Author's collection.

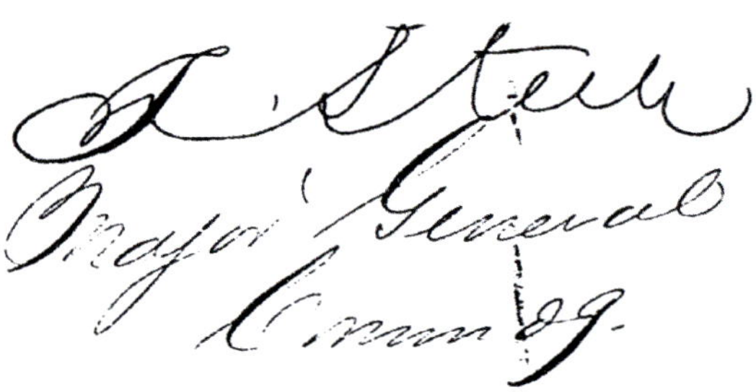

Steele, Frederick (1819-1868) was born in New York. Steele was admitted to the Military Academy in 1839, graduating thirtieth in the class of 1843 along with his lifelong friend, Ulysses Grant. He was commissioned in the 2nd Infantry and won brevets to captain in the war with Mexico. Before the Civil War he served in frontier posts, including three in California from 1849 to 1853, when he returned to Carlisle Barracks, Pennsylvania, for two years. At the outset of war he was serving at Fort Leavenworth, Kansas, and was promoted to major in the 11th Infantry. While marching with a battalion of regulars to Missouri and fighting at the Battle of Wilson's Creek he was appointed colonel of the 8th Iowa in September 1861, and then brigadier-general of volunteers in 1862. He commanded the Southeast District of Missouri from February 1862 to April 1862. He was then given command of a division in General Samuel Curtis' Army of the Southwest in its movement south from Batesville to capture Helena, Arkansas, on the Mississippi River. Steele then led a division in the XIII Corps in Sherman's Yazoo Expedition, sometimes referred to as "First Vicksburg". He was engaged in assaulting and being repulsed at Chickasaw Bluffs, and a month later participated in the federal capture of Arkansas Post. In the Vicksburg campaign he commanded a division in the XV Corps and was engaged at Grand Gulf, the capture of Jackson, and the siege of Vicksburg. In July 1863 he was placed in command of the Army of Arkansas as a major-general of volunteers with the purpose of clearing scattered Confederate forces from Arkansas. From July to September 1863 he moved through central Arkansas and occupied Little Rock. In the spring of 1864 he was ordered to cooperate with General Nathaniel Banks, who was to move his forces, including a fleet of gunboats, up the Red River to Alexandria from New Orleans. Steele's role was to move toward Alexandria overland from Little Rock. The Red River Expedition was an abject failure in conception, planning, and execution. Steele's part of the expedition at Camden, Arkansas, ran into poor weather and problems with supply lines. He was defeated at the Battle of Jenkin's Ferry and suffered other heavy losses in actions, retreating back into Little Rock. In February 1865 Steele was transferred to the Department of the Gulf and led a division in General E.R.S. Canby's operations against Mobile, Alabama. He was mustered out of volunteer service in January 1867. He died in San Francisco in January 1868 as a result of a carriage accident. At the time he was commanding the Department of the Columbia.

STEVENS

Stevens, Isaac. *Carte de visite* by unidentified photographer probably Brady. Author's collection.

Stevens, Isaac Ingalls (1818-1862) was born in Massachusetts. He attended Phillips-Andover Academy before being admitted to the Military Academy in 1835, graduating first in the class of 1839. Commissioned in the Corps of Engineers, he served in engineering assignments on the east coast. In the Mexican War Stevens served on General Winfield Scott's staff and was engaged in engineering actions, being severely wounded in the capture of Mexico City. For gallantry he received brevets of first-lieutenant and captain. After the Mexican War he returned to engineering and construction duties, but resigned from the army in March 1853. He was appointed Governor and commissioner of Indian Affairs in the Washington Territory in 1853. Stevens, ever an opportunist, on his way west to Washington superintended a 120 man exploration survey for the Northern Pacific Railroad. His primary objective in Washington was to open up the territory to settlement. To accomplish this he made numerous treaties with Indian tribes, but his personal style, oftentimes abrasive, egotistical, and dictatorial, made him few friends among many whites and Indians. He also made governmental decisions that put him in conflict with the commander of the Department of the Pacific and the United States Attorney. From 1856 to 1857 Stevens mishandled Indian hostilities in eastern Washington, but in spite of these near disasters he was elected as territorial delegate to Washington. He was defeated in 1860 due to his being the campaign chairman of pro-slavery presidential candidate John C. Breckinridge and vice presidential candidate Joseph Lane, a close personal friend. At the outbreak of Civil War hostilities he traveled back to Washington and offered his services, but could not find a command until July 30, 1861, when he was appointed Colonel of the 79th New York Highlanders. When Stevens took command of the regiment it was in near mutiny, however, the five foot one inch colonel soon restored order and morale. He was appointed brigadier-general of volunteers in September 28, 1961, and accompanied General Thomas Sherman's Expedition to South Carolina and was distinguished in the actions near Port Royal. Stevens was then transferred to North Carolina, commanding a division. He made, under protest, an unsuccessful attack on Secessionville in a failed attempt to take Charleston, South Carolina. He returned to General John Pope's Army of the Virginia, and during the Second of Bull Run commanded a division in the IX Corps led by General Jesse Reno as a major-general of volunteers. At the Battle of Chantilly, where Confederate forces were attempting to get in between Pope and Washington, Steven's troops were attacked on September 1, 1862, by those of General Stonewall Jackson, and he was instantly killed by a bullet to the head. At the time of his death there existed rumors in Washington that he was in line to be appointed commander of the Army of the Potomac. Despite his occasional Napoleonic posturing he was a perceptive and aggressive general, a type not always found in the federal army.

Stevens, Isaac. *Carte de visite* by Griffin, Beaver, Pennsylvania. General Stevens and his staff shortly before his death. His son, Brevet Brigadier General Hazard Stevens, stands to his right. Author's collection.

STONEMAN

Stoneman, George. *Carte de visite* by Brady, Washington. Author's collection.

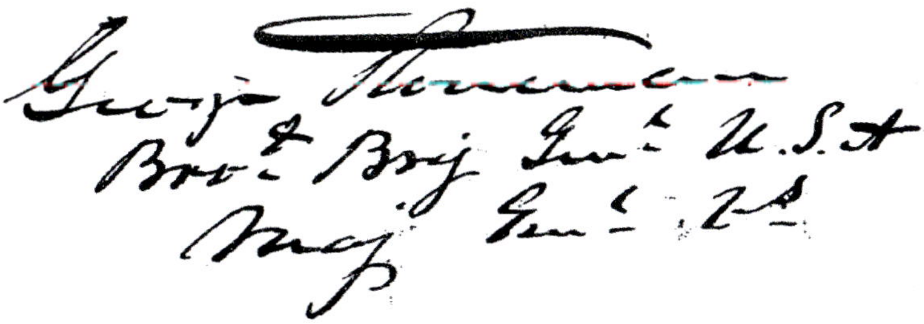

Stoneman, George. *Carte de visite* by Brady, Washington. Author's collection.

Stoneman, George (1822-1894) was born in New York. He entered the Military Academy in 1842, graduating thirty-second in the class of 1843 along with George McClellan and Thomas J. Jackson. He was commissioned in the 1st Dragoons, his first assignment being as assistant quartermaster to the Mormon Battalion during its 1846 march from Fort Leavenworth to Santa Fe, and later through New Mexico, finally ending in San Diego, California. He was stationed in California from 1846 to 1855, when he was promoted to captain in the 2nd Cavalry, then stationed in Texas. He was stationed at the cavalry school at Carlisle Barracks, Pennsylvania, at the beginning of the Civil War. Stoneman was promoted to major in the 1st Cavalry in May 1861, and soon commanded mounted troops in the capture of Alexandria, Virginia. Afterwards he received appointment to the staff of his former classmate and friend, General George McClellan, then operating in West Virginia. When General McClellan received command of the Army of the Potomac Stoneman was made his chief of cavalry and a brigadier-general of volunteers. He commanded cavalry during the 1862 Virginia Peninsula campaign and brought on the Battle of Williamsburg when his units collided with Confederate troops retreating from Yorktown. At the Second Battle of Bull Run Stoneman moved from the cavalry to command General Philip Kearny's division in the III Corps, which did not take part in the Antietam campaign. In November 1862 he was appointed major-general of volunteers and fought in the Battle of Fredericksburg. Under new Army of the Potomac commander General Joseph Hooker, he reorganized and refitted the Army of the Potomac cavalry into an offensive force of nearly 10,000 men. On April 13, 1863, he led the cavalry corps in a raid toward Richmond with the objective of operating behind General Robert E. Lee's lines, while General Hooker and the rest of the Army of the Potomac would move forward, thus putting Lee between Stoneman and Hooker. Due to incessant rain and high water in the rivers the raid was delayed nearly two weeks. When it finally did get underway its military effects were minimal, although highly publicized both in the south and the north. It's most important effect was to deprive General Joseph Hooker of his eyes and ears and flank protection during his defeat at the Battle of Chancellorsville. Stoneman was replaced in May 1863 as the Army of the Potomac's chief of cavalry by General Alfred Pleasonton. Assigned to the Bureau of the Cavalry in Washington, Stoneman was displeased with the assignment and was unable to stop the incessant corruption in the bureau's purchasing of cavalry horses and supplies. In January 1864 he received command of the XIII Corps in the Army of the Ohio, and in April 1864 was shifted to command the cavalry corps of the Army of the Ohio. In the Atlanta campaign he mounted a raid to free union prisoners at Andersonville and Macon, but instead was himself captured at Clinton, Georgia, and held prisoner for three months. During the last months of the war he commanded the District of East Tennessee and made a successful raid into southwestern Virginia to support Sherman's movements in the Carolinas. He mustered out of volunteer service in September 1866 and was appointed colonel of the 21st Infantry, then reluctantly served as Department of Arizona commander till his retirement for ill health in 1871. He retired to his ranch in Southern California and later was elected Governor of California. Stoneman was an old time frontier cavalryman, always obeying orders and not often showing ingenuity and aggressive behavior. It is quite likely his chronic ill health affected his performance. While suffering with acute hemorrhoids the life of a cavalryman could not have been pleasant.

STRONG

George Crockett Strong. *Carte de visite* by Brady, Washington. Author's collection.

Strong, George Crockett (1832-1863) was born in New York, but grew up in Massachusetts, from which he was appointed to the Military Academy in 1853, graduating fifth in the class of 1857. He was commissioned in the Ordnance Branch and served at several arsenals until the beginning of the Civil War. In July 1861 he was appointed chief ordnance officer on the staff of General Irvin McDowell, and was praised for his conduct at the Battle of Bull Run. Upon the removal of McDowell he joined General George McClellan's staff until he was selected as chief ordnance officer for General Benjamin Butler's Expedition to New Orleans. After the capture of the city he remained with Butler, now commanding the Department of the Gulf, as both his chief ordnance officer and chief of staff. He was on sick leave from December 1862 to June 1863, most likely suffering from malaria. Apparently his first field command was the Expedition to Ponchatoula, Louisiana, in September 1862, sent there to destroy the headquarters and supplies of Confederate General Jeff Thompson. In June 1863 Strong was appointed a brigadier-general of volunteers, and in November 1862 was sent to South Carolina to command a brigade in the X Corps in the Department of the South. The X Corps moved against Charleston in July 1863, first making a descent on Morris Island and laying siege to Fort Wagner. In assaulting the fort on July 18, 1863, Strong received a severe wound to his thigh and died in New York twelve days later of lockjaw. He was posthumously appointed by President Lincoln a major-general of volunteers on July 31, 1863, but this appointment was never confirmed by the Senate.

SUMNER

Sumner, Edwin (Bull). *Carte de visite* by Brady, Washington. Author's collection.

Sumner, Edwin (Bull). *Carte de visite* by Brady, Washington. Author's collection.

Sumner, Edwin Vose (1797-1863) was born in Massachusetts. Sumner received a direct appointment to the Army in 1819 and joined the 2nd Infantry as a second-lieutenant. He served in the Black Hawk War and became a captain in the 2nd Dragoons in 1833 and major in 1846. His duty stations were typically on the frontier and at the cavalry school at Carlisle Barracks, Pennsylvania. In the Mexican War he led a furious cavalry charge at the Battle of Cerro Gordo and acquired the sobriquet "Bull Head" for allegedly having a musket ball bounce off his head. He received brevets to lieutenant-colonel and colonel, and returned to frontier duty as the acting governor of New Mexico. He was promoted to colonel of the 1st Cavalry in 1855 and was sent to Fort Leavenworth, Kansass, during the "Bleeding Kansas" conflict between pro-slavery and anti-slavery groups fighting over Kansas statehood. He campaigned in 1857 against the Cheyenne and was in charge of the Department of the West from 1858 to 1861, when he was selected by General Winfield Scott to escort President Lincoln to Washington. When General David Twiggs was dismissed from the army for illegally surrendering San Antonio and his command to Texas insurrectionists in 1861 Sumner became one of three brigadier generals in the regular army. Prior to the Peninsula campaign President Lincoln ordered, over the objections of General George McClellan, the establishment of an army corps comprised of multiple divisions as the organization base of the Army of the Potomac. General Sumner was placed in command of the II Corps, with General McClellan praising his performance at the Battle of Seven Pines, as well as his judgment and energy during the campaign. He was appointed to major-general of volunteers in May 1862 and commanded the II Corps at the Battle of South Mountain and at the Battle of Antietam, where he received both a wound and criticism for leading his corps, like an old cavalry colonel, from the front rather than the rear, where he could better direct operations. He was also accused of committing his divisions into the battle piecemeal. At the Battle of Fredericksburg he commanded both the II Corps and IX Corps, which made bloody assaults on Marye's Heights. His divisions nearly broke through the Confederate lines, but took a devastating number of casualties. When General Burnside was removed from command of the Army of the Potomac Sumner requested relief, and was given command of the District of Missouri, but he died of pneumonia before arriving in St. Louis. General Sumner, at the times of his death in March 1863, was exhausted and in ill health. He was most assuredly a brave soldier, and faithfully served his country for 44 years. However, his critics were probably correct in that he was best fitted to be a colonel of cavalry on the western plains.

SWAYNE

Swayne, Wager. *Carte de visite* by Witt, Columbus, Ohio. Author's collection.

Swayne, Wager (1834-1902) was born in Ohio. He graduated from Yale University in 1856 and entered the Cincinnati law school, from which he graduated in 1859. He practiced law in Columbus, Ohio, until the Civil War with his father, Noah Swayne, who was later appointed by Lincoln to the United States Supreme Court. He entered the Civil War in August 1861 as a major in the 43rd Ohio, and soon was promoted to lieutenant-colonel. His regiment constituted part of General John Pope's forces that were victorious at the battles of New Madrid and Island No. 10. It also accompanied Pope on General Henry Halleck's slow advance on Corinth, and in October 1862 fought at the Battle of Corinth, where he won the Congressional Medal of Honor. Swayne was promoted to Colonel of the 43rd Ohio, then commanded the 2nd Brigade, 4th Division in the XVI Corps. His brigade mainly performed garrison duty in Tennessee until General Sherman's 1864 Atlanta campaign. His brigade, as part of the XVI Corps, fought at Resaca, Dallas, Kennesaw Mountain, and the Battle of Atlanta. Swayne's brigade, during Sherman's March to the Sea, was part of the XVII Corps, and in the crossing of the Salkehatchie River in South Carolina Swayne received a severe leg wound that required amputation. He received appointment to brigadier-general of volunteers in March 1865, and in June 1865 General O.O. Howard, in charge of the Freedman's Bureau, asked that General Swayne be appointed to handle the bureau's operations in Alabama. His responsibilities encompassed not only civil, but military command of the state. In May 1866 he was appointed to major-general of volunteers with rank from June 1865. He was also commissioned as Colonel of the newly organized 45th Infantry. In 1868 he was recalled from Alabama for duty in Washington, and in the 1869 army reorganization the 45th Infantry was consolidated with the 14th Infantry, leaving Swayne was without a command. In 1870 he was placed on the retired list at his own request and returned to Ohio to practice law. He was the last appointed major-general of volunteers appointed and confirmed in the Civil War.

SYKES

Sykes, George. *Carte de visite* by Brady, Washington. Author's collection.

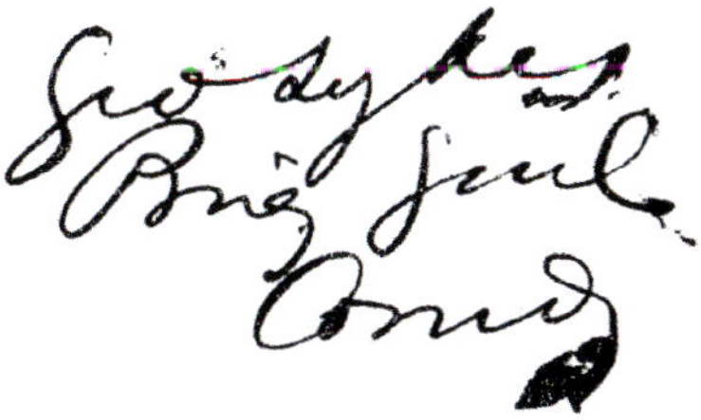

Sykes, George (1822-1880) was born in Delaware, and was admitted to the Military Academy in 1838, graduating thirty-ninth in the class of 1842. He was commissioned in the 3rd Infantry and served in the Seminole wars and on frontier duty until the Mexican War, where he was present at six battles, winning a brevet to captain at Cerro Gordo. Between 1849 and 1860 Sykes was stationed at a number of posts in Arizona and New Mexico. He participated in the 1854 expedition against the Apaches and the 1859 expedition to subdue the Navahos. At the opening of the Civil War Sykes was stationed at Fort Clark, Texas, as captain in the 14th U.S. Infantry. At the beginning of the Civil War he was able to escape Texas and, arriving in Washington, was soon promoted to major in the 14th Infantry. Sykes took part in the Battle of Bull Run, commanding the regulars. His battalion stood firm in the midst of the panic stricken volunteers and covered the retreat back to the Washington defenses. He was promoted to brigadier-general of volunteers in September 1861 and placed in command of a brigade, and later a division in General Fitz John Porter's V Corps. Sykes always preferred to command regulars, and his division was comprised of nine regular and two volunteer regiments. Sykess' regulars fought hard at the Battle of Gaines Mill and on Malvern Hill during the 1862 Virginia Peninsula Campaign, with Sykes receiving a brevet to colonel in the regular army for gallant actions at Gaines Mill. Sykes' regulars were heavily engaged at the Battle of Second Bull Run, and he was appointed to major-general of volunteers in November 1862. His division was partially used at Antietam and held in reserve at the Battle of Fredericksburg. Sykes assumed command of the V Corps in May 1863 when General George Meade took command of the Army of the Potomac. Sykes' corps at the Battle of Gettysburg fought well on the left of the union line on the second day of the battle, trying to save the hard pressed III Corps. The V Corps units also seized and held the key defensive position on Little Round Top. After Gettysburg he received a brevet to brigadier-general in the regular army. Sykes was removed from command after the Mine Run campaign, in which General Meade claimed that he was too slow when aggressive action was needed. Even though Sykes' nickname in the "old" army was "Tardy George", Meade was probably trying to shift some of the blame for the Army of the Potomac's slow pursuit of Lee after Gettysburg. Sykes was relieved in April 1864 and took command of the Department of Kansas, remaining there until the end of the war. After the war he reverted back to his rank of lieutenant-colonel of the 5th Infantry, and in 1868 was promoted to colonel of the 20th Infantry. He continued mostly on frontier duty until he died at Fort Brown, Texas, in 1880.

Sykes, George. *Carte de visite* by Brady, Washington. Author's collection.

TERRY

Terry, Alfred. *Carte de visite* by Beers and Mansfield, New Haven, Connecticut. Author's collection.

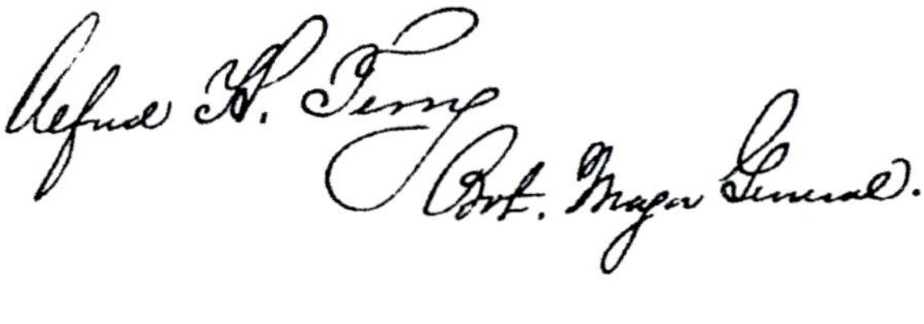

Terry, Alfred. *Carte de visite* by Anthony, New York. Author's collection.

Terry, Alfred Howe (1827-1890) was born in Connecticut. He attended Yale University, and in 1849 began the practice of law. From 1854 to 1861 he served as clerk of the superior and supreme courts of Connecticut. In command of the 2nd Connecticut Militia, he was present with General Erasmus Keyes' brigade at the Battle of Bull Run. In September 1861 he organized and became colonel of the 7th Connecticut Volunteers, accompanying General Thomas Sherman's expedition that captured Port Royal, South Carolina. He also was engaged with General Quincy Gilmore in the siege and capture of Fort Pulaski, Georgia. In April 1862 he was appointed brigadier-general of volunteers and remained in the Department of the South, taking part in actions against Charleston, Fort Wagner, James Island, and Stono River. He was awarded command in April 1864 of the X Corps in the Army of the James, then led by General Benjamin Butler, and was engaged in actions before Petersburg and Richmond. In December 1864 he participated in Butler's unsuccessful movement to capture Fort Fisher, which guarded the city of Wilmington and was the last significant Confederate port. Butler's secret weapon of a barge full of explosives failed to destroy or even damage Fort Fisher, moving Butler to call off the operation. The failure of Butler's attack was the last straw for General Ulysses Grant, and he removed Butler from command of the Army of the James. He then selected Terry to work cooperatively with Admiral David Porter to devise a joint plan of attack to capture Fort Fisher. Terry's 8,000 infantry, with Porter's forty-four ships, were able in two days of bombardment and assaults to capture Fort Fisher in a brilliant example of effective army and navy cooperation. He received the thanks of Congress and promotion to brigadier-general in the regular army, as well as appointment to major-general of volunteers. From January 1865 until the surrender at Appomattox Terry commanded a provisional corps in North Carolina, cooperating with the advance of the armies under General William T. Sherman. After the Civil War he served in various western departmental commands. In 1876 he commanded the Department of Dakota and was in personal command of the three columns constituting the Little Bighorn Expedition, in which a portion of lieutenant-colonel George Custer's 7th Cavalry was annihilated. General Terry, much to the consternation of the press and Custer's friends, never commented on whether Custer disobeyed his orders to not engage the Sioux until joined by General Gibbon's column. In 1886, due to seniority, he was made major-general, and in 1888 was placed on the retired list. Terry was one of the few non-graduates of the Military Academy to attain the full rank of major-general.

THOMAS

Thomas, George. *Carte de visite* by Griers, Nashville, Tennessee. Author's collection.

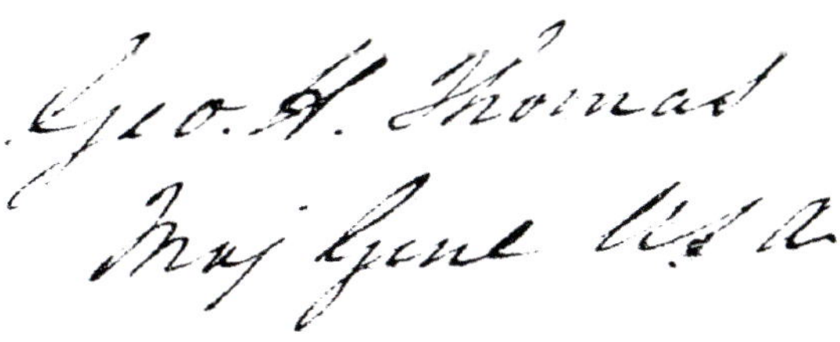

Thomas, George Henry (1816-1870) was born in Virginia. He entered the Military Academy in 1836, graduating twelfth in the class of 1840, along with his friend, William T. Sherman. He was commissioned in the 3rd Artillery and served against the Seminoles in Florida and in various artillery posts until the outbreak of the Mexican War. For his actions in Mexico he was breveted to captain for gallantry at the Battle of Monterey and to major for gallantry at the Battle of Buena Vista. In 1848 he returned to the United States to again fight Seminole Indians in Florida. From 1851 to 1854 he served as an instructor in artillery and cavalry at the Military Academy before returning to duty in the west. He was promoted to captain in 1854 while serving at Benecia Barracks, California, and Fort Yuma, Arizona Territory. In 1858 he was promoted major in the 2nd Cavalry, stationed in Texas, and took part in the Red River Country conflict and the Kiowa Expedition. In a skirmish on the Clear Fork of the Brazos River he was seriously wounded and went on leave of absence until 1860. In 1861 he most likely watched the coming of the Civil War with unease, as his family all resided in Virginia. Governor Letcher of Virginia offered Thomas a position in the Virginia forces that he declined, and on the day the American flag was lowered at Fort Sumter he relinquished his leave and reported for duty at Carlisle Barracks, Pennsylvania. With the resignations of colonel Robert E. Lee and Albert Sidney Johnston, Thomas moved from being a major to Colonel of the 2nd Cavalry. He served with General Robert Patterson in the Shenandoah Valley during the campaign of First Bull Run and defeated the forces of Stonewall Jackson at the minor battle at Falling Waters. General Robert Anderson, commander of the Department of the Cumberland, requested his services, and in late 1861 he transferred as a brigadier-general of volunteers, taking charge of organizing troops at Camp Dick Robinson, Kentucky. These regiments were organized into a division that formed the initial Army of the Cumberland. In January 1862 General Thomas defeated the Confederate forces of General Felix Zollicofer at the Battle of Mill Spring and prevented the Confederate movement toward Lexington, Kentucky, from being successful. Thomas' victory at Mill Springs was the first victory for federal forces in the western theater. From November 1862 to October 1863 he commanded a division under General Don Carlos Buell in the Army of the Ohio, except for a period when he commanded the right wing of General Henry Halleck's and later General William Roscrans' forces at Corinth, Mississippi. He had fought at Shiloh as part of General Buell's forces and was promoted in May 1862 to major-general of volunteers, and then credibly fought in the battles of Perryville and Stone's River. General William Rosecrans, upon taking command of the Army of the Cumberland, organized it into three wings, with the newly formed XIV Corps commanded by Thomas to be the center wing during the Tullahoma campaign, in which Rosecrans outmaneuvered General Braxton Bragg, forcing him to leave Chattanooga and retreat south.

At the Battle of Chickamauga, Thomas' determined stand on Horseshoe Ridge saved the Army of the Cumberland from being annihilated by Bragg's forces. His last ditch stand deservedly earned him the fame of being the "Rock of Chickamauga". When Rosecrans was removed Thomas became commander of the Army of the Cumberland and was appointed to brigadier-general in the regular army. In November 1864 General Thomas' troops, under the watchful eye of General Ulysses Grant, stormed up Missionary Ridge, driving General Braxton Bragg's army south to Dalton, Georgia. In the 1864 Atlanta campaign Thomas' Army of the Cumberland contained nine infantry divisions and three cavalry divisions, performing the hardest work in the campaign, most particularly at the Battle

Thomas, George. *Carte de visite* by Morse, Nashville, Tennessee. General Thomas's signature appears on the front of the carte. Author's collection.

of Kennesaw Mountain. After the fall of Atlanta and movement of General John B. Hood toward Alabama and Tennessee, General William T. Sherman ordered General Thomas back to Nashville with 35,000 troops to check Hood. Another 35,000 troops were gathered from other commands, including a cavalry force of 10,000 commanded by General James Wilson. The first battle to stop Hood by Thomas' forces was at Franklin, Tennessee, where General John Schofield was forced to confront Hood while on his way to join Thomas in Nashville. The ensuing Battle of Franklin was six hours of the most bloody fighting in the war. Hood's army was significantly weakened, but it gathered reinforcements and continued towards Nashville. Schofield reached Nashville ahead of Hood and joined with the rest of Thomas' forces in preparing to repel the Confederate army. Thomas' break-out of Nashville was constantly delayed due to ice and snow until December 16, 1864, when he attacked Hood and sent the Confederates reeling back to Alabama, and for all practical purposes put Hood's army out of the war. The two day Battle of Nashville was one of the most decisive battles of the Civil War. Thomas came close to being relieved by Grant just before the Battle of Nashville, thinking he was too slow in confronting Hood. There were also doubts in Washington, especially from Secretary of War Stanton, about Thomas' loyalty to the federal cause. At war's end he was one of the three most important generals in the federal forces. He remained in Nashville, commanding the Military District of Tennessee, and then in several other departmental commands until he asked for and received a transfer to the Department of the Pacific, where he died of a stroke in 1870.

Thomas, George. *Carte de visite* by unknown photographer. Author's collection.

Thomas, George. *Carte de visite*. Brady, Washington. Author's collection.

WALLACE

Wallace, Lew. *Carte de visite* by Brady, Washington. Author's collection.

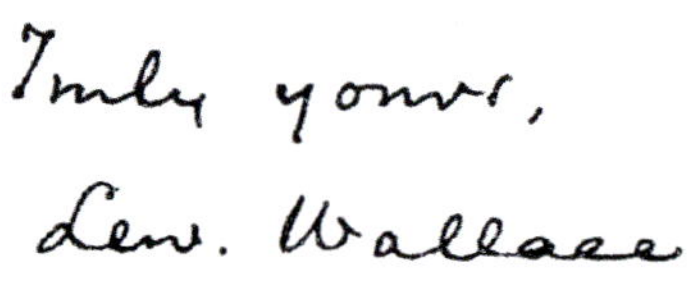

Wallace, Lewis (1827-1905) was born in Indiana. At twenty years of age he served in the Mexican War as a first lieutenant in the 1st Indiana Volunteers. He saw limited action and returned to Indianapolis to study law. Wallace began the practice of law in tandem with a career in politics. He moved his residence to Crawfordsville, Indiana, and was elected to the Indiana state senate in 1856. At the start of the Civil War, Indiana Governor Oliver Morton appointed Wallace as state adjutant general and later named him Colonel of the 11th Indiana Volunteers. Wallace and the 11th Indiana briefly served in West Virginia before being transferred to the District of Missouri at Cairo. He was appointed brigadier-general of volunteers in September 1861 and given the 3rd Division in the Army of the Tennessee under General Ulysses Grant. He took part in the capture of Fort Henry and Fort Donelson, and was appointed major-general of volunteers dated from March 1862. At the Battle of Shiloh, Wallace's division was camped six miles downstream from General William Sherman's division. At the onset of battle General Grant ordered Wallace to move his division to the battleground with all possible haste. Wallace chose to move his division on a road that was three miles longer than if he had taken one along the river. His choice of road put him in the rear of the Confederate lines, where he could have been easily captured or destroyed. Fortunately he realized his mistake, and then in a blundering manner finally reached Grant, who was furious and never forgave him his mistake that could have lost the battle. On the second day of the battle Wallace made a cautious attack and again drew Grant's displeasure. Grant was probably also displeased with the theatrical posturing and personality of Wallace. He was later removed from field command and held administrative posts until he helped organize the defenses of Cincinnati against the raid of Confederate General E. Kirby Smith. In March 1864, while in command of the Middle Department in Maryland, he was able, with a scratch force, to delay the progress of General Jubal Early in reaching and attacking Washington. Wallace's twenty-hour delaying action at the Battle of Monocacy allowed the movement of General Horatio Wright's VI Corps to reach the Washington defenses with just several hours to spare. Wallace was a member of the court-martial for the Lincoln conspirators and presided over the trial of Henry Wirz, former commander of the Andersonville prison. Always fascinated with Mexico, in late 1865 he traveled to Mexico to financially assist the forces of Juarez against the French supported Maximilian. He even accepted a major-generalship in the revolutionary Republican forces, but for some reason his efforts in Mexico failed to financially prosper and he returned to the United States. In the 1870s he served as governor of the New Mexico Territory and later as Minister to Turkey. While in diplomatic service he wrote the best-selling novel *Ben Hur: The Life of Christ.* He lived for many years in Crawfordsville, Indiana, and became one of the nation's most prominent authorities on fishing.

WARREN

Warren, Gouverneur. *Carte de visite* by Brady, Washington. Author's collection.

Warren, Gouverneur Kemble (1830-1882) was born in New York. Warren entered the Military Academy at the age of sixteen in 1846 and graduated second in the class of 1850. He was commissioned in the Topographical Engineers and served in normal engineering assignments until 1854, when he was the topographical engineer assigned to the Sioux Expedition, participating in a skirmish at Blue Water. He continued to perform topographical surveys and was the first explorer into the Black Hills of South Dakota. In 1859 he was assigned to the Military Academy as Assistant Professor of Mathematics. In May 1861 Warren left the engineers, becoming lieutenant-colonel and then Colonel of the 5th New York Volunteers and seeing action at the Battle of Big Bethel. Following the 1862 Virginia Peninsula Campaign Battle of Yorktown he was given command of a brigade in the division of General George Sykes, and was slightly wounded at the Battle of Gaines Mill. Warren was appointed to brigadier-general of volunteers in September 1862 and led his brigade at the Battles of Second Bull Run, Antietam, and Fredericksburg. Upon taking command of the Army of the Potomac, General Joseph Hooker made Warren his chief engineer. At Gettysburg on July 2, 1863, he contributed to the Federal victory by his recognition of the threat to Little Round Top and quickly organizing troops for its defense against Hood's repeated attacks. In August 1863 he was confirmed as a major-general of volunteers and was placed in temporary command of the II Corps. On October 14, 1863, Warren repulsed General D.H. Hill at the Battle of Bristoe Station and was praised by General Meade for "skill and promptitude". At Mine Run he unilaterally aborted an attack that Meade agreed should not have been made, but the incident developed a rift between the two generals. The reorganization of the Army of the Potomac in March 1864 brought Warren the command of the V Corps for Grant's Overland Campaign. He fought competently at the battles of the Wilderness, Spotsylvania, Cold Harbor, and North Anna. At the siege of Petersburg he was criticized for not holding the enemy in place and allowing them to reinforce Confederate forces at the Battle of the Crater. In the final Virgina campaign Warren's V Corps was placed under the direction of General Philip Sheridan, and soon the two generals, with very different temperaments, clashed. Sheridan had been given authority by Grant to remove Warren, and at the Battle of Five Forks Sheridan felt the V Corps had made a disorganized attack due to improper information that was actually provided by Sheridan. Warren had gone to the front to personally sort out the difficulties, allowing the attack to be successful. When Sheridan could not find Warren at his headquarters he was furious and abruptly relieved him from command. Warren was then assigned to duties in Mississippi, but in May 1865 he resigned his volunteer rank and returned to the Corps of Engineers in his regular army rank. He remained in the Corps of Engineers till his retirement in 1879 with the rank of lieutenant-colonel. After his removal by Sheridan he asked for a court of inquiry that was never granted until 1879. Its findings were that, although a bit slow, he contributed greatly to the substantial victory at Five Forks. The manner of his dismissal in the hearing was lightly touched upon, but the essence of it was that he been wronged by Sheridan. This verdict did little for Warren, as he had died a few months earlier. Warren was a good general, but due to unfortunate character traits he was unable or unwilling to foster good working relationships with superior officers, such as Meade, Grant, and Sheridan.

WASHBURN

Washburn, Cadwallader. *Carte de visite* by Fredricks, New York. Author's collection.

Washburn, Cadwallader Colden (1818-1882) was born in Maine, but eventually moved to Wisconsin and became a practicing lawyer and businessman in Mineral Point. One of six brothers in a politically oriented family, Washburn and two of his brothers served simultaneously in Congress. At the opening of the Civil War Washburn, who had accumulated a huge fortune in land, banking, railroading, and lumbering, held and remained in his seat in Congress during the first year of the war. Though at least partially attributable to the efforts of his brother Elihu, an intimate friend of Lincoln and Grant's chief political sponsor, Washburn was appointed Colonel of the 2nd Wisconsin Cavalry in February 1862. In July 1862 he was appointed brigadier-general, of volunteers and major-general of volunteers in March 1863. In December 1862 he commanded a cavalry division under General Eugene Carr in the District of Eastern Arkansas, and then in February 1863 a cavalry division in the XIII Corps of the Army of the Tennessee. He commanded the land side of the first attempt to take Vicksburg and a detachment of three divisions of the XVI Corps in the siege of Vicksburg. Washburn then commanded the XIII Corps in the Department of the Gulf and was successful in capturing Fort Esperanza on Matagorda Bay, Texas. Beginning in April 1864 until the end of the war he commanded the District of West Tennessee, headquartered at Memphis. He was successful in protecting rail lines and administering Memphis commerce and government, as well as containing, if not preventing, the frequent raids of Confederate General Nathan Bedford Forrest. After the war he resumed his career in politics and served two more terms in Congress and as Wisconsin governor before founding a business that was later renamed the General Mills Corporation. There is little doubt that Washburn's political connections influenced his assignments in the Civil War. However, he appeared to render a competent performance in each assignment.

WEITZEL

Weitzel, Godfrey. *Carte de visite* by Brady, Washington. Author's collection.

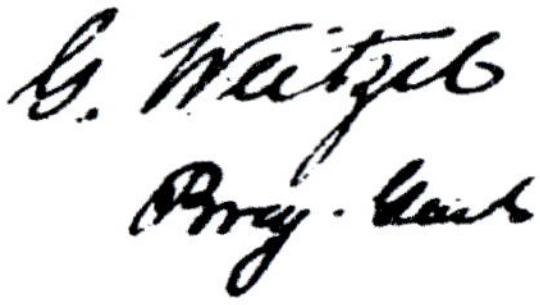

Weitzel, Godfrey (1835-1884) was born in Ohio. He entered the Military Academy in 1851 and graduated second in the class of 1854. Weitzel was commissioned in the Corps Engineer, and was assigned between 1855 and 1860 to work in the construction of the defenses located below the city of New Orleans. He was serving as an assistant professor of engineering at West Point at the opening of the Civil War. Weitzel performed engineering duties in the defenses of Washington and Cincinnati, Ohio, before being selected in March 1862 as chief of engineers for General Benjamin Butler's expedition to New Orleans . After the occupation of the city Butler named Weitzel acting mayor, as well as military commander. He was appointed a brigadier-general of volunteers and commanded infantry forces at the Battles of Lefourche and Thibeaudox, where he was breveted to major. He also participated in General Nathaniel Banks' movement against Port Hudson and led a division making two gallant assaults, gaining him a brevet of lieutenant-colonel. Weitzel was engaged and was complimented for his part in the unsuccessful 1862 Sabine Pass expedition. In 1864 he again joined Butler in the Army of the James as chief of engineers, and later commander of the XVIII Corps, which was engaged at the Battle of Drewry's Bluff. He supervised the construction of the fortifications at the Bermuda Hundred and Deep Bottom that bottled up Butler's army and prevented it from assisting Grant's movement on Richmond. He helped to repel the later attack on Fort Harrison and participated in the attacks on the Confederate entrenchments on the Williamsburg and Nine Mile Roads, for which he was likely appointed to major-general of volunteers. Commanding the XXV Corps, he was second in command to Butler on the blundering attempt to capture Fort Fisher. After Butler's removal Weitzel took command of all troops north of the Appomattox during the movement against Richmond. On April 3, 1865, his troops entered Richmond, and Weitzel had the honor of announcing its capture to President Lincoln in a telegram, stating "We entered Richmond at 8:00 this morning". Weitzel was transferred to the District of the Rio Grande during the government's campaign in late 1865 to discourage the French supported Maxmillian from remaining in Mexico. He mustered out of the volunteer service in March 1866, and by August that year was promoted to major, and in charge of the construction of Fort Knox. His close relationships with failed political Generals Butler and Banks probably hurt his career in the post-war army.

Whipple

Whipple, Amiel. *Carte de visite* by Addis, Washington. Author's collection.

Whipple, Amiel Weeks (1816-1863) was born in Massachusetts. He attended Amherst College before being admitted to the Military Academy in 1837, graduating fifth in the class of 1841. He initially was commissioned in the 1st Artillery in July 1841, but transferred to the Corps of Engineers in September of that year. Whipple was engaged in surveys establishing the borders with Canada and Mexico, as well as surveying for a future railroad near the 35th parallel extending from the Mississippi River to the Pacific Ocean. His first assignment in the Civil War was as chief topographical engineer for the Washington defenses south of the Potomac. As chief of engineers on the staff of General Irvin McDowell he fought at the Battle of Bull Run on July 31, 1861. Afterwards, he received a brevet of lieutenant-colonel for his gallantry in the Manassas Campaign. He returned to the Washington defenses and remained there as chief engineer. During this time he became involved and responsible for the formation of the federal army's balloon corps under the civilian leadership of Thaddeus Lowe. On April 14, 1862, he was appointed brigadier-general of volunteers and given a brigade, and then a division in the III Corps that was engaged in the Rappahannock Campaign. While in command of the 3rd Division of the III Corps he fought at the Battle of Fredericksburg as part of General Joseph Hooker's Center Grand Division and at Chancellorsville, where he was mortally wounded and died on May 7, 1863. He was appointed major-general of volunteers to date from May 6, 1863, but the appointment was never confirmed by the Senate. Whipple Barracks near Prescott, Arizona, is named for him.

WILSON

Wilson, James Harrison. *Carte de visite* by Morse, Nashville, Tennessee. Author's collection.

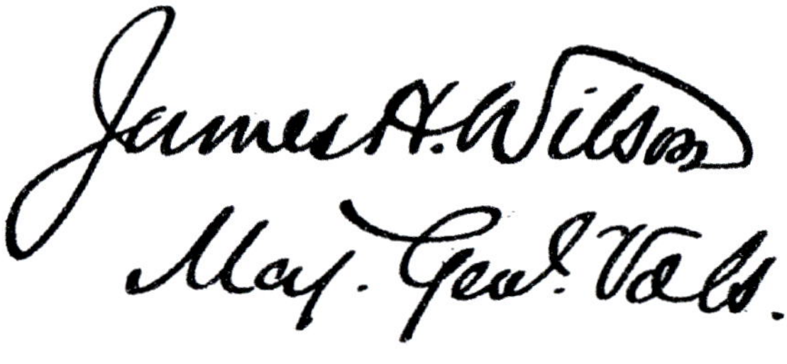

Wilson, James Harrison (1837-1925) was born in Illinois. He entered the Military Academy in 1855, graduating sixth in the class of 1860. Wilson was commissioned in the Topographical Engineers and was stationed in the Department of Oregon at the beginning of the Civil War. He rushed back to Washington in time to accompany General Thomas Sherman's Port Royal Expedition as chief engineer, and then, while still in the Department of the South, assisted General Quincy Gilmore in the reduction of Fort Pulaski. During the Maryland Campaign at the Battle of Antietam Wilson acted as aide to General George McClellan. In late 1862 he was sent west to join the staff of General Ulysses Grant as assistant engineer and inspector general for the Army of the Tennessee. During the Vicksburg campaign he was active in devising engineering projects, and soon became prominent on Grant's personal staff. He won a brevet for gallantry at the Battle of Chattanooga and accompanied General William Sherman's relief of Knoxville. Appointed brigadier-general of volunteers, he was assigned as head of the Cavalry Bureau in Washington and largely stopped the corruption on the part of dealers selling horses to the government. When Grant assumed command of the federal army he named Wilson to be a division commander in the Cavalry Corps of the Army of the Potomac under General Philip Sheridan. Wilson, showing tactical ability. was highly complimented for numerous fights and skirmishes during the 1864 Overland Campaign and in Sheridan's battles in the Shenandoah Valley. Prior to the Battle of Cedar Creek, Wilson was ordered west as chief of cavalry to General William T. Sherman. His first organizational task was in the equipping and prepartion of the cavalry force of General Judson Kilpatrick that would accompany General Sherman on the Atlanta campaign. Next he organized the remaining cavalry in the western theater to be the single largest force of cavalry in the war. He led this corps at the battles of Franklin and Nashville. In the pursuit after the Battle of Nashville that nearly destroyed Hood's army Wilson's forces captured thousands of Confederate troops. In the spring of 1864 he led his corps south and overwhelmed and dispersed the cavalry of General Nathan Bedford Forrest near Selma, Alabama. He then turned his 13,500 cavalry troops across Alabama, finally ending the expedition at Macon, Georgia, on April 20, 1865, when learning of Lee's surrender. A few days later one of Wilson's regiments captured Confederate President Jefferson Davis. He was appointed a major-general of volunteers in June 1865 with date of rank to be May 5, 1865. General Wilson mustered out of the volunteer service in January 1866 and was designated colonel of the 35th Infantry, but did not command his regiment, as he received engineering assignments till his retirement in 1870. Wilson became a successful railroad executive, but in 1898 he returned to active duty as a major-general of volunteers in Puerto Rico and Cuba during the Spanish-American War. He also traveled to China and commanded troops in the relief of American forces engaged in the Boxer Rebellion. Wilson also wrote several books on Grant and the Civil War.

Wilson, James Harrison. *Carte de visite* by unidentified photographer probably Brady. The glass plate used to print this *carte* was damaged. Author's collection.

Wood

Wood, Thomas. *Carte de visite* by Morse, Nashville, Tennessee. Author's collection.

Wood, Thomas John (1823-1906) was born in Kentucky. He entered the Military Academy in 1841, graduating fifth in the class of 1845. Commissioned in the Topographical Engineers, he was immediately sent to the occupation of Texas. During the Mexican War he took part in the battles of Buena Vista and Monterey as a lieutenant in the 2nd Dragoons. He served in Texas with the 2nd Dragoons until 1855, when promoted to captain in the 1st Cavalry. After seeing service in the field during the Kansas troubles he accompanied the Utah Expedition, and was then posted in the Indian Territory. Wood was on leave in Europe when the Civil War began, and upon his return received promotion in May 1861 to major in the 1st Cavalry. He was assigned till March 1861 organizing Indiana troops, and was promoted to lieutenant-colonel of the 1st cavalry May 9, 1861. Wood was later appointed brigadier-general of volunteers in October 1861 and placed in command of a brigade Army of the Ohio in General Alexander McCook's Department of the Cumberland . He later participated in General Don Carlos Buell's support of General Grant at the Battle of Shiloh. At the battles of Perryville and Murfreesboro he credibly led a division. At the Battle of Stone River his three brigades were instrumental in saving the day for federal forces. At the Battle of Stone River he was wounded but refused to leave the field till the conclusion of the day's fighting. Wood served in General William Rosecrans' Tullahoma Campaign, culminating in the Battle of Chickamauga, which was a near disaster for the federal forces. Wood's division was positioned in the near center of the federal line when he received an order delivered by one of Rosecrans' aides to close a gap between his lines and those of General Joseph J. Reynolds. Wood was aware the supposed gap did not exist, as General John Brannan's 3rd Division was positioned there. He protested the order, but in doing so did not sufficiently inform Rosecrans of the location of Brannan's troops. He had been criticized earlier by Rosecrans for being slow, and he now obeyed his orders to the letter and moved his division, creating a real gap that was quickly discovered and exploited by General James Longstreet. The Confederates poured through the gap in the federal lines and would have likely destroyed Rosecrans' entire army if not for the determined defense on Muleshoe Ridge by General George Thomas. General Wood later fought in the Battle of Missionary Ridge, and his division was one of the first Federal forces overrunning Confederate lines. On the Atlanta Campaign Wood was seriously wounded with a shattered leg at the Battle of Lovejoy's Station in September 1864. Wood's division was selected to accompany General George Thomas back to Nashville after the Battle of Atlanta to counter General John B. Hood's drive towards Tennessee and Kentucky. The division was engaged at the Battle of Franklin and at the Battle of Nashville with Wood in temporary command of the IV Corps, which played a key role in the destruction of Hood's army. In February 1865 he was appointed major-general of volunteers and served the remainder of his career in the Departments of Tennessee, Arkansas, and Texas. He mustered out of volunteer service in September 1866 and on June 9, 1868, was retired for disability from his leg wound.

WOOL

Wool, John Ellis. *Carte de visite* by Fredricks, New York. Author's collection.

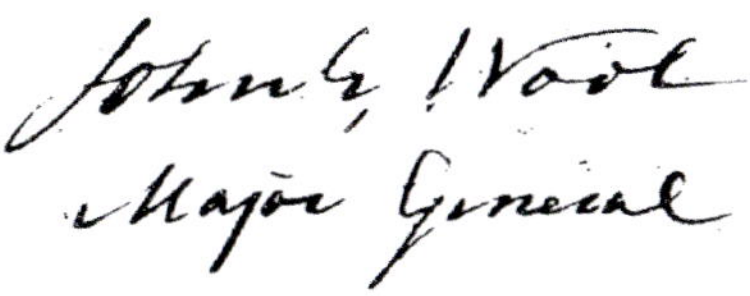

Wool, John Ellis. *Carte de visite* by Anthony, New York. Author's collection.

Wool, John Ellis (1784-1869) was born in New York. Wool was a bookseller and law student at Troy, New York, in his early years. At the opening of the War of 1812 he raised a company and was later appointed a captain in the 13th U.S. infantry upon the recommendation of New York Governor DeWitt Clinton. He was seriously wounded at the Battle of Queenstown and made a major. In 1816 he was appointed a colonel and inspector general of the army. Wool had the disagreeable task in 1836 of removing by the orders of President Andrew Jackson the Cherokees from their homes in Georgia to the Indian Territory. He was made brigadier-general in 1841, and in the war with Mexico organized 12,000 volunteers from the Midwestern states and followed them to Mexico, where he became second in command to General Zachary Taylor. At the Battle of Buena Vista he chose the ground, disposed his forces, and led them during the early stages of the battle. For action at Buena Vista he received a brevet to major-general and presentation swords from New York and congress. He was in charge of the Department of the Pacific 1854 to 1857, and effectively managed a series of Indian wars. In April 1861 General Wool telegraphed state governors from Maine to Illinois to immediately take control of federal arsenals and prevent any arms being shipped south. He then expedited the movement of federal troops from New York to Washington. Wool also quickly saw to the reinforcement of Fortress Monroe, and in August 1861 was placed there as commander of the Department of Virginia and soon moved to occupy Norfolk and Portsmouth. He was appointed major-general of volunteers, and in June 1862 was placed in command of the Middle Military Department, headquartered in Baltimore. His last duty assignment was commanding the Eastern Department with headquarters in New York City and in suppressing the draft riots. He was retired on August 1863 as one of the oldest generals to serve in the Federal or Confederate armies.

WRIGHT

Wright, Horatio. *Carte de visite* by Golden, Washington. Author's collection.

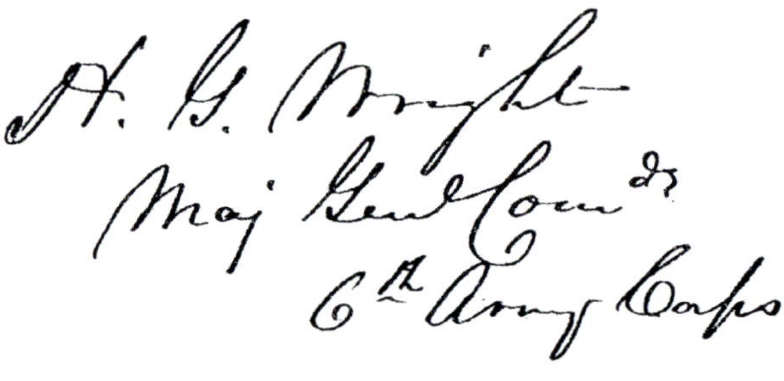

Wright, Horatio Gouverneur (1820-1899) was born in Connecticut. He entered the Military Academy in 1837, graduating second in the class of 1841. Wright was commissioned in the Corps of Engineers and served on various engineering projects, including the construction of Fort Taylor and the Naval Coal Depot at Key West, Florida. Between 1842 and 1844 he was assigned to the Military Academy teaching French and engineering. Promoted to captain in 1855, Wright served on commissions examining aspects of using selected large ordnance in and against fortifications. His first service in the Civil War was as chief engineer with an expedition to destroy the Norfolk Navy Yard. The effort was a failure, and Wright was captured but soon released. He next accompanied General Samuel Heintzeleman's Division as chief engineer at the Battle of Bull Run. Wright then played a key role in the development and construction of the Washington defenses, and in July 1861 was assigned as chief engineer of General Thomas Sherman's Port Royal Expedition. In September 1861 he was appointed brigadier-general of volunteers and placed in command of a brigade that was present at the capture of Hilton Head. From February to June 1861 he commanded the land forces in the Florida Expedition that captured Jacksonville and St. Augustine. Given division command under fellow engineer General Henry Benham, his troops made a determined but futile assault in the federal defeat at the Battle of Secessionville, South Carolina. In June 1862 he took command of the Department of the Ohio when General John Foster was injured in a fall from his horse. In March 1863 Wright, as commander of the District of Louisville, coordinated federal efforts to prepare and mass forces at Louisville to counter Bragg's invasion of the state. Wright was sent to be a division commander in the VI Corps of the Army of the Potomac after being appointed major-general of volunteers in July 1862. The appointment was not confirmed by the Senate in March 1862 due to Wright's poor performance at Louisville, and he was not to be a major-general until 1864. His division at the Battle of Gettysburg saw minimal action, but was engaged in the actions at Rappahannock Bridge and Mine Run. For his action at Mine Run he was given a brevet to lieutenant-colonel. In the 1864 Overland Campaign Wright fought at the Battle of the Wilderness and was wounded, but recovered quickly and assumed command of the VI Corps at the Battle of Spotsylvania when General John Sedgwick was killed by a sniper. He continued to command the VI Corps for the rest of the campaign and received promotion to colonel of engineers. Wright and the VI Corps, in July 1864, were rushed to protect Washington from a raid by General Jubal Early, and on July 12th, engaged Early and forced his retreat. Wright made a slow and cautious pursuit, allowing Early to preserve his forces for future actions in the Shenandoah Valley. General Wright and the VI Corps then served under General Philip Sheridan in the Valley Campaign of 1864. At Cedar Creek in October 1864, Wright was in command of the federal forces in the absence of General Sheridan when they were surprised by General Jubal Early's forces. Some authorities claim the wounded Wright was able to regroup the Federal forces before the dramatic arrival of General Sheridan, who then led them to victory. The VI Corps returned to the Petersburg line in December 1864, and his troops were the first to break the Confederate lines. He was present at the surrender at Appomattox. and for a year commanded the Department of Texas before being mustered out in September 1866. He returned to engineering duties as a lieutenant-colonel.

President Lincoln, Cabinet Officers, and Governors

Lincoln, Abraham. *Cartes de visite* by Brady, Washington. Author's collection.

Lincoln, Abraham. *Carte de visite* by Brady, Washington. President Lincoln is shown with his most prominent major-generals and admirals. Author's collection.

Union Generals killed in action during the Civil War. From a Meserve negative. Author's Collection.

Bates, Edward. *Carte de visite* by Brady, Washington. Lincoln's Attorney General. Author's collection.

Blair, Montgomery. *Carte de visite* by Brady, Washington. Lincoln's Postmaster General. Author's collection.

Cameron, Simon. *Carte de visite* by Brady, Washington. Lincoln's first Secretary of the War. Author's collection.

Hamilin, Hannibal. *Carte de visite* by Brady, Washington. Lincoln's first Vice President. Author's collection.

Chase, Salmon. *Carte de visite* by Brady, Washington. Lincoln's first Secretary of the Treasury. Author's collection.

Johnson, Andrew. Carte de visite by Brady, Washington. Lincoln's second term Vice President. Author's collection.

Holt, Joseph. *Carte de visite* by E. Anthony, New York. Lincoln's Judge Advocate General. Author's collection.

McCulloch, Hugh. *Carte de visite* by Brady, Washington. Lincoln's comptroller of the currency and then became Secretary of the Treasury. Author's collection.

Seward, William H. *Carte de visite* by Alexander Gardner, Washington. Lincoln's Secretary of State and chief advisor. Author's collection.

Smith, Caleb. *Carte de visite* by Brady, Washington. Lincoln's Secretary of the Interior. Author's collection.

Stanton, Edwin. *Carte de visite* by Brady, Washington. Lincoln's second Secretary of War. Author's collection.

Usher, John. *Carte de visite* by Bruening, Indianapolis, Indiana. Lincoln's second Secretary of the Interior. Author's collection.

Welles, Gideon. *Carte de visite* by Brady, Washington. Lincoln's Secretary of the Navy. Author's collection.

Brown, Benjamin Gratz. *Carte de visite* by unidentified photographer. Radical Republican United States Senator from Missouri. Author's collection.

Brownlow, William (Parson) *Carte de visite* by Anthony, New York City. Newspaper Editor and Reconstruction Governor of Tennessee. Author's collection.

Chandler, Zachariah. *Carte de visite* by Brady, Washington. Radical Republican Senator from Michigan and a leader of the Committee on the Conduct of the War. Author's collection.

Harlan, John. *Carte de visite* by Brady, Washington. Radical Republican Senator of Iowa. Author's collection.

Pomeroy, Samuel. *Carte de visite* by Brady, Washington. Radical Republican Senator of Kansas. Author's collection.

Trumbull, Lyman. *Carte de visite* by Brady, Washington. Republican Senator of Illinois as Chair of the Senate Judiciary Committee he was strongly opposed to slavery. Author's collection.

Wade, Benjamin. *Carte de visite* by Brady, Washington. Radical Republican Sentor of Ohio served as chair of the Joint Committee on the Conduct of the War and played a key role in selection and removal of generals.

Wilson, Henry. *Carte de visite* by Case and Getchel, Boston. Radical Republican Senator of Massachusetts served as chair of the Senate Military Affairs committee where each Lincoln appointed general had to be confirmed.

Andrew, John. *Carte de visite* by Brady, Washington. War Governor of Massachusetts. Strong supporter of Lincoln and the war. Author's collection.

Bradford, Augustus. *Carte de visite* by Brady, Washington. Governor of Maryland and Lincoln supporter. Author's collection.

Buckingham, William. *Carte de visite* by Jennings, Norwich, Connecticut. War Governor of Connecticut and a loyal Lincoln and union supporter. Author's collection.

Curtin, Andrew. *Carte de visite* by Brady, Washington. War Governor of Pennsylvania and supporter of Lincoln. Author's collection.

Magoffin, Beriah. *Carte de visite* by Anthony, New York. Governor of Kentucky in the first year of the war and tried to keep the state neutral. Author's collection.

Morgan, Edwin. *Carte de visite* by Fredricks, New York. War Governor of New York and strong supporter of Lincoln and the war.

Morton, Oliver. *Carte de visite* by Fredricks, New York. War Governor of Indiana and a strong supporter of the individual soldier in the war. Author's collection.

Rice, Henry. *Carte de visite*. By Brady, Washington. Senator of Minnesota on the Military Affairs Committee and usually a Lincoln supporter. Author's collection.